THE BRITISH PARTICULAR BAPTISTS

BENJAMIN KEACH IN THE PILLORY.

THE BRITISH PARTICULAR BAPTISTS
1638-1910

Volume I

Edited by

Michael A. G. Haykin

Particular Baptist Press
Springfield, Missouri

Haykin, Michael A. G.
 The British Particular Baptists, 1638-1910. Two
 Volumes.
ISBN 1-888514-05-1 (Acid-Free Paper)
1. Haykin, Michael A. G. 2. Baptists—Great Britain—
Biography 3. Particular Baptists — History I. Title.

First Edition

Particular Baptist Press
2766 W. Weaver Road
Springfield, Missouri 65810

Printed in the United States of America

To
Jim Elliff and Don Whitney,
dear brothers in Christ
who esteem our
Calvinistic Baptist forebears

CONTENTS

ACKNOWLEDGMENTS

I owe a tremendous debt of gratitude to Pastor Gary Long for his friendship, encouragement and support over the entire time that this book has been in the process of being prepared for publication. Without his vision and enthusiasm, this book would never have seen the light of day. I would also like to thank Mr. S. J. Taylor, the Librarian of the Evangelical Library, London, England, for the help that he gave me in procuring portraits of many of the figures discussed in this volume.

I must also extend my thanks to a number of churches who have helped make this book possible: Sovereign Grace Baptist Church of Springfield, Missouri, Reformed Baptist Church of Memphis, Tennessee, Barnes Chapel Baptist Church of Columbia, Missouri, and Clearwater Baptist Church of Roanoke, Virginia. I would also like to thank various friends from the following cities and towns who have generously contributed to this project of making our Baptist forebears known: Springdale, Arkansas; Cerritos, California; Greeley, Colorado; Longmont, Colorado; and Palm Harbor, Florida.

Finally, a hearty thanks to all of the contributors to this work—may God own your labours for the glory of his Son.

Michael A. G. Haykin,
Dundas, Ontario.

NOTES ON CONTRIBUTORS

Michael A.G. Haykin is presently Professor of Church History at Heritage Baptist College and Heritage Theological Seminary in Cambridge, Ontario. Among his publications are *One heart and one soul: John Sutcliff of Olney, his friends, and his times* (Evangelical Press, 1994) and *Kiffin, Knollys, Keach: Rediscovering our English Baptist Heritage* (Reformation Today Trust, 1996).

Barry H. Howson is presently completing a Ph. D. at McGill University, Montreal, where his thesis is on "Seventeenth-Century Particular Baptist Thought: The Case of Hanserd Knollys." He has served as the pastor of Lachute Baptist Church and Dalesville Baptist Church, both of which are in Quebec. He also serves as the Copy Editor of *The Baptist Review of Theology*. He is marrried with two girls.

Gary W. Long is pastor of the Sovereign Grace Baptist Church in Springfield, Missouri. He heads up Particular Baptist Press, coordinates the bi-annual Spurgeon Pastor's Conference held at William Jewell College, Liberty, Missouri, and is on the board of "Friends of the Spurgeon Library."

Peter Naylor is the minister of the Tabernacle Baptist Church, Wellingborough, Northamptonshire, and the author of *Picking up a Pin for the Lord: English Particular Baptists from 1688 to the Early Nineteenth Century* (Grace Publications, 1992).

Tom J. Nettles currently serves as Professor of Historical Theology at The Southern Baptist Theological Seminary in Louisville, Kentucky. He has published several works in the history of Baptist theology, including *By His Grace and For His Glory* (Baker, 1986).

Robert W. Oliver is currently pastoring a Baptist church in Bradford on Avon, England, where he has served since 1971. After research into early English Strict Baptist History under the supervision of Harold Rowdon and Barrie White, he was awarded a Ph.D. by the Council for National Academic Awards in 1987. Since 1989 he has also been Lecturer in Church History at the London Theological Seminary.

B. A. Ramsbottom is the present Editor of *The Gospel Standard*. He became the Editor at the beginning of 1971. He has been pastor at Bethel Strict Baptist Chapel, Luton, England, since 1967, and is the author of several books and booklets on Particular Baptist History, including *Stranger Than Fiction: The Life of William Kiffin* (Gospel Standard Trust, 1989) and *The Puritan Samson: The Life of David Crosley 1669-1744* (Gospel Standard Trust, 1991).

James M. Renihan is Dean of the Institute of Reformed Baptist Studies at Wetsminster Theological Seminary in California, Escondido, California. He receieved his Ph. D. in Theological Studies from Trinity Evangelical Divinity School, Deerfield, Illinois, having written a dissertation entitled "The Practical Ecclesiology of the English Particular Baptists, 1675-1705: The Doctrine of the Church in the Second London Baptist Confession as Implemented in the Subscribing Churches." He has been pastor of Reformed Baptist Churches in New York and Massachusetts, and is married with five children.

Allen E. Smith, a native of Alabama, was ordained to the ministry in 1956 and has served in four pastorates. He founded and was pastor of Clearview Baptist Church, Roanoke, Virginia, from 1969 until his retirement at the end of 1998. He has done extensive study and writing in the area of Baptist church polity and the relationships of Baptist Churches and their Associations.

Kirk Wellum is the founding and present pastor of Sovereign Grace Community Church in Sarnia, Ontario, Canada, and the chairman of the Sovereign Grace Fellowship of Baptist Churches in Canada. He is a graduate of Ontario Bible College (now Tyndale College and Seminary) and Waterloo University. He is married and blessed with four children.

Paul Wilson is the Director of General Education at Heritage Baptist College, Cambridge, Ontario. He holds a Ph. D. in History from the University of Western Ontario. Dr. Wilson is an historian who specializes in Canadian religious history. He has written a number of articles on Canadian Baptist businessmen.

FOREWORD

Gary W. Long

It is to be hoped that this book will serve to re-introduce many of today's Baptists to their illustrious and largely forgotten forebears, whose learning, struggles and faith are needed now more than ever. The "Particular Baptists" of Great Britain were men and women who embraced the historic Calvinistic faith (the term "Particular" denoting their commitment to particular redemption or, as it is sometimes termed, limited atonement) and were godly examples in character and demeanor. A considerable number of them were also first-rate scholars, second to none.

All of the authors who have contributed to this book have graciously written on their subjects in the spirit of "giving honor to whom honor is due." It needs to be noted, though, that their contributions to this book is not a complete endorsement by Particular Baptist Press of the subjects on whom they write. But if we have the great honor to be of edification to any through this work, we then joyfully count all the hardships of putting together a book like this as delight and offer a sincere heavenward "Thanks" for having this privilege to serve.

Springfield, Missouri,
February, 1998.

A

SERMON

Occafioned by the

DEATH

O F

ELIZABETH GILL,

W H O

Departed this Life *May* 30th. 1738.
having entred the 13th Year of her Age.
Preached *June* 4th.

To which is added,

An ACCOUNT of fome of her CHOICE
EXPERIENCES.

By JOHN GILL.

LONDON:

Printed and Sold by AARON WARD, *at the* Kings
Arms *in* Little Britain. M.DCC.XXXVIII.

PRICE *Six Pence.*

BRITISH PARTICULAR BAPTIST BIOGRAPHY

Michael A. G. Haykin

From the origins of Christianity, the Church has recognized the important role that Christian heroes and heroines play in modelling for other believers what Christianity is all about. The author of Hebrews, for example, can point his readers to a long line of "faith-full" men and women who, he is clearly hoping, will act as an encouragement to his readers to persevere in their Christian commitment (Hebrews 11; see also Hebrews 13:7). The early acts of the martyrs, written between the second and early fourth centuries, served a similar function: strengthening their readers in the face of persecution from the Roman state. A good example in this regard is the account of the martyrs of Lyons, which may well have been drawn up by the second-century divine Irenaeus of Lyons (d. *c.*200).[1]

For a lengthy period of time, the Middle Ages, some of these heroes acquired a status that was not rightly theirs, that of acting as mediatorial figures between God and men. The Reformation rightfully cleaned out these so-called "saints" from the Church and restored Christian heroes to their proper place and function: men and women, who, though flawed sinners, could serve as role models for other Christians as they sought to be faithful followers of Christ. *The Acts and the Monuments of the Church* of John Foxe (1516-1587), better known as *Foxe's Book of Martyrs*, is an excellent illustration of this Reformation understanding of the nature of Christian heroes and the importance of Christian biography.

Now, the British Particular Baptist community is a direct product of the Reformation. Over the years historians have had long debates about

---

[1] See Eusebius of Caesarea, *Ecclesiastical History* 5.1.

the roots of the Baptist movement. Some have wanted to find them in the soil of the Mennonites and Hutterites of the Reformation era. Others, more ambitious, have maintained that there is an unbroken chain of Baptist churches from the time of the Apostles. That God has always had his people in every period of history is undoubtedly true. The argument that there have always been Baptist churches for the last two thousand years, though, is more a product of wishful thinking than solid historical research.

What is absolutely clear from the historical record about Baptist origins is this: they emerged from the womb of English Puritanism in the early to mid-seventeenth century. The Puritans had appeared on the scene of history in the 1560s, confident that they could fully purify the Church of England from what they considered to be unbiblical practices of worship that had sprung up during the Middle Ages. But they were mistaken. Their programme of reform and renewal was met with fierce opposition from both church authorities and the English monarch, Queen Elizabeth I (r. 1559-1603).

Consequently, in the latter part of the sixteenth century, a number of Puritans came to the conviction that the Church of England would never be fully reformed, and they decided to separate from the state church and organize their own congregations. It was among these Separatists, as they came to be known, that believer's baptism was rediscovered, and Baptist congregations subsequently formed in the first half of the seventeenth century.[2]

As they developed a distinct community, the Particular Baptists, like other Christian groups, recognized the vital importance of Christian heroes and Christian biography. Thus, the earliest Baptist histories by Thomas Crosby (c. 1683-c. 1752)[3] and Joseph Ivimey (1773-1834)[4] made abundant use of biography as they sought to explain to their readers who exactly were the Baptists and what was the nature of their theological

---

[2] For further discussion of Baptist origins, see Michael A. G. Haykin, *Kiffin, Knollys, Keach: Rediscovering our English Baptist Heritage* (Leeds: Reformation Today Trust, 1996).

[3] His four-volume *The History of the English Baptists* (1738-1740).

[4] His four-volume *A History of the English Baptists* (1811-1830).

convictions. Baptist preachers also used the opportunity of funeral sermons to set forth deceased members of their community as role models for the Christian life.

A marvellous example in this regard is the funeral sermon of John Gill (1697-1771) for his daughter Elizabeth, who died at the age of twelve on May 30, 1738. After preaching on 1 Thessalonians 4:13-14, he gave what he called "An Account of Some Choice Experiences of Elizabeth Gill."[5] He gave some facts about his daughter's birth and temperament, and her early delight in books by Puritan writers like John Bunyan (1628-1688) and James Janeway (1636-1674). He developed at some length the account of her conversion, giving examples of "her sense of sin, and the tenderness of her conscience, as well as of God's sealing his pardoning grace to her soul."[6] Gill tells us of her Christian life, especially taking note of her humility and "very great ...respect for the hearing of the word, and other ordinances of the Gospel," as well as her inclination to "retire into corners, to read good books, and to desire of God to give her his grace."[7]

Elizabeth was disturbed, when on her death-bed, she had never been able to partake of the Lord's Supper. Her father's church was closed communion in its convictions and she would had to have been baptized before she could have partaken of the Supper. Her father's response was that though baptism and the Supper are "ordinances of Christ, and ought to be complied with, and submitted to by all that believe in Christ,...yet salvation does not depend upon them; persons may be saved without them, through the grace of Christ."[8] Gill takes note of the fact that "death was no king of terrors to her." She knew herself to be in the hands of a Sovereign God, and was content to die if he so willed it.[9]

As Gill recounts these aspects of his daughter's brief Christian pilgrimage, there is no doubt that he himself is deriving comfort and

---

[5] *A Sermon Occasioned by the Death of Elizabeth Gill* (London, 1738), 33-44.
[6] *Ibid.*, 36.
[7] *Ibid.*, 38-39.
[8] *Ibid.*, 41.
[9] *Ibid.*, 42-43.

strength from his daughter's example. At the beginning of the sermon, for instance, he says to the congregation: "You must permit me, this afternoon, to preach rather to my self and family than to you."[10] Yet, the very fact that he published the material about Elizabeth at a later date indicates that he hoped others would be strengthened and encouraged by it.

The Particular, or Calvinistic, Baptist tradition abounds in such heroes and heroines, and yet for a variety of reasons relatively few of them are well known today. Oh yes, three of them are sufficiently famous to regularly find a place in biographical dictionaries: Bunyan, William Carey (1761-1834), and C. H. Spurgeon (1834-1892). John Gill and Andrew Fuller (1754-1815), the two leading eighteenth-century theologians of the community, are also fairly well known. In fact, the names of these two latter figures can still serve today as rallying-points for differing, and at times opposing, perspectives on Calvinism. But many other figures like Benjamin Beddome, Caleb Evans, Samuel Pearce, and Christopher Smith are virtual unknowns. Yet, the lives of such individuals have much to teach us if we had accounts of them.

The goal of this two-volume work is to introduce the lives of a number of these men to a generation that is rediscovering the biblical attractiveness of the Calvinistic Baptist tradition. Unfortunately, the constraints of space have meant that a number of figures have not been included. There are no separate chapters in this work, for example, on Hercules Collins (d.1702), David Crosley (1669-1744),[11] John Brine (1703-1765),[12] Anne Dutton (1692-1765), Daniel Turner (1710-1798), Benjamin Wallin (1711-1782), Anne Steele (1717-1778), John Ash

---

[10] *Ibid.*, 3.

[11] See B. A. Ramsbottom *The Puritan Samson: The Life of David Crosley 1669-1744* (Harpenden, Hertfordshire: Gospel Standard Trust, 1991).

[12] See the brief account by Walter Wilson, *The History and Antiquities of Dissenting Churches and Meeting Houses, in London, Westminster, and Southwark; including the Lives of Their Ministers, From the Rise of Nonconformity to the Present Time* (London, 1808), II, 574-579.

(1724-1779), and John Hirst (1736-1815).[13] And there should be. Hopefully these two volumes will be well received and whet the appetite for more. Then it may well be possible to add a third and include such figures as these.

One final point that needs to be mentioned is the fact that nearly all of the contributors to these two volumes would see themselves as heirs to the Particular Baptists depicted in these pages and they would joyfully own the name "Calvinistic" or "Reformed Baptist." Yet, within the ranks of present-day Calvinistic Baptists there are differences of opinion over a number of issues, one of which has to do with the two theologians mentioned earlier, Gill and Fuller. Was Gill a cause of Particular Baptist decline in the eighteenth century and Fuller a catalyst for renewal? Or was Gill's theology a landmark that should never have been tampered with, and Fuller's writings, therefore, an instrument of declension? These are not easy questions to answer. Nor will the reader find a definitive answer in these two volumes. What he or she will find are differing perspectives on these questions. In other words, contributors have been given liberty to differ with regard to this issue which historically has been quite divisive.

It is the editor's and publisher's fervent hope that these two volumes would be used by God to enlighten modern-day Baptists, and other Christians, to the richness of the Particular Baptist tradition, and ultimately, be a vehicle of bringing glory to the Triune God of grace.

---

[13] See Kenneth Dix, "John Hirst—Pastor at Bacup", *Grace Magazine*, 49 (October 1974), 7-10.

THE
CONFESSION
OF FAITH,

Of thofe CHURCHES which are
commonly (though falfly) called ANABAPTISTS;

Prefented to the view of all that feare
GOD, to examine by the touchftone of the Word
of Truth : As likewife for the taking off thofe
afperfions which are frequently both in Pulpit and
Print, (although unjuftly) caft upon them.

ACTS 4. 20.

Wee cannot but fpeake the things which wee have feene and heard.

ISA I. 8. 20.

*To the Law and to the teftimony, if they fpeake not according to
this Rule, it is becaufe there is no light in them.*

2 COR. I. 9, 10.

*But wee had the fentence of death in our felves, that wee fhould not
truft in our felves, but in the living God, which raifeth the dead;
who delivered us from fo great a death, and doth deliver, in whom
wee truft that he will yet deliver.*

LONDON,
Printed in the yeare of our Lord, 1 6 4 4.

JOHN SPILSBURY (1593-*c.* 1662/1668)

James M. Renihan

The emergence of distinctively Calvinistic, or as they are more commonly known, Particular Baptist churches in the late 1630s and early 1640s is a development of the greatest importance in Baptist history. In most ways, the principles and practices of modern churches have been molded and shaped by the theological and practical principles advocated among those early churches. They set the contours which have ever since distinguished Baptist churches from their evangelical paedobaptist counterparts.

Though few men may legitimately be called pioneers, John Spilsbury[1] deserves that title.[2] As the first pastor of the original Particular Baptist Church in London, he stands at the head of a long and worthy line of Calvinistic Baptists. His leadership among the London churches may be evidenced by the frequent appearance of his name in the public documents of his era, and his importance is acknowledged by the fact that the

---

[1] Spilsbury's surname is variously spelled "Spilsbery" and "Spilsberie." For the sake of consistency, I have (with two exceptions) used "Spilsbury" throughout this paper. In all other cases, spelling and punctuation have been left as in the original sources.

[2] Murray Tolmie has called him "the pioneer of ultra-separatist rebaptism as well as of believer's baptism among the London separatists." Cp. Murray Tolmie, *The Triumph of the Saints: The Separate Churches of London 1616-1649* (Cambridge: Cambridge University Press, 1977), 24. Spilsbury would have rejected the notion that he practiced "rebaptism." Ernest Kevan says that some have called him the " 'Founder of the Baptists,' but such a statement is not strictly accurate" [*London's Oldest Baptist Church* (London: The Kingsgate Press, 1933), 23].

Calvinistic Baptists across the ocean in New England communicated with him in time of trouble.[3]

Few details of his life remain, and thus it is necessary to piece together various tidbits in order to catch a glimpse of the man.

Spilsbury's life and ministry

Apparently born in 1593, Spilsbury was a cobbler[4] in London.[5] In the 1630s, he was involved with a secession from the London church under the ministry of Henry Jessey (1601-1663), and formed what was probably the first Particular Baptist church in 1638. Ancient records state

---

[3] In John Clarke's *Ill Newes from New-England: Or A Narrative of New-Englands Persecution. Wherein is Declared That while old England is becoming new, New-England is become Old* (London, 1652), 17-23, is found a letter from Obadiah Holmes addressed "Unto the well beloved Brethren Iohn Spilsbury, William Kiffin, and the rest that in London stand fast in that Faith, and continue to walk stedfastly in that Order of the Gospel which was once delivered unto the Saints by Iesus Christ." Clarke, Holmes and John Crandall had been the subjects of prosecution by the authorities for their refusal to participate in a Congregationalist worship service in Lynn, Massachusetts. The letter details the difficulties Holmes had encountered, and urges his "dearly beloved brethren" to press on in their principles.

[4] He also seems to have been a "weigher of hay." See Robert Oliver, *From John Spilsbury to Ernest Kevan: The Literary Contribution of London's Oldest Baptist Church* (London: Grace Publications Trust, 1985), 8, and also the poem by John Taylor cited below.

[5] For a brief summary of his life, see Richard L. Greaves, "Spilsbury, John" in his and Robert Zaller, eds., *Biographical Dictionary of British Radicals* (Brighton, Sussex: Harvester Press, 1984), III, 193-194. He should not be confused with two paedobaptists, father and son, of the same name. John Spilsbury Sr. was a fellow of Magdalen College, Oxford, and was for many years minister in Bromsgrove, Worcestershire. His son was a dissenting minister in Kidderminster. See Walter Wilson, *The History and Antiquities of Dissenting Churches and Meeting Houses in London, Westminster and Southwark* (London, 1808), 2:55-56. The son apparently married the daughter of John Eckels, the Particular Baptist pastor in Bromsgrove. See Greaves and Zaller, eds., *Biographical Dictionary*, III, 194.

that several individuals "being convinced that Baptism was not for Infants, but professed Beleivers joyned wth Mr. Jo: Spilsbury."[6] This
church drew the notice of several of the more radical opponents of the
so-called "sectaries," and even called forth the following scurrilous
rhyme from the pen of a certain John Taylor:

> Also one Spilsbery rose up of late
> (Who doth, or did dwell over Aldersgate)
> His office was to weigh Hay by the Trusse
> (Fit for the pallat of Bucephalus)
> He in short time left his Hay-weighing trade,
> And afterwards he Irish Stockings made:
> He rebaptiz'd in Anabaptist fashion
> One Eaton (of the new found separation)
> A zealous Button-maker, grave and wise,
> And gave him orders, others to baptize;
> Who was so apt to learne in one day
> Hee'd do't as well as Spilsbery weigh'd Hay.[7]

Deviations from the established norm did not go unnoticed, especially
when the adherents to the new doctrines were ever increasing in number.
In 1643, Spilsbury published a book on baptism, defending the increasing number of Calvinistic Baptist churches against the charge that their
baptisms were invalid. In 1644, he, along with fellow church members
George Tipping and Samuel Richardson, signed the *First London Confession of Faith*,[8] and in 1646 published a second book defending the

---

[6] Cited W. T. Whitley, "Rise of the Particular Baptists in London, 1633-
1644", *Transactions of the Baptist Historical Society*, 1 (1908-1909), 231. At
this point, the church practiced believer's baptism, but had not yet adopted
immersion as the mode of baptism.

[7] Cited W. T. Whitley, "Records of the Jacob-Lathrop-Jessey Church 1616-
1641", *Transactions of the Baptist Historical Society*, 1 (1908-1909), 221.
The poem was published in 1641.

[8] William L. Lumpkin, *Baptist Confessions of Faith* (Valley Forge: Judson
Press, 1969), 156.

practice of baptism as well as asserting that Christ's death was specific
and intended only for the elect.

Spilsbury's relationship to the origin of the *First London Confession*
is unknown, though several authors hypothesize that he was its primary
author. A. C. Underwood, for instance, cites an anonymous writer who
called him the "great Patriarch of the Anabaptist Confession," and R. L.
Greaves says that "he was a signatory and probably the principal author
of the Particular Baptist confession."[9] W. L. Lumpkin's suggestion that
"he must have played a prominent part in its preparation" is probably
correct. He then suggests that "if the Confession was the product of
joint authorship, [he] probably had the assistance of William Kiffin and
Samuel Richardson."[10] Given the importance of these men, the proposed
scenario is highly possible.

The few surviving records indicate that John Spilsbury was regarded
as a prominent leader throughout the 1640s and 1650s. He signed such
public documents as the 1650 anti-Ranter tract *Heart Bleedings for
Professors Abominations*, the 1654 letter to Irish Baptists appealing for
a calm recognition of the government of Oliver Cromwell, the 1657 pe-
tition to Cromwell appealing to him to refuse the Crown, and the 1660
Humble Apology addressed to Charles II (r.1660-1685) in response to
the rebellion of Thomas Venner (d.1661).[11] As a result of the letter sent
to Ireland, Henry Cromwell (1628-1674) attempted to bring Spilsbury to
Ireland in order to help maintain calm among the Baptists there, but he
replied that he could not come because "he had accepted a call from 'a
very great people'."[12]

---

[9] A. C. Underwood, *A History of the English Baptists* (London: The Baptist Union Publication Department, 1947), 60; Greaves, "Spilsbury" in his
and Zaller, eds., *Biographical Dictionary*, III, 193-194.

[10] Lumpkin, *Baptist Confessions*, 145-146.

[11] Each of these documents may be consulted in E. B. Underhill, *Confes-
sions of Faith, and other Public Documents, Illustrative of the History of the
Baptist Churches of England in the 17th Century* (London: Hanserd Knollys
Society, 1854), 293-310, 322-326, 335-338, 343-352.

[12] Underwood, *History*, 60. See also Greaves, "Spilsbury" in his and
Zaller, eds., *Biographical Dictionary*, III, 194. Apparently, the Irish Baptists

Outside of London, he was also recognized as a leader. In 1653, the Abingdon Association sent a letter to Spilsbury, William Kiffin, and the London churches, informing them of the formation of their association and seeking correspondence between the assemblies.[13] His stature seems to have been sufficiently great as to persuade these men to treat him as something of a leader among the London churches. In 1657, another mention of Spilsbury is found in the Abingdon records, indicating that messengers from the London churches met weekly at Spilsbury's home in "Cole-Harbour in Thames Street."[14] In this decade, he and Kiffin seem to have been the *de facto* leaders of the churches in the metropolis. His date of death is unknown, but is thought to have been as early as 1662 or as late as 1668.[15]

Spilsbury's theological contributions

The emergence of a Calvinistic Baptist community brought forth many polemicists who published their criticisms of the new churches and their practices. Spilsbury acted as an apologist (along with others[16]) for the

---

were heavily influenced by Fifth Monarchy ideas, and were agitating against Cromwell's rule. Spilsbury and Kiffin sought to encourage loyalty and maintain the peace. On the Fifth Monarchist movement, see below, pages 59-60.

[13] B. R. White, *Association Records of the Particular Baptists of England, Wales and Ireland to 1660* (London: The Baptist Historical Society, 1974), 131. The wording of the address in the letter is tantalizing: "To the church of Christ of which our brethren John Spilsberie and William Kiffin are members..." Does this indicate that Spilsbury and Kiffin were co-pastors of the same church? If it does, it would require a re-evaluation of some of the early pastor-church relationships.

[14] *Ibid.*, 175.

[15] Greaves, "Spilsbury" in his and Zaller, eds., *Biographical Dictionary*, III, 194.

[16] Benjamin Coxe (d. 1688) and Hanserd Knollys immediately come to mind. Coxe, who wrote an appendix to the 1646 edition of the *First London Confession,* also authored a brief work refuting Pelagianism, *Some Mistaken Scriptures Sincerely Explained In answer to one infected with some Pelagian Errours. Written by Benjamin Cox when he was first Prisoner in Coventrie.*

principles and actions of the young assemblies. His two major works were written in response to the scruples of paedobaptist successionists and apologists, Seekers, and Arminians.

The first of these, *A Treatise Concerning the Lawfull Subject of Baptisme*[17] is a reply to objections raised by paedobaptists against the new practice of believer's baptism by immersion. It was not simply a theoretical work—it was a sober defense of principles so controversial that Spilsbury at one point admits "men [are] so incensed against me, as to seek my life, as some have done."[18] The pressing need for a theological apologetic was very real. The title page provides a summary of the contents of the book:

> The Baptizing of *Infants* confuted, and the Grounds to prove the same answered.
> The Covenant God made with *Abraham* and his seed handled, & how the same agrees with the Gentiles & their seed.

Now Published by the Author for the clearing of the truth. Licensed and entered according to Order (London, 1646), and participated with William Kiffin and Hanserd Knollys in the publication of *A Declaration Concerning The Publike Dispute which should have been in the Publike Meetinghouse of Alderman-Bury the 3d of this instant moneth of December, Concerning Infants Baptism,* (London, 1645). Knollys defended the Particular Baptists in the 1640s in his *A Moderate Answer unto Dr. Bastwicks Book, called Independency Not God's Ordinance* (London, 1645), and *The Shining of a Flaming fire in Zion. Or, A clear Answer unto 13 Exceptions, against the Grounds of New Baptism, (so called) in Mr. Saltmarsh his Book, Intituled, The Smoke in the Temple,* (London, 1646). On Coxe, see W. T. Whitley, "Benjamin Cox", *Transactions of the Baptist Historical Society,* 6 (1918), 50-59. On Knollys, see below, pages 39-62.

[17] J[ohn] S[pilsbury], *A Treatise Concerning the Lawfull Subject of Baptisme,* (London, 1643). *The Epistle to the Reader* is signed "John Spilsbury." B. R. White calls this "the first known publication on the subject by a Calvinist." See B. R. White, *The English Baptists of the Seventeenth Century* (London: The Baptist Historical Society, 1983), 71.

[18] *Treatise,* 43.

> The Baptisme administered by an Antichristian Power confuted, as no Ordinance of God, and the Grounds to prove the same answered.
>
> If either Church, or Ordinance be wanting, where they are to be found, and how recovered.
>
> The Covenant and not Baptisme formes the Church, and the manner how.
>
> There is no succession under the New Testament, but what is spiritually by faith in the Word of God.

The book naturally divides into two sections, the first being a response to several paedobaptist objections to the rejection of infant baptism, and the second in reply to the notion that the new baptism must of necessity be invalid because it is not in succession from the Apostles. It concludes with a brief ten-point confession of the author's faith.

In *The Epistle to the Reader*, Spilsbury sets the field for his arguments. Though his opponents "mock and deride" believer's baptism by immersion as "a new found way," he argues that, while it is in fact "a new found truth, in opposition to an old growne errour," it is the principle that the elements of worship must be regulated by the Word of God that has brought the new practice into the churches.[19]

The first portion of the work is of interest in that it gives evidence of the early lines of thinking which produced the rejection of infant baptism and recovery of believer's baptism by immersion. Spilsbury acknowledged, in the first paragraph of the body of his argument, that he was committed to the same covenantal theology as was held by the paedobaptists, but differed with them in that "the abolishing of the old Covenant or Testament, reached unto all that outward form of worship, under any type or shadow, by which the people professed their faith and obedience to God."[20] The paedobaptist argument failed to reckon with the true newness of the new covenant. All of the positive ordinances of the old covenant have passed away, and the church now has to do with the positive ordinances revealed in the new covenant.

---

[19] *Ibid.*, unnumbered page 2 of *The Epistle to the Reader*.
[20] *Ibid.*, 1 (sigla A3).

In the development of their doctrine of baptism as exemplified in Spilsbury, the Baptists insisted that the New Testament alone was the final basis for their practice. They believed that infant baptism was a remnant of Romanism, unwarranted by the clear teachings of Jesus and the Apostles. No line could be drawn from the practice of circumcision under the Old Covenant to include the children of believers in the initiatory rite of the New Covenant. This type of reasoning brought forth an immediate criticism from Stephen Marshall (c.1594-1655), a prominent member of the Westminster Assembly.[21] He asserted that the Baptist rejection of infant baptism by insistence on "an expresse institution or command in the New Testament" similarly enervated the theological basis for an ongoing Sabbath (Lord's Day) observance.[22] Both paedobaptism and Sabbath-keeping were, in Marshall's mind, dependent on theological continuity between the covenants. To reject one would *ipso facto* eliminate the other.

John Tombes (1603-1676) effectively responded to this objection by pointing out that the two were fundamentally different. Sabbath observance is moral, and thus a universal obligation for humanity. Baptism is of positive institution, and would not be known apart from Apostolic directive. That which is moral is a common duty for all, while that which is merely positive is ceremonial. In this way, the Baptists early in their history maintained the validity of the Lord's Day Sabbath while rejecting paedobaptism.[23] The Covenant of Grace remained in place, while the

---

[21] For Marshall, see Greaves and Zaller, eds., *Biographical Dictionary*, II, 217-219; William S. Barker, *Puritan Profiles: 54 Influential Puritans at the time when the Westminster Confession was written* (Fearn, Ross-shire: Christian Focus Publications, 1996), 120-127.

[22] *A Sermon of the Baptizing of Infants, Preached in the Abbey-Church at Westminster, at the Morning Lecture, appointed by the Honorable House of Commons* (London: Richard Cotes, 1645), 6. Marshall calls this a "great mischiefe" implied in Baptist theological reasoning.

[23] John Tombes, *Two Treatises and an Appendix to them Concerning Infant-Baptisme* (London: George Whittington, 1645), 27-31. This material is found in the second "Treatise," which is entitled "An Examen of the Sermon of Mr. Stephen Marshall, About Infant-Baptisme, in a Letter sent to him." Though Tombes was not himself part of the separate Baptist churches, he

positive institutions associated with its differing manifestations changed. Baptism was not symmetrically parallel with circumcision. While seeking to defend the validity of believer's baptism as practiced by the young churches against paedobaptist criticism that it was spurious because of the lack of a proper administrator in succession from the Apostles, Spilsbury wrote,

> By vertue of this union they [i.e. the local church] have with their head Christ, the body thus joyntly considered, hath the power & authoritie of Christ within her selfe, to chuse and make use of any one, or more of her members, as occasion offers, and authorises him or them to administer baptisme upon the whole body, and so upon themselves in the first place, as a part of the same. ...Where a thing is wanting, there must be of necessitie a beginning to reduce that thing againe into beeing.[24]

Spilsbury argued that the church had a right to appoint its own administrator(s) of baptism, who were thus authorized to restore the ordinance without prior baptism. In the second edition of the book (1652), he altered his language and expanded the defense by arguing that approved preachers, though themselves at first unbaptized, may administer the ordinance to others. Their warrant for so doing does not depend on succession from the Apostles, but from Scripture:

---

spoke of their position saying, "For that which is naturall or morall in worship, they [i.e. the Particular Baptists] allow an institution or command in the old Testament as obligatory to Christians, and such doe they conceive a Sabbath to be, as being of the Law of nature, that outward worship being due to God, dayes are due to God to that end, and therefore even in *Paradise*, appointed from the creation; and in all nations, in all ages observed: enough to prove so much to be of the Law of nature, and therefore the fourth Commandment justly put amongst the Morals" (*ibid.*, 28, emphasis his). Tombes should technically be designated an antipaedobaptist. While he was the major seventeenth-century polemicist for the practice of believer's baptism, he also believed in a national church and never severed his relationship to it. On Tombes, see Greaves and Zaller, eds., *Biographical Dictionary*, III, 245-46.
    [24] *Ibid.*, 38.

If any object, How can such receive others into the Gospel order, that never were in it themselves?

The answer is, where there is a beginning, some must be first, and our obedience to God depends only upon his word, that gives being to all order of worship, and the Gospel order once instituted stands firm for ever unalterable, for all that believe to obey and submit themselves thereunto, by a practical profession of the same, 2 Tim. 3:15, 16, 17. Rev. 22.18, 19. Mat. 28.19, 20.[25]

For Spilsbury, the lack of an administrator in succession from the Apostles was no difficulty. Scripture provides the warrant for the recovery of the lost ordinance. His words could not be more plain:

The Scriptures remaining in the place of the Apostles for us to have recourse unto, and serve as the mouth of Christ to all believers, as the Apostles did before they were written, Mat. 28.20. 2 Pet. 1.19, 20, 21. Rom. 10.6, 7, 8. And as the people of old conferred with the Prophets and Apostles about their great affairs, so have the Lords people now Moses and the Prophets, Christ and his Apostles in their writings, as Luk. 16.29, 30, 31. Which are to us with the spirit of life in them as effectual, as their personal presence, if not more, as Joh. 6.62, 63. 2 Pet. 1.18, 19. Rev. 11.3. 5.11. And thus all succession from the beginning came to Christ, and from Christ to the Apostles, and from them to the Scriptures, which are the headspring of all to us, so that, all succession now is onely spiritual, according to faith, and follows not the personal succession of any, but onely the word, that gives being to all order and ordinances that are of God.[26]

---

[25] John Spilsbury, *A Treatise Concerning the Lawfull Subject of Baptism.* (2nd ed. corrected and enlarged by the Author; London: Henry Hills, 1652), 63.

[26] *Ibid.*, 67.

The possession of the Scriptures is akin to the personal presence of Christ and the Apostles, and provides a sufficient basis upon which the recovery of baptism may proceed. When it, or any other ordinance has been lost, the church has the authority to turn to the Scriptures and institute that which is commanded there. Anything more is superfluous, unnecessary, and goes beyond Scripture. The "gospel order" was established by Christ and the Apostles, and that establishment is sufficient for re-institution.

This idea is closely related to Spilsbury's view of the role of a covenant in the formation of a church. In 1643, he argued that a covenant was the initiating document of a church. It preceded baptism, and enchurched those who committed themselves to it. Basing his argument on an analogy with the priority of the covenant of grace, which was the first "forme" God used to bring his people into relationship with himself, Spilsbury sought to demonstrate that the same type of form was necessary when people join together as a church. He said, "the covenant is the forme."[27]

Spilsbury was attempting to exonerate himself and the other new Baptist assemblies from the allegation that their baptism was a novelty and a nullity. His opponents charged that the recovery of believer's baptism by immersion was invalid, as it implied that the unbaptized, of necessity, must have been the administrators at the time of recovery, an unthinkable condition according to their presuppositions. Spilsbury's retort was that the church had temporal priority over baptism, and being in existence, could appoint some of its own, though unbaptized, as proper administrators of the ordinance. "The covenant and not baptism formes the church."[28] In this way, he argued that the gathered assembly had, in itself, sufficient authority to recover a lost ordinance apart from any kind of succession.

---

[27] *Treatise* (1643), 41.
[28] This phrase was used on the title page as a summary of one of the "particulars" addressed in the book. See *Treatise* (1643), 40-43.

The second of Spilsbury's works, *God's Ordinance, The Saints Priviledge*,[29] is a combination of two essays. The first attempts to prove, as its subtitle indicates, *The Saints Interest by Christ in all Priviledges of Grace; Wherein their right to the use of Baptisme, and the Lord's Supper, even now during the reigne of Antichrist, is cleared, and the objections to those that oppose the same, are answered.* This treatise is evidently an attempt to answer the objections of the so-called Seekers to the re-institution of baptism by immersion. They were an unorganized, but nevertheless influential, group, who argued that the ordinances, and even the true church, were lost during the ascendancy of Rome and its apostasy. In order for the church and its ordinances to be valid, there must be a genuine apostolic succession, but this was interrupted during "the apostasy" and thus there was no longer a true church on the earth. Those who loved the truth should seek after its restoration, which would only come with a new Pentecost, and living Apostles.[30]

The Seekers had a certain amount of success in attracting converts to their views from out of the Baptist churches.[31] Their position was in some ways similar to the paedobaptist argument: a lineal succession is necessary in order for an ordinance to be true and valid. The difference is that the paedobaptists were willing to argue that there was an uninterrupted succession, though admittedly through a corrupt church, while the Seekers replied that the corruptions were so great the succession was lost. The Baptists were caught in the middle. They had no succession—believer's baptism by immersion had only just been re-instituted in

---

[29] *God's Ordinance, The Saints Priviledge* (London: M. Simmons for Benjamin Allen, 1646).

[30] See Michael Watts, *The Dissenters* (Oxford: Oxford University Press, 1978), I, 185; T. L. Underwood, *Primitivism, Radicalism, and the Lamb's War: The Baptist-Quaker Conflict in Seventeenth-Century England* (Oxford: Oxford University Press, 1997), 13-14.

[31] Tolmie states that the paedobaptist successionist arguments contributed to the development of Seeker views, and eventually "wrecked" one of the original Particular Baptist congregations, namely the one organized under Richard Blunt (*Triumph of the Saints*, 54). Watts notes that George Fox was successful in cultivating some "shattered Baptists" into his growing movement of Quakers (*Dissenters*, I, 204).

January, 1642[32]—and yet they were convinced that their actions were right and proper. Spilsbury's *God's Ordinance* was an attempt to reply to the Seeker polemic.
   Spilsbury states,

> I present to thy view the subject I deale upon, endeavouring to maintaine the right & priviledges purchased by Christ, and freely given to all that believe in him for salvation, against such as oppose the same: who under pretence of seeking the truth, doe by cunning and craftie enquiries undermine the same, and (as they of old did) overthrow the faith of some: who deny unto such as do believe in Jesus Christ for eternall life, Church fellowship and communion with Christ in his Ordinances of the new Testament, for want (as they say) of a Ministry with power from God to call and fit a people for Ordinances, and to administer the same.[33]

The argument of the essay is built upon six particulars. The first is an assertion of the foundational nature of the apostolic ministry. They were the eye-witnesses of Christ's ministry, responsible "to disannul and make voyd" the positive institutions of the old covenant, and "to set up and establish another way of worship in the place thereof." They were "layers of the foundation, and the ministeriall instituters of the whole state and order of Christ's Church to be observed to the end of the world." They left a record in the "holy Scriptures of the new Testament...by which all both persons and actions shall be tryed and judged." Because a foundation is only laid once, there are no more "instituters or beginners" of the work, the obligation of all now being "to learn their way, and to walk in the same."[34] While the Seekers argued that the apostasy broke any succession from the apostles, and thus a new Pentecost was required, Spilsbury countered that "the Church, Ministery, and

---

[32] See James M. Renihan, "An Examination of the Possible Influence of Menno Simons' *Foundation Book* upon the Particular Baptist Confession of 1644", *American Baptist Quarterly*, 15, No. 3 (September 1996), 191-95.
[33] *God's Ordinance*, unnumbered page 3 of "To the Christian reader."
[34] *Ibid.*, 2-3.

Ordinances, are not lost to the Scriptures, the Spirit, and faith, but onely to the world."[35]

The second argument turns to the Scriptures, and asserts that in them Christ has left an "absolute rule" by which "to know such as are sent of God to the work of the Ministery." This is simply the token of God's blessing on preachers who bring the gospel to lost men, see conversions under their preaching ministry, and gather these new believers into church order according to the Scriptural pattern. Nothing extraordinary is necessary beyond this validation. The Scriptures are a sufficient "rule of truth."[36]

Spilsbury's third argument is so basic that he acknowledges that it is self-evident: there is still, in spite of the apostasy, true salvation for all who believe. But the obvious nature of this fact belies its importance. If there is still genuine salvation, then there must be genuine instruments who are able to bring this message of salvation to individuals, hence there must be a genuine ministry remaining in the world. True "preaching the Gospel is now afoote." Since preaching itself is an ordinance, the door is opened for the use of other ordinances as well.[37]

The fourth argument is also basic. Spilsbury asserts that there is no time in which "man is freed from obedience to the Scriptures since the new testament came in force." The gospel must be believed, and all of its attendant obligations obeyed, in every age. This obviously includes the ordinances of Baptism and the Supper. The abiding authority of the Word of God requires believing obedience to all of its continuing commands.[38]

Next, Spilsbury is concerned to demonstrate that the New Testament scriptures are "equall with, if not above, the authoritie of the old Testament." Once this is demonstrated and granted, he is able to contend that there is a universal obligation to submit to the Gospel contained in them,

---

[35] *Ibid.*, 6.
[36] *Ibid.*, 7-18.
[37] *Ibid.*, 18-22.
[38] *Ibid.*, 22-23. This is the briefest of the six principles.

and thus to all of its attendant duties. All men and nations are to submit to the rule of Christ expressed in Scripture.[39]

Finally, the author declares that Christ requires a public confession from all those who believe in him. This is to be a clear acknowledgment of his lordship and his offices, a professed subjection to Jesus Christ. He states: "The Rule of which professed subjection and confession, is the instituted order and administration of Christs Testament, for no other confession doth he approve of ... This confession doth Christ therefore require of such as believe in him, and ownes no believing unto salvation in his new Testament... where this is refused." Of course, this confession involves submission to the ordinances of the New Testament. To refuse to observe them is "to pull Christs scepter out of his hand, his crowne from his head, and himselfe from the throne."[40]

Together, these six principles form a powerful argument against the Seeker view. A true church, a true ministry, and true ordinances were still in existence in the world, without succession from the apostles. The foundation of Christ and the apostles, and the abiding obligation to obey Scripture provide a sufficient basis upon which to build the Baptist practices.

The latter portion of *God's Ordinance* is subtitled *The peculiar Interest of the Elect in Christ, and his saving Grace: Wherein it is proved that Christ hath not presented to his Fathers justice a satisfaction for the sinnes of all men; but only for the sinnes of those that doe, or shall believe in him; which are his Elect onely: And the objections of those that maintaine the contrary, are also answered.*[41] It is an explication of the doctrine of definite atonement, most likely issued in reply to the General Baptist Henry Denne's 1646 book *The Dragnet of the Kingdom of Heaven, or Christ's Drawing all Men.* Spilsbury explicitly mentions Denne's book on page 46, speaking of him as an "adversary." In all probability, Spilsbury (and Coxe) were very concerned that no one identify their churches with the Arminian views being promulgated by

---

[39] *Ibid.*, 23-26.

[40] *Ibid.*, 27-38.

[41] According to the title page, the second part of the book was "transcribed, and somewhat enlarged, by Benjamin Coxe."

the General Baptists. A casual observer might have noticed a resemblance because of the common view of baptism, while missing the more profound theological differences separating the two parties. By publishing this work, they could ensure that their orthodoxy would not be questioned.

The doctrine of Christ's particular redemption rests on three propositions: (1) Christ has not by his death taken away the sins of all men, for many are still under the wrath of God, only believers being free from it; (2) Christ did not intend by his death to save all men, but only the elect; and (3) Christ has not "presented to his Fathers justice a satisfaction for the sinnes of all men; but onely for the sinnes of those that doe, or shall believe in him."[42] After establishing these three propositions, a lengthy series of objections arising (mostly) from specific texts are handled and answered. Throughout this work Spilsbury maintains that the opposite view "brings forth evil fruits" such as a denial of divine predestination, the robbing of God's glory in his special love and mercy to "his chosen ones," the robbing of God's people of assurance of perseverance and thus of salvation, and "holds forth God as making a shew of being equally loving to all, when indeed in his purpose he is not so."[43] There can be no doubt concerning the Calvinism of Spilsbury and the early Particular Baptists.

These treatises reflect Spilsbury's attempt to position the Particular Baptists as over against three distinct groups: the paedobaptists, the Seekers, and the General Baptists. The first replies to the successionist arguments proposed by men such as Praisegod Barbone (c.1596-1679); the second to the objections raised by those who argued that lost ordinances could not be restored apart from living apostles; and in its latter half is an attempt to distance the Particular Baptists from their Arminian counterparts.

---

[42] *Ibid.*, 39.
[43] *Ibid.*, 80.

The influence of John Spilsbury

At the end of the twentieth century, John Spilsbury's name is not so generally well known as his contemporaries William Kiffin and Hanserd Knollys. But in his own day, he was held in high esteem both within and without the Particular Baptist movement. It is no exaggeration to assert that his personal leadership, as well as his written treatises gave substance and direction to the developing churches.

In terms of his involvement as a leader among the assemblies, he is clearly identified with the major confession of his era, the *First London Confession of Faith*, and with both the London and Abingdon Associations. He was known to the government of the day, and considered sufficiently important to be asked to represent their interests in Ireland. Even after the return from exile of Charles II, Spilsbury is involved in the attempt to distance the Baptists from rebels and to assure the King of their loyalty.

His two major publications addressed some of the most pressing issues facing the new churches. As the author of the first Calvinistic Baptist defense of believer's baptism, Spilsbury provides important clues concerning the theological background against which this new practice was understood by its adherents. His attempts to reply to charges from the paedobaptist successionists as well as Seeker objections provided the churches with important polemics and apologetics for the contemporary scene. In addition, his concern to reject publicly the Arminian views of the General Baptists serves to underscore the essential unity that these churches shared with the broader Independent/Congregational church movement.

In these ways, John Spilsbury was indeed a pioneer among the Particular Baptists. His leadership provided an important contribution to their developing movement, and laid down a foundation upon which many modern churches are still building.

Hopwood Sc.

Hanserd Knollys

Ob.t 1691.

From a rare Print.

HANSERD KNOLLYS (c.1598-1691)

Barry H. Howson

Hanserd Knollys was born at Cawkwell, just south of Louth in Lincolnshire, about the year 1598.[1] His father, Richard Knollys, was probably "the resident clergy man of the parish," a God-fearing man but most likely not a Puritan.[2] Up to the age of ten Hanserd was home-schooled and later briefly attended Grimsby free school.[3] When he was fourteen years old his father was appointed the Anglican rector of Scartho near Grimsby. Consequently, the family moved to Scartho, not too far from Cawkwell.[4] Sometime afterwards he studied at Cambridge and, in particular, Catharine Hall, where such Puritans as John Arrowsmith (1602-1659) and Thomas Goodwin (1600-1680) attended at approximately the same time as he did.

During these early years Knollys had several experiences in his life that he later considered significant. One occurred at the age of six when he was rescued from drowning by his father.[5] Another had to do with his father's counsel against strong drink and the making of vows.[6] A third

---

[1] His birthdate is unknown. We know that he died on September 16, 1691 in his ninety-third year [*The Life and Death of that Old Disciple of Jesus Christ and Eminent Minister of the Gospel, Mr. Hanserd Knollys*, ed. William Kiffin (London: E. Huntington, 1812), 4, 7]. Henceforth, this book will be referred to in these notes as *Life*.

[2] James Culross, *Hanserd Knollys, "A Minister and Witness of Jesus Christ" 1598-1691* (London: Alexander and Shepheard, 1895), 2-3, 9.

[3] *Life*, 9.

[4] Culross, *Hanserd Knollys*, 9. The Record Office has recorded "Ricus Knolles R. 17 Feb., 11 Jacobi. Yearly value 40."

[5] *Life*, 8.

[6] *Ibid.*, 8-9.

involved a fight with his brother after which he felt convicted of sin before God and his father.[7] And a fourth occurred after hearing several sermons at Cambridge on a particular Lord's day when he became quite convinced of his sinful state. He tells us,

> I was much more convinced of my sinful condition, and that I was a child of wrath, without Christ, and grace, &c. which work of conviction remained upon me above one year; under which I was filled with great horror, fears of hell, sore buffettings and temptations of the devil, and made to possess the sins of my youth: but yet I prayed daily, heard all the godly ministers I could, read and searched the holy scriptures, read good books, got acquainted with gracious christians then called Puritans, kept several days of fasting and prayer alone, wherein I did humble my soul for my sin, and begged pardon and grace of God for Christ's sake; grew strict in performing holy duties and in reformation of my own life, examining myself every night, confessing my sins and mourning for them, and had a great zeal for God, and indignation against actual sins, both committed by myself and others.[8]

After he had taken his degree at Cambridge he was appointed Master of Gainsborough Free school. While in Gainsborough he became aquainted with an elderly, pious widow who helped him in the Christian walk and put him in touch with a Nonconformist who held a conventicle in his own house. Knollys often attended the meetings and spent valuable time with this man.[9]

After a few years Knollys left Gainsborough and on March 30, 1629, he became a pensioner at Catharine Hall, Cambridge, with a view to ordination in the Church of England. During his time at the Hall he was under the tutelage of the influential Puritan Richard Sibbes (1577-1635). After only three months Knollys was ordained deacon and the following day ordained a presbyter of the Church of England by the bishop of

---

[7] *Ibid.*, 9-10.
[8] *Ibid.*, 10-11.
[9] *Ibid.*, 12; Culross, *Hanserd Knollys*, 12-13.

Peterborough, Thomas Dove (1555-1630).[10] Two years later the bishop of Lincoln gave Knollys a small living at Humberston, near his father's parish in Scartho.[11]

It was during his time at Humberston that he witnessed an unusual act of God in the life of a widow who appeared to be close to death. She had lain speechless for two or three days when Knollys visited her in her home. While he was with her, the "devil set upon me with a violent suggestion, that the scriptures are not the word of God." "Satan, thou art a liar," he responded, "a deceiver, and a false accuser. The holy scriptures are the word of God, and the scriptures of truth; and seeing thou hast often tempted me in this kind, and now dost assault me again, that I may for ever silence thee thou wicked and lying devil, I will trust in God, and act faith in the name of Christ in that very word of his truth which thou hast now suggested."[12] Knollys then went to the woman's bedside and prayed for her healing in order that the devil might be revealed to be a liar. While he was praying she began to recover and eventually was completely restored. According to Knollys, he was never tempted by the devil on that issue again.

In 1631 Knollys married Anne Cheney, a woman ten years younger than himself, the daughter of a John Cheney, Esq. In Knollys' words, she was "a holy, discreet woman, and a meet help for me in the ways of her household, and also in the way of holiness."[13] Not long after his marriage Knollys became convinced that some of the elements of Anglican worship—things such as wearing a surplice, the use of the cross in baptism, and indiscriminate admission of all and sundry to the Lord's Supper—were sinful. He thus resigned his living but was permitted for several years to continue preaching.

---

[10] *Life*, 11; Culross, *Hanserd Knollys*, 13. Knollys writes, "[I] preached above sixteen sermons before I was ordained, by way of trial of my ability for that great work of the ministry" (*Life*, 11-12). He was ordained deacon on June 29. It should be noted that by his own admission he was as yet to experience the saving work of God in his life.

[11] *Life*, 12. He preached twice on Sunday and once every feast day.

[12] *Ibid.*, 13-14.

[13] *Ibid.*, 16; Culross, *Hanserd Knollys*, 14.

Subsequently, he became convinced that his ordination itself was invalid and that he "had not received any seal from Christ of [his] ministry; for though many had been reformed and moralized, yet [he] knew not that [he] had been instrumental to convert any souls to God." He was determined not to preach anymore "until [he] had a clear call and commission from Christ to preach the gospel."[14] He began to pray "day and night" for several weeks, pleading "that Christ would count me worthy, and put me into the ministry." After a time of prayer one day in the woods at Anderby, Lincolnshire, he found his pleas were answered while he was walking home engaged in meditation. He neither heard an audible voice nor saw a visible form, but the following was "plainly and articulately spoken" to his heart and mind: "Go to Mr. Wheelwright, and he shall tell thee, and shew thee how to glorify God in the ministry."

The very next morning he went to see John Wheelwright (c.1592-1679),[15] a Puritan minister who had just moved to a village three miles from Humberston. After Wheelwright had asked Knollys some penetrating questions, he told Knollys plainly that he was building his "soul upon a covenant of works, and was a stranger to the covenant of grace." This conversation proved to be a major turning-point in Knollys' life. As he later recorded, Wheelwright had exposed his attempt to seek "righteousness as it were by the works of the law." After a few days of intense soul-struggle, Knollys experienced what he described as "joy and

---

[14] *Life*, 17.

[15] John Wheelwright, was ordained in 1619, and was vicar of Bilsby, Lincolnshire, from 1623 to 1633. He was silenced for his nonconformity and lived privately in Lincoln for three years. He then sailed to Boston, Massachusetts, arriving in May 1636. A year and a half later (November 1637) he was banished from Massachusetts for Antinomianism. His second wife was the sister of the husband of Anne Hutchinson (1591-1643), the key figure in the Antinomian controversy in New England in the 1630s. Wheelwright appears to have gotten into trouble along with her on this issue. However, he was reconciled to the pastoral leadership of the New England churches in May 1644 and later became the minister at Hampton, New Hampshire, where he served until his death [B. R. White, *Hanserd Knollys and Radical Dissent in the 17th Century* (London: Dr. Williams's Trust, 1977), 7, 25].

peace in believing." For the next three or four years Knollys preached in a number of Lincolnshire villages and knew the blessing of the Lord on his preaching, "whereby very many sinners were converted and many believers were established in the faith."[16]

In 1633 the situation worsened for the Puritans in England with the ascension of William Laud (1573-1645) to the Archbishopric of Canterbury. Laud aggressively pursued a policy of conformity to Anglican worship for all citizens. He left no room for dissent and persecuted any who dared to defy him. Among those arrested at this time was Knollys. While he was preaching in Lincolnshire in 1636 he was arrested on a warrant from the Court of High Commission. Knollys managed, though, to convince the man who issued the warrant to let him go. With his family Knollys made his way to London and from there to Boston, Massachusetts. The voyage across the Atlantic took twelve weeks and Knollys and his wife suffered much hardship, including the loss of their only child. They probably arrived in Boston in the summer of 1638.

Meanwhile, Knollys' former mentor, John Wheelwright, who had earlier made his way over to New England, had become involved in the Antinomian controversy surrounding the views of Anne Hutchinson, and was consequently banished from the plantation for Antinomianism.[17] On Knollys' arrival the magistrates were informed by the ministers that Knollys was also an Antinomian.[18] Before any action could be taken

---

[16] *Life*, 26. During these years he preached at Anderby, Fulletby, and at Wainfleet All Saints.

[17] *Ibid.*, 26-27; White, *Hanserd Knollys and Radical Dissent*, 6. Wheelwright was banished in November 1637 and Hutchinson was excommunicated in March 1638. For a historical account of this controversey see David D. Hall, *The Antinomian Controversy, 1636-1638: A Documentary History* (Middletown, Connecticut: Wesleyan University Press, 1968). For a detailed theological account of this controversy see William K.B. Stoever, *A Faire and Easie Way to Heaven* (Middletown, Connecticut: Wesleyan University Press, 1978).

[18] John Winthrop (1588-1649), the Governor of Massachusetts Bay Colony, states that Knollys was rejected "for holding some of Mrs Hutchinson's opinions" [*Winthrop's Journal*, ed. James Kendall Hosmer

against him, however, he was asked to come to Piscattuah (now Dover, New Hampshire) to preach. He formed a church there and ministered in it until September 1641 when he returned to England to care for his aged father. Knollys, his wife and their three-year-old child arrived in London on December 24, 1641, in the midst of the struggle between King and Parliament that would lead to the outbreak of the Civil War the following year. Upon his return to England Knollys took up teaching in order to provide for his family—first, by teaching as a schoolmaster on Great Tower Hill and then as Master of Mary-Axe free school.[19]

When the Civil War began, his sympathies were with the Parliamentary cause. He left off teaching and joined the army, preaching regularly to the common soldiers. However, he soon became disenchanted with the commanders who "sought their own things, more than the cause of God and his people, breaking their vows and solemn engagements," and so he eventually quit the army.[20] Knollys thus returned to London to continue his teaching.

It was during this time after his return to London that Knollys began to seriously question infant baptism and consider that only believers were the proper recipients of this ordinance. In January 1644 he told Henry Jessey—Knollys was regularly worshipping with Jessey's congregation—that he was not prepared to have his child baptized and requested that some meetings take place that "they [the church] might satisfye him, or he rectify them if amiss herein." Out of the discussion that ensued a couple of Particular Baptist churches were formed, one led by Knollys and one by William Kiffin.[21] In 1645 Knollys' congregation

---

(New York: Charles Scribner's Sons, 1908), I, 295]. See also *ibid.*, I, 309, 328; II, 27-28.

[19] *Life*, 30. At the latter school he taught 140 day-students and 16 boarders.

[20] *Ibid.*, p. 30. Thomas Edwards (1599-1647), the Presbyterian divine, in his *Gangraena* says Knollys "wrought a great deal of mischief" in the army.

[21] For Kiffin, see below, pages 65-77. These churches would have been founded between March 17, 1644 and June 29, 1645. On June 29, 1645, Knollys baptized Henry Jessey. Knollys probably came to Baptist convictions in 1644. He did not sign the *First London Confession of Faith* published in that same year.

was meeting next door to St. Helen's Church where it was reported by some neighbours that as many as a thousand attended his services. He was eventually turned out of there by the landlord and moved to Finsbury Fields. During his years as pastor of this church he says,

> I received from the church always according to their ability, most of the members of the church being poor; but I coveted no man's gold nor silver, but chose rather to labour, knowing, 'It is more blessed to give than to receive:' nor did I neglect the whole of my duty as a pastor, but preached two or three times in the week, and visited the members of the church from house to house, especially when they were sick.[22]

During the year of 1645, Knollys answered John Bastwick's *Independency not God's Ordinance* with *A Moderate Answer unto Dr Bastwicks book.* In this work he denied Bastwick's assertion that Scripture taught a Presbyterian, synodical church government, and asserted instead that it taught a Congregational, independent one. In addition, Knollys maintained that people were to be brought into membership of a local church upon their profession of faith, repentance and baptism as in the Apostles' days. In December Knollys, in company with Benjamin Coxe and William Kiffin, published *A Declaration concerning the Publicke Dispute... concerning Infant Baptism.* A debate had been arranged between the three Baptists and some Presbyterians, including Edmund Calamy, Sr. (1600-1666), for December 3 on the subject of baptism. However, it was cancelled by the Lord Mayor for fear that there might be violence. Unable to state their position by means of a public discussion, the Baptists turned to the medium of print to make their views more widely known.

The following year Knollys published two more works in defence of the Baptist cause.[23] The first was the second edition of the *First London*

---

[22] *Life*, 34-35.

[23] During this year he was also imprisoned in Ipswich (White, *Hanserd Knollys and Radical Dissent*, 13) and wrote a foreword to Robert Garner's

Confession of Faith. This second edition contained a few changes that were the result of criticism made by Presbyterians like Daniel Featley (1582-1645).[24] Later that year *An Appendix to a Confession of Faith* was attached to this *Confession.* The author of the *Appendix* was Benjamin Coxe but the internal evidence shows that the entire group of men who signed the revised *Confession,* including Knollys, agreed with it.[25] It espoused a High Calvinist soteriology and a closed communion ecclesiology. The other work that Knollys published in the course of this year was *The Shining of a Flaming fire in Zion* in response to *The Smoke in the Temple* by John Saltmarsh (d.1647) which totally denied the need for the ordinances of baptism and the Lord's Supper.[26] In this work Knollys emphasized that the church after the Apostles was to continue in the practice of the ordinances of Christ. He also argued that only those who had the gifts of the Spirit to preach the gospel, and who were approved by the church, were permitted to administer the ordinances of baptism and the Lord's Supper.

All of his life Knollys kept up the study of the original languages of the Scriptures, and in 1648 he published his first grammar entitled, *The rudiments of Hebrew grammar in English.* He would eventually produce seven more grammatical tools to help former students of his, now teachers themselves, review what they had been taught.[27]

Mysteries Unvailed that attacked Arminian teaching. A High Calvinistic soteriology is taught in the latter.

[24] See W. L. Lumpkin, *Baptist Confessions of Faith* (Philadelphia: Judson Press, 1959), particularly, 165, 166, 167.

[25] For this *Appendix* see E. B. Underhill, *Confessions of Faith and other Public Documents illustrative of the history of Baptist Churches of England in the 17th Century* (London: Haddon, Brothers, and Co., 1854), 49-60.

[26] Saltmarsh, though not a Seeker, took the position of a Seeker in his argument against the Baptists.

[27] *Grammaticae Graecae compendium* (1664), *Grammaticae Latinae compendium* (1664), *Grammaticae Latinae, Graecae, & Hebaicae* (1665), *Linguae Hebricae delineatio* (1664), *Rhetoricae adumbratio* (1663), *Radices simplicium vocum* (1664), and *Radices Hebraicae omnes* (1664). In the first General Assembly of Particular Baptists, which took place in London in 1689, a central fund was to be collected so that, among other things,

In the 1640s and 1650s the Particular Baptists experienced tremendous growth as they spread their message far beyond the limits of London. Knollys played a key role in this expansion. For example, in 1649 Kiffin and Knollys were authorized by Parliament to go to Ipswich to preach. The early 1650s found him in Wales, travelling the countryside as an evangelist appointed by the London churches. In the mid-1650s Knollys helped to organize a church in Cornwall.

It should also be noted that in these halcyon years of the 1650s Knollys was also deeply involved in civil affairs. For instance, he held the office of examiner of customs and excise under the Commonwealth at a salary of 120 pounds a year, but resigned in March 1653 "by reason of more beneficial employment calling him away."[28] Up until 1655 he was also employed as a clerk in the Navy, maintaining a register of the men employed on board ships as well as navy artificers in the port of London.[29] Then, Knollys engaged in politics when he felt it was necessary. In 1657 when Oliver Cromwell was offered the crown Knollys along with the Independent John Goodwin (*c*.1594-1665) and Calvinistic Baptists John Spilsbury and Henry Jessey petitioned him with the *Address of the Anabaptist Ministers in London, To the Lord Protector*, encouraging him not to take it.[30] They did not want a return to monarchial government, but were convinced that it would be in the greater interest of the Kingdom of God that England remain a republic.

Knollys did little writing in the 1650s. The only work he published during this decade was *An Exposition of the first chapter of the Song of Solomon* (1656). Based on various spoken messages, the chief concern

---

assistance might be given to for those who wanted to study Latin, Greek and Hebrew (White, *Hanserd Knollys and Radical Dissent*, 22-23). In addition, at the 1691 Assembly Knollys signed an epistle to the churches recommending the institution of a freewill offering, so "that godly young men whom God hath gifted, and who are approved of, may be instructed in the tongues wherein the Holy Scriptures were written" (Culross, *Hanserd Knollys*, 106). Knollys probably played a key role in initiating such recommendations.

[28] State Papers relating to the Navy (cited Culross, *Hanserd Knollys*, 75).

[29] *Ibid.*, p. 75.

[30] Underhill, *Confessions of Faith*, 335-338.

of the book was the communion between Christ and his church. But Knollys also touched on such things as the Lord's Supper and the Christian's relationship to the civil government. Concerning the latter he clearly teaches that the saints are only to use spiritual weapons in their warfare against the enemy. This clearly undermines the oft-made assertion that Knollys agreed with the Fifth Monarchy position of taking up arms against the government.[31]

After Oliver Cromwell died in 1658 and his son Richard stepped down from leadership, the crown was returned to Charles II in 1660. A number of Fifth Monarchists led by the Baptist Thomas Venner, believing the Lord's Coming was at hand, attempted an insurrection in London. It failed miserably and resulted in the arrest of four hundred people who were suspected of taking part in the uprising. Knollys was one of those imprisoned in Newgate for eighteen weeks because he "refused to take the oaths of allegiance and supremacy." He was released when a pardon was issued to celebrtate the king's coronation. This imprisonment was the foretaste of twenty-eight years of brutal persecution for all who dissented from the worship of the Church of England.

After Knollys was released from Newgate prison he preached with millenarians Henry Jessey and John Simpson (d.1662) at All Hallows Church, and then shortly after made his way to Holland and then to Germany with his wife and two children. Two or three years later he and his family returned to London, having sold all their goods to make the trip. He took up teaching in London again in order to provide for his family.

Little of his activities during the 1660s is known. We do know that during the London Plague of 1665 Knollys remained in the city to

---

[31] There were a number of people in Knollys' own congregation that signed the Anti-protectorate Fifth Monarchy manifesto of 1654 entitled *A Declaration of several of the churches of Christ*. Knollys was also good friends with Fifth Monarchists Henry Jessey and John Simpson.

minister to the suffering and bereaved.[32] We also know that on June 28, 1666, he and Edward Harrison (d.1673) were involved in the ordination of Thomas Patient (d.1666) as an elder in William Kiffin's congregation. And when Patient died Knollys helped to set apart Daniel Dyke (1617-1688) in the same church as a replacement for Patient.[33] Moreover, it was during these years that he published the first of six eschatological works. This first book, written in 1667, was entitled *Apocalytptical Mysteries*. In it he expounded the historicist view of the Book of Revelation, discussing the meaning of the seven trumpets and the seven vials, and the nature of Christ's coming kingdom.

A little more is known of Knollys' activities in the 1670s. On May 10, 1670, shortly after the passing of the Second Conventicle Act he was apprehended at a meeting in George Yard and incarcerated in the Compter at Bishopsgate. The jailer, though, proved to be well-disposed towards Knollys and he was allowed to preach twice a day to the prisoners.[34] During this decade Knollys' wife, two grand-children, three sons, and possibly another grandchild and a daughter-in-law, died. Moreover, he also fell seriously ill and thought he was dying. But he called for Kiffin and the Welsh Baptist leader Vavasor Powell (1617-1670) to pray over him and anoint him with oil according to James 5:14-15. As a result of this and the fervent prayers of others he recovered.[35] We also know that in 1672 he officiated at the marriage of Benjamin Keach to his second wife Susannah Partridge.[36]

Towards the end of this decade, in 1677, Knollys and the London Particular Baptists churches anonymously published a new confession of faith. It was made public in 1689 when William III (r.1688-1702) and Mary II (r.1688-1694) came to the throne and a measure of toleration was given to Dissenters in the Act of Toleration. At that time Knollys with over seventy other elders signed this *Confession* which was a Baptist revision of the Presbyterian *Westminster Confession of Faith*

---

[32] Culross, *Hanserd Knollys*, 92.
[33] White, *Hanserd Knollys and Radical Dissent*, 19.
[34] *Ibid.*, 20.
[35] *Ibid.*, 20.
[36] *Ibid.*, 20. On Keach, see below, pages 95-130.

and Congregationalist *Savoy Declaration*. It is known to history as the *Second London Confession of Faith*.[37] No doubt Knollys and others would have signed this *Confession* in 1677 but refrained from doing so because of persecution. In 1689 Knollys and Kiffin were the only Particular Baptist leaders who were a part of the movement in its early years to sign this *Confession* and the only two to sign both the *First* and *Second London Confessions*.

There is little material on the life of Knollys in the 1680s. He signed a foreword with Kiffin, Dyke, and Coxe, among others, for John Russell's book *A brief narrative of some considerable passages concerning the first gathering and further progress of a church of Christ in Gospel-order in Boston in New England*. Knollys and his fellow Baptists were seeking to encourage toleration for the Baptist cause in Boston. During the spring of 1684 Knollys was imprisoned again in Newgate for breaking the Conventicle Act. He was eighty-six at the time and remained there for sixteen months. And again he was allowed to preach daily to the prisoners "the things that concern the kingdom of God."[38] Four years later Knollys published his last and crowning work on eschatology, his *Exposition of the Book of the Revelation*. It was formed from messages he had preached to his congregation over the years.

In 1689 Knollys and other London Particular Baptist leaders sent out a letter calling for a general assembly of the churches to gather in September of that year. Two of the reasons given for calling this meeting were to address "the great neglect of the present ministry" and the "raising up of an honourable ministry for the time to come."[39] More than one hundred churches were represented with over one hundred and fifty messengers.

In his final years Knollys was embroiled in a controversy over congregational hymn-singing. Knollys' concern about this issue, however, had begun years before. In 1663 he penned a foreword to Katherine Sutton's *A Christian Womans Experiences of the glorious working of God's free grace*, in which he commends the singing of

---

[37] See Lumpkin, *Confessions of Faith*, 235-295.
[38] Culross, *Hanserd Knollys*, 100.
[39] White, *Hanserd Knollys and Radical Dissent*, 22.

hymns and spiritual songs along with the psalter as an ordinance of God's worship. Over the next number of years he contended for the singing of both hymns and psalms in the public worship of his congregation. Thus, when controversy over hymn-singing erupted among the London Baptist churches, Knollys quickly took the offensive with two books, both published in 1691: *An Answer to I.[saac] M.[arlow] "A brief discourse concerning singing in the public worship of God in the Gospel-Church"*, which is still extant, and *A small piece in defence of Singing ye Praises of God*, which is not.

In addition to this controversy Knollys also got embroiled in one over Antinomianism when he and twelve other ministers commended the publication of the complete sermons of Tobias Crisp (1600-1643). On the basis of these sermons, Crisp had been accused of Antinomianism in the 1640s. Samuel Crisp, his son, decided to republish these sermons in 1690.[40] Knollys died in the midst of the controversy.

During the last two years of his life Knollys was limited in what he could do, but he did attend the 1690 and 1691 General Assemblies of the Particular Baptists. Not long after the 1691 Assembly on September 19 he died in his ninety-third year. Like many of his fellow Particular Baptists, he was buried in Bunhill Fields, the burial ground for Dissenters in London. At his funeral, Thomas Harrison well summed up Knollys' character with these words.

> He walked with that caution, that his greatest Enemies had nothing against him, save only on the matter of his God; That holy Life which he lived, did command Reverence even from those who were Enemies to the holy Doctrine which he preached. He was a Preacher out of the Pulpit as well as in it... He had a great respect to Christ's New Commandment, which he gave to his Disciples, to love one another. He loved the Image of God wheresoever he saw it. He was not a man of a narrow and private, but of a large and

---

[40] The attribution of Antinomianism to Crisp is debatable. After Knollys died the other ministers who signed the commendation made known that their signatures were intended primarily to certify that the editor, Samuel Crisp, had correctly transcribed eight previously unpublished sermons.

publick spirit. The difference of his fellow Christians' Opinions from his, did not alienate his affections from them. He lov'd all his fellow Travellers, tho' they did not walk in the same particular path with himself... He chearfully went about suffering as well as preaching work. He was not unwilling to take up his cross and follow his Lord and Master in the Thorny road of Tribulation.

Knollys authored or co-authored over twenty-five books in his lifetime, most of which are extant.[41] They are a marvellous, and little-used, source to understand the thought of this early Baptist pioneer on a wide varitey of theological topics. In what follows, we will look at them with regard to two particular areas: Knollys' doctrine of salvation and his eschatology.

The doctrine of salvation

Knollys came into contact with Puritanism and thus Calvinism during his years at Catharine Hall in Cambridge. By the time he became a Baptist his Calvinistic soteriology, from which he never departed, was firmly established. Theologically, Knollys was a High Calvinist similar to other contemporary Puritans like John Owen (1616-1683) and Thomas Goodwin. His High Calvinism is most clearly seen in the two Baptist *Confessions* he signed in 1646[42] and 1689.[43] It is also seen in his

---

[41] There are three that are lost: *An essay of sacred rhetoric used by the Holy Spirit in scripture of truth* (1675); *Miscellanae sacra; or a New Method of considering so much of the history of the Apostles as is contained in Scripture* (1665); and *A small piece in defence of Singing ye Praises of God* (1691).

[42] Knollys signed the revised edition of the 1644 *Confession* in 1646.

[43] The 1644 and 1689 *Confessions* both teach that Christ died for the elect only (1644: Article 17, 21; 1689: Chapter 8.5, 11.4, 30.2). The 1689 *Confession* teaches that salvation for the elect comes by means of the active and passive righteousness of Christ (Chapter 8.4, 5). Both *Confessions* place predestination at the beginning where the doctrine of God is taught (1644: Article 3; 1689: Chapter 3.3-7). The 1689 *Confession* teaches that Adam's guilt was imputed to his descendants (Chapter 6.3). For a comparison of these

personal writings.[44] For instance, in 1646 concerning the atonement he stated, "Christ as a Saviour [was] made sinne, made a Curse and crucified to redeem his Elect from the Curse due to sinne."[45] Many years later, in 1681, he wrote that Christ has made full satisfaction for the sins of all whom the Father had given him to redeem.[46] And only three years before his death, he wrote that Christ will own the one who overcomes, "That he is one of the Election of Grace, whom God the Father gave unto his Son Jesus Christ, for whom Christ laid down his life; unto whom Christ hath given *Spiritual* life, and hath promised him Eternal life."[47] Later in the same book he states: "Christ by his precious blood obtained *eternal* Redemption for us, (not for all,) *Heb.* 9.12. for Gods elect; *that is*, Christ hath bought them."[48]

Two important questions concerning his soteriology need to be answered, though. Was Knollys an Antinomian[49] and was he a Hyper-Calvinist?[50] He was accused of being an Antinomian in the 1630s,

---

two *Confessions* on the atonement, see Barry Howson, "A Study of the 1644 and 1689 Particular Baptist Confessions of Faith" (Unpublished M.A. Thesis, McGill University, 1995), 68-71.

[44] It should be noted that Knollys' writings are primarily and passionately pastoral, and not strictly doctrinal works per se.

[45] *Christ Exalted: A Lost Sinner Sought; and saved by Christ: Gods people are an Holy people* (London: 1646), 23.

[46] *The World that now is, and the world that is to come* (London, 1681), 6, 7.

[47] *An exposition of the whole Book of Revelation* (London, 1689), 49.

[48] *Ibid.,* 76.

[49] Antinomians in England in the seventeenth century believed that though the moral law has a pedagogical use (convincing sinners of their sin and need of Christ) it has no place in the life of the believer who is not under the law but under grace. See Hugh J. Blair, "Antinomianism," in J. D. Douglas, ed., *The New International Dictionary of the Christian Church*, Revised Edition (Grand Rapids: Zondervan Publishing House, 1979), 48, and Gertrude Huehns, *Antinomianism in English History* (London: The Cresset Press, 1951), 37-148.

[50] Hyper-Calvinism is that teaching which went beyond High Calvinism and developed in England in the early part of the eighteenth century. The two

having been associated with John Wheelwright and implicated in the Hutchinson controversy in New England.[51] And he was accused of the same in the 1690s after signing the reprint of the sermons of the so-called Antinomian Tobias Crisp. Notwithstanding these allegations, there is no evidence at all in his writings that he was either a doctrinal or practical Antinomian. In fact, there is much evidence to the contrary.

It can be seen that Knollys was no doctrinal Antinomian from his sermon on Luke 19:10, where he addressed the subject of the law in the believer's life. Knollys declared that Christ saves sinners from sin, the law, Hell, and Satan's temptations.[52] Salvation from the law includes freedom from the ceremonies of the law, its penalties and curse, its school-mastership, and the use of the law as a means of righteousness.[53] Once freed from the law the believer now serves God under a new

---

doctrines of Hyper-Calvinists that distinguished them from High Calvinists were: (1) the gospel is not to be offered to the unregenerate until there is evidence of the regenerating grace of God working in them; and (2) only the elect are required to exercise evangelical repentance and saving faith in Christ when they hear the gospel message. Other doctrines taught by, or emphases of, the Hyper-Calvinists include eternal justification, eternal adoption and the eternal covenant of grace; little distinction between the revealed and secret will of God; and excessive emphasis on the doctrine of irresistible grace where the elect person is passive in conversion. Some of the factors that led to this development in the eighteenth century were the loss of High Calvinism in Presbyterianism after the Restoration in 1660; the Antinomian controversy of the 1690s; the effect of rationalism on the thought of High Calvinists which made their teaching go beyond the teaching of Scripture; and the emphasis, due to Enlightenment attacks on orthodoxy, of these Calvinists on the preservation and defence of the faith rather than on evangelism and conversion.

[51] As has already been noted (see above, page 43, n.18), John Winthrop states that Knollys was "rejected by us for holding some of Mrs. Hutchinson's opinions." For a history of the Antinomian Controversy, see Emery Battis, *Saints and Sectaries* (Chapel Hill: University of North Carolina Press, 1962), and David D. Hall, ed., *The Antinomian Controversy, 1636-1638: A Documentary History* (2nd ed.; Durham: Duke University Press, 1990).

[52] *Christ Exalted*, 21-25.

[53] *Ibid.*, 23-24.

schoolmaster, the Lord Jesus Christ. According to Knollys the difference between the old and new schoolmaster is not the moral duties but the power and wisdom to do them. He writes: "Moses in the Law commands his Disciples to do this, and forbeare that, but gives no power, nor communicates no [sic] skill to performe any thing: Christ commands his Disciples to do the same morall duties, and to forbeare the same evills, and with his Command he gives power, and wisedome, for he workes in us both to will and to do according to his good pleasure."[54] The Christian is taught by Christ to yield obedience to his Father's will and to serve him in newness of spirit. Moreover, though the Old Covenant of the law is now done away with and abolished, Knollys observes, "we do not hereby make voide the Law, but establish it, Rom. 3.31. For we say that we ought to yeeld obedience of Faith, in newnesse of spirit, and so fulfill the Royall law according to the Scripture, James 2.8....Neither are we without Law to God, but under the Law to Christ, 1 Cor. 9.21."[55]

Nor was Knollys a practical Antinomian. Throughout his writings and sermons he calls professing Christians to be holy and to live according to the will of God. For example, in his sermon on Ephesians 1:4, he states: "Those people, that are ungodly, unsanctified, are not the people of God, such may boast of their justification, but they deceive themselves, for God hath not justified unsanctified people, 1 Cor. 6.9, 10, 11."[56] Knollys' concern for believers to lead holy lives is also evident in his last major work, his commentary on Revelation. The difference between the true and false church according to Knollys is that the former is governed by Christ's "Institutions, Laws, and Ordinances."[57] In addition to these quotes we may add the example of his life. As is evident from the biographical section he sought to live a godly life and was known by others for it. Knollys was no practical Antinomian.

The second question has to do with whether or not Knollys was a Hyper-Calvinist. It has been suggested that his High Calvinistic

---

[54] *Ibid.*, 24.
[55] *Ibid.*, 24-25.
[56] *Ibid.*, 33.
[57] *Revelation*, 106.

soteriology was a precursor to the Hyper-Calvinism of the eighteenth-century Particular Baptists.[58] It is true that the High Calvinism of Knollys and the Particular Baptists of the seventeenth-century led to the Hyper-Calvinism of the next century. Certain factors, though, were necessary for that transition to take place.[59] Knollys and other seventeenth-century Particular Baptists were by no means Hyper-Calvinists in their theology and ministry. For example, in 1675 when Andrew Gifford Sr. (*c*.1641-1721) of the Pithay Baptist Church in Bristol asked the London Baptist pastors for advice concerning prayer by, and exhortation to, unconverted people, Knollys and others stated that all people are obligated to pray and fulfil whatever duties God calls them to do.[60] Knollys believed that all people are required to obey the commands of God, including that to believe in Christ. In a sermon on Colossians 3:11 he could plainly state, "This word of the gospel God will have preached to every creature in all parts of world, Mark 10.15. None are exempted or prohibited from hearing the gospel preached, but every one that hath an eare is required to heare, Revel. 2.7."[61]

Knollys also believed that the church ought to call all and sundry to repentance and faith in Christ. For example, commenting on Revelation 22:17 where the "Spirit and the bride say Come," Knollys writes: "The Church of God, and all converted persons, do invite all sorts of sinners, *especially*, thirsty sinners, without exception against any Persons, that are willing, and without any price, to take Christ freely, *Isa*. 55. 1, 2, 3."[62]

Moreover, Knollys did not teach eternal justification, a view characteristic of Hyper-Calvinism. When Knollys deals with the subject

---

[58] Michael A. G. Haykin, "Hanserd Knollys (*ca*. 1599-1691) on the Gifts of the Spirit", *Westminster Theological Journal*, 54 (1992), 100. Cp. Peter Toon, *Puritans and Calvinism* (Swengel, Pennsylvania: Reiner Publications, 1973), 77-83.

[59] See above, pages 53-54, note 50.

[60] The letter may be found in Joseph Ivimey, *A History of the English Baptists* (London, 1811), I, 416-420.

[61] *Christ Exalted*, 12.

[62] *Revelation*, 242-243.

of the sinner's conversion in his 1681 tract *The World that now is, and the world that is to Come*, he plainly states that the sinner is justified, adopted and sanctified when God works faith in his heart.[63] Knollys was no Hyper-Calvinist.

The doctrine of last things

The most that Knollys wrote on any one subject was on that of eschatology, the doctrine of last things. It is noteworthy that he did not begin to write on this topic until he was sixty-eight years old, and for the next twenty-four years of his life his interest was absorbed by this subject. In all he produced six treatises on it.

Knollys was typical of many seventeenth-century pastors who believed that God's work in history, especially in the final days, was vital sermonic material. He sincerely believed that the end was near and that his generation was living in the last days of the latter times.[64] While he was confident that no one knew the exact hour or day of Christ's return, the London Baptist was equally sure that certain signs would indicate the end was near. Of these signs the most vital were: the apostasy of professing believers; the growth of iniquity among the profane of the world; a great tribulation; and the gospel being preached throughout the earth to all of the nations.[65]

In 1667 Knollys felt confident enough about his end-time calculations that he reckoned there were only twenty-one years left before history would begin to wind down to the final judgment.[66] Knollys was certain that when the end comes three important things would transpire: mystical Babylon would fall;[67] the Ottoman Empire would be

---

[63] *World that now is*, I, 36.

[64] *Apocalyptical Mysteries* (London, 1667), "Preface."

[65] *World that now is*, I, 81ff, 92-94; *Revelation*, 135, 144.

[66] *Apocalyptical Mysteries*, I, 10. Other places that Knollys mentions 1688 are *Revelation*, 130, and *An Exposition of the Eleventh Chapter of the Revelation* (London, 1679), 13.

[67] *Revelation*, 149ff., 189.

destroyed;[68] and the Spirit would be poured out upon the Jewish people
and they would be restored to their land.[69]

For Knollys, like numerous other Protestant interpreters of Scripture
of his day, mystical Babylon was Papal Rome, the Papacy itself was the
Beast who comes out of the bottomless pit, the Church of Rome was the
Great Whore who rides the Beast, and the False Prophet was the Roman
Church's priesthood.[70] When the entire papal system fell, Christ would
come for his church, as a bridgroom for his bride, and set up a spiritual
kingdom on earth for a thousand years.[71] This coming would be
spiritual, and the saints who were then living on the earth would
experience it through the Spirit of Christ, but, Knollys believed, it would
not be a personal coming.[72] At the end of this millennial kingdom, when
the realms of this world have submitted to the rule of Christ, then Jesus
would return, visibly and personally, with all his of saints.[73] At this time
Satan would be finally defeated, the general resurrection of the dead and
the final judgment would take place, and the handing over of the
kingdom to God the Father and the creation of the new heavens and new
earth would transpire.[74]

These particulars of Knollys' post-millennial eschatology were not
peculiar for his time. Much of what he espoused was rooted in the
eschatology of divines like Thomas Brightman (1562-1607), Joseph
Mede (1586-1638) and Thomas Goodwin.[75] However, there are two
questions which need to be dealt with concerning Knollys' eschatology.
The first has to do with the time of his writing. Why did he write on this

---

[68] *Ibid.*, 196-197, 198; *Apocalyptical Mysteries*, II, 33-34.
[69] *World that now is*, II, 20, 43; *Revelation*, 197. Concerning the return to
the land, see *Apocalytical Mysteries*, II, 26-27.
[70] These are the four propositions asserted and proven in *Mystical Babylon
Unvailed* (London [?], 1679).
[71] *The Parable of the Kingdom of Heaven Expounded* (London, 1674), 85.
[72] *Ibid.*, 68.
[73] *Ibid.*, 75-77.
[74] *Revelation*, 225, *Parable*, 72.
[75] For an excellent study of English Protestant eschatology to 1660 from a
theological perspective see Bryan W. Ball, *A Great Expectation* (Leiden: E. J.
Brill, 1975).

subject at the end of his life when the eschatological fervour of the pre-Restoration days had somewhat diminished? While we do not have a definitive answer to this question, a couple of suggestions may be offered. First, Knollys believed the end was coming around 1688, and so, professors of faith in the midst of persecution and England in the grip of a state church needed to be warned and ready for the coming of Christ. If others were not as ready as in former days to believe, write, and preach that the end was near, Knollys felt compelled for the welfare of professing believers, and of England itself, to do so. Second, with the fear of Roman Catholicism re-entering the country through the religious predilections of the crown, Knollys felt it necessary to warn England and its people of the judgment of God if they did not repent.[76]

The second question concerns Knollys' links to the Fifth Monarchy movement. Was he a Fifth Monarchist? There are some reasons to think he may have been. In 1654, for instance, fourteen members of his church signed the Fifth Monarchist manifesto *A declaration of several churches of Christ*. He also moved in the same circles as such well-known Fifth Monarchy men as Henry Jessey and John Simpson.[77] He not only believed in an earthly millennium,[78] but, based on the vision of the five kingdoms in Daniel 2, he taught that the fifth monarchy would begin in the final years of the fourth monarchy and that during the millennium the saints will put down by force those who will not submit to Christ's rule.[79]

Nevertheless, the evidence does not lead us to believe he was a Fifth Monarchist in practice or in doctrine. First of all, there is no overt

----

[76] According to Knollys God would judge England by re-establishing Catholicism in the land. It should be noted that *Mystical Babylon Unvailed* and *An Exposition of the Eleventh Chapter of the Revelation* were written in the aftermath of the Popish Plot scare. Moreover, Knollys sincerely believed England would hold a special place in the plan of God to the end of history.

[77] White, *Hanserd Knollys and Radical Dissent*, 17.

[78] Though, it should be noted that this is not exceptional. Many who were not Fifth Monarchists believed in such a millennium. See Ball, *Great Expectation, passim*.

[79] *Apocalyptical Mysteries*, III, 14, 16-18.

evidence that he espoused Fifth Monarchist views. Second, there is evidence that he flatly rejected one of their chief teachings, namely, that the millennial kingdom will be inaugurated by physical force before Christ comes. In his commentary on Revelation he plainly tells his readers that the "Ecclesiastical Power ordained by Christ and given to his Ministers, is not Magisterial, but Ministerial; not the Power of the Sword but of the Word."[80] In his *An Exposition of the first chapter of the Song of Solomon* (1656), written at a time when Fifth Monarchist views were being aired throughout Great Britain, Knollys makes some comments that clearly contradict the distinctive tenets of the Fifth Monarchists. With what weapons will the saints fight during the final conflict between Christ and his enemies? Through those of the Spirit, Knollys states— prayer and preaching:

> The spirit of faith in prayers and prophecyings of the Saints, will certainly effect the ruin and utter destruction of all their Enemies Zac. 4.6, 7. ... O ye Saints! Pray in faith, and prophesie in faith by the Spirit of the Lord, and your Enemies will fall; ye shall not need to fight, for Christs Enemies and yours will every one help to destroy another. ...The worm Jacob is Christs Battle-Axe, Jer. 51.20. whereby he will destroy kingdomes, his praying Saints, and prophesying Servants; are the Lords company of Horses, though now in Pharoah's Chariot, under the powers of the Earth, who lord it over the Lords Heritage.[81]

The significance of Hanserd Knollys

Knollys was an important figure in the British Particular Baptist community for the first fifty years of its existence, giving it both doctrinal and pastoral stability. He not only signed its first two

---

[80] *Revelation*, 129.
[81] *An Exposition of the first chapter of the Song of Solomon* (London, 1656), 44-45.

Confessions and gave it wise counsel and leadership, but he also faithfully pastored one of its leading London churches throughout this period of time. There are at least three areas concerning which note should be taken of Knollys' significance for his own time and for following generations. The first is his High Calvinism. Although some eighteenth-century Particular Baptists crossed over from High Calvinism to Hyper-Calvinism, Knollys in his day did not. His Calvinism sought the biblical balance of the sovereignty of God and human responsibility in the matter of salvation. While he was unshaken in his confidence that God alone saves, he never hesitated to call sinners to repentance and faith in Christ.

A second area of significance relates to his eschatology. Knollys' doctrine of last things makes three important theological contributions. The first concerns his date-setting of Christ's coming. Succeeding generations should have learned from him and others of his day that predicting the time of Christ's coming or confidently seeing the fulfilment of end-time signs in their own generation was not wise. On the other hand, Knollys' concern for, expectation of, and preaching about the coming of Christ is entirely commendable and reminiscent of the Early Church's anticipation of this great event. And third, as British Baptist historian Barrie White has noted, Knollys' spiritual rather than political eschatological emphasis set, and might I add, ought to continue to set, a pattern for all who look for the blessed hope of our Lord Jesus Christ.[82]

Finally, Knollys' personal example of faithfulness in the midst of fiery trials is a model for all believers. His faith and walk remained constant through persecution, imprisonment, reproachment, personal pain, family deaths, denominational growth, denominational problems, times of want, and times of plenty. The stability of the Particular Baptist movement at the end of the seventeenth century owed not a little to the personal integrity and sparkling witness of this London Baptist pastor named Hanserd Knollys.

---

[82] *Hanserd Knollys and Radical Dissent.* 24.

Further reading

James Culross, *Hanserd Knollys, "A Minister and Witness of Jesus Christ" 1598-1691* (London: Alexander and Shepheard, 1895) is the longest and most detailed biography of Knollys' life. By means of considerable, careful research, Culross sets Knollys' career against the political and religious background of his day. A much briefer look at Knollys' life is Pope A. Duncan, *Hanserd Knollys: Seventeenth-Century Baptist* (Nashville: Broadman Press, 1965). Duncan also includes an examination of certain areas of his thought, in particular, the doctrine of redemption, ecclesiology, and religious liberty. In the last chapter of this booklet, Duncan examines the relationship of Baptists like Knollys to more radical movements of the day such as the Quakers.

B. R. White's *Hanserd Knollys and Radical Dissent in the 17th Century* (London: Dr. Williams's Trust, 1977) is a detailed account of Knollys' life from his Anglican ordination to his death. White's extensive knowledge of seventeenth-century Baptist history makes this the best and most up-to-date work on Knollys' career. See also White's article, "Knollys, Hanserd (c.1599-1691)" in Richard L. Greaves and Robert Zaller, eds., *Biographical Dictionary of British Radicals in the Seventeenth Century* (Brighton, Sussex: Harvester Press, 1983), II, 160-162.

For a study of Knollys' teaching on the gifts of the Spirit, see Michael A. G. Haykin, "Hanserd Knollys (ca.1599-1691) on the Gifts of the Spirit", *Westminster Theological Journal*, 54 (1992), 99-113. A modified version of this study is found in Haykin's *Kiffin, Knollys, Keach: Rediscovering our English Baptist Heritage* (Leeds: Reformation Today Trust, 1996), 54-61.

THE
Shining of a Flaming fire
IN ZION

Or,

A clear A n s w e r unto 13. Exceptions,
against the Grounds of New B a p t i s m ;
(fo called) in Mr. *Saltmarſh* his Book, Intituled,
The Smoke in the Temple, p. 13, &c.

Which Exceptions,
Were tendered by him to all Believers, to ſhew
them, how little they have attained; and that there
is a more glorious fulneſſe to be revealed.

ALSO,

A POSTSCRIPT;

Wherein (to the like end) fome Queries are
propounded unto Believers.

By H a n s e r d K n o l l y s , a Miniſter, and a
Witneſſe of J e s u s C h r i s t.

I s a i a h 4. 5.

*And the Lord will create upon every dwelling place of Mount Zion
and upon her Aſſemblies a Cloud, and a Smoke by day, and The ſhining
of a Flaming fire by Night, &c.*

M a t t h. 21. 24, 25.

*I alfo will ask you one thing, which if ye tell me, I likewife will tell you
by what authority I do thefe things. The Baptifme of John, whence was
it ? From Heaven, or of Men ?*

LONDON, Printed by J a n e C o e, *according to Order*, 1646.

Hopwood Sculpt

William Kiffin.

Ætat 50, Anno, 1667.

From an original Painting.

WILLIAM KIFFIN (1616-1701)

Paul R. Wilson

William Kiffin is one of the most influential and important Particular Baptist leaders of the seventeenth century. Born in London in 1616, evidence concerning Kiffin's early life is scant. What is available indicates that in his early years William Kiffin experienced tragedy and hardship. In 1625, at the tender age of nine, young William suffered the loss of both parents when the great plague swept through London. He was also afflicted with the plague but, as Kiffin later recalled, "it pleased God, of his great goodness, to restore me."[1] By 1629, at the age of thirteen Kiffin became an apprentice "to a mean calling" under the mastership of John Lilburne (who became a leader of the Levellers) a Porter Brewer and Cooper in London.[2] Eventually, he completed his apprenticeship and after a brief time as a glover he decided by the early 1640s to strike out on his own as a merchant in the Dutch woollen trade.[3]

In his new vocation Kiffin exercised what he modestly termed a "small talent" for business with an acumen that proved most profitable. By seizing the expanded trade opportunities offered by the English government in the late 1640s William Kiffin had, by the early 1650s, amassed a fortune. In his characteristic manner he cited God's providence as the source of his material success. "It pleased God so to

---

[1] William Orme, ed., *Remarkable Passages in the Life of William Kiffin: Written by Himself, and Edited from the Original Manuscript, with Notes and Additions* (London: Burton and Smith, 1823), 2.

[2] *Ibid.*

[3] For a thorough but undocumented account of Kiffin's business career, see B. A. Ramsbottom, *Stranger Than Fiction: The Life of William Kiffin* (Harpenden, Hertfordshire: Gospel Standard Trust Publications, 1989), 34-44.

bless our endeavours," Kiffin noted, "that, from scores of pounds, he brought it to many hundreds and thousands of pounds: giving me more of this world than ever I could have thought to enjoy."[4] In his business endeavours then, Kiffin realized outstanding results.

With the combination of wealth and religious Nonconformity, however, came both benefits and challenges. Wealth gave Kiffin the opportunity to devote himself to biblical studies and pastoral ministry. It also enabled him to "give without receiving," thereby encouraging many Particular Baptists who did not have sufficient material resources to meet the challenges associated with persecution or economic hardship.[5] Finally, wealth gave Kiffin access to powerful people who could intervene on behalf of Baptists caught in the web of religious intolerance. In 1664, for example, when ten men and two women were seized from a General Baptist meeting at Aylesbury and subsequently sentenced to die, William Kiffin presented their case to Lord Chancellor Hyde (1609-1674) who then laid their case before King Charles II. The King granted an immediate royal reprieve and the lives of the Baptists were spared.[6]

On the negative side, however, wealth and religious Nonconformity made Kiffin a target for those who sought to discredit the Baptist cause by attacking one of its most respected supporters. By the end of his life Kiffin was able to recall numerous occasions when his own physical well-being had been at risk. On one such occasion Kiffin was arrested at midnight by George Villiers (1628-1687), the second Duke of Buckingham, and accused of plotting to kill the King. After two trips to prison and intervention by Lord Chancellor Hyde, Kiffin was granted his freedom. "This great deliverance," proclaimed Kiffin, "was a cause for wonder to all that heard of it."[7] Indeed, God was faithful, but with wealth and notoriety came many personal and spiritual challenges.

Like so many of his contemporaries, William Kiffin's spiritual journey began when he was young. Sometime in 1631, while he was still

[4] Orme, *Remarkable Passages*, 23.
[5] *Ibid.*
[6] Barrie R. White, "William Kiffin—Baptist Pioneer and Citizen of London", *Baptist History and Heritage*, 2, No. 2 (July 1967), 101.
[7] Orme, *Remarkable Passages*, 43.

an apprentice of John Lilburne (c. 1614-1657), Kiffin came under the Puritan preaching of Thomas Foxley. Kiffin began to attend Puritan services. As he sat under the teaching of various Puritan preachers Kiffin began to wrestle with his own sinfulness and his need for personal salvation. Eventually, after many weeks of "great distress" Kiffin was able to find rest for his soul through a personal conversion experience.[8]

In 1638, Kiffin became convinced that policies pursued by the Archbishop of Canterbury, William Laud, were unbiblical and he decided to join "an Independent congregation."[9] Historians have debated long and hard the questions of how and when William Kiffin became a Baptist. One view is that in 1638, Kiffin joined the Independent church pastored by Henry Jessey. At some point later he became a member of the Particular Baptist church at Wapping. Finally, Kiffin led a group out of the Wapping church to form a new Baptist congregation in the Devonshire Square area of London where he was to serve as Pastor for the rest of his life. The second interpretation argues simply that Kiffin and the Independent church that he joined in 1638 grew together to embrace Particular Baptist beliefs and practices.[10] Clearly, whatever version that one chooses to hold is secondary to the fact that between his decision to join an Independent congregation in 1638 and his signing of the *First London Confession of Faith* in 1644, Kiffin's beliefs and practices became those of the Particular Baptists.

From the scant evidence available, it appears that as a pastor Kiffin proved himself a worthy shepherd. He not only paid careful attention to the needs of his large London congregation, but he also travelled widely on behalf of the Particular Baptist cause. As B. A. Ramsbottom has pointed out, the stresses and strains placed on Kiffin's "time and talents" required that co-pastors share in the responsibilities of ministry at

---

[8] *Ibid.*, 1-21. One should also consult Ramsbottom, *Stranger Than Fiction*, 9-17.

[9] Orme, *Remarkable Passages*, 14.

[10] For an excellent summary of the two views, see Barrie R. White, "How did William Kiffin join the Baptists?", *Baptist Quarterly*, 23 (1969-1970), 201-207 and Murray Tolmie, *The Triumph of the Saints* (Cambridge: Cambridge University Press, 1977), *passim*.

Devonshire Square.[11] The able assistance provided by Thomas Patient, Daniel Dyke and Richard Adams (d.1719) meant that Kiffin could rest assured that the daily spiritual needs of his flock would not go unattended.

In his family life William Kiffin knew both great joy and deep sorrow. While he worshipped with the Independent congregation "it pleased God to provide for me a suitable yoke-fellow," noted Kiffin, "who was one with me in judgement, and joined to the same congregation."[12] Hannah Kiffin proved to be a most wonderful companion and an exemplary follower of Christ. Her death after almost forty-four years of marriage and ministry brought a moving tribute from her husband:

> It pleased the Lord...to take to himself my dear and faithful wife, with whom I had lived nearly forty-five years. Her tenderness to me, and faithfulness to God, were such as cannot by me be expressed. She sympathized with me in all my afflictions, and I can truly say I never heard her utter the least discontent under all the various providences that attended myself or her. But owning the hand of God in them, she was a constant encourager of me in the ways of God. Her death was to me the greatest sorrow I ever met with in this world. She departed this life on October 5, 1682.[13]

The sting of death was a reality that William Kiffin knew all too well. His wife was predeceased by three of the Kiffin children. The eldest son, William, died at the tender age of twenty on August 31, 1669. Kiffin later recorded his response to this tragic loss:

> It pleased God to take out of the world to Himself my eldest son, which was no small affliction to me and my dear wife. His obedience to his parents, and forwardness in the ways of God, were so conspicuous as to make him very amiable in the eyes of all who knew him. The grief I felt for his loss did greatly press me down

---

[11] *Stranger Than Fiction*, 78-81.
[12] Orme, *Remarkable Passages*, 14.
[13] *Ibid.*, 50.

with more than ordinary sorrow; but in the midst of my great distress it did please the Lord to support me by that blessed word being brought powerfully to my mind: 'Is thine eye evil because I am good? Is it not lawful for Me to do what I will with Mine own?' These words did quiet my heart so that I felt a perfect submission to His sovereign will.[14]

Even in the midst of his deep sorrow Kiffin allowed the reality of God's sovereignty to bring him the peace that passes all understanding.

Had the death of his eldest son been Kiffin's only trial it would have been painful enough, but other tragedies followed. Soon after the death of William, a second son was poisoned by "a Popish priest" while he visited Venice on his way home from a trip to the continent. Kiffin's response to this murderous act was nothing short of remarkable. "I pray God," wrote Kiffin concerning the priest who had killed his son, "that this sin may not be laid to his charge!" Furthermore, on March 15, 1679, one of his daughters, Priscilla, also died. Finally, in 1698 his son Harry died at the age of forty-four.[15] Yet, even these sorrows paled when compared to the suffering Kiffin experienced in 1685.

After the death of his son-in-law, Benjamin Hewling, William Kiffin took charge of the Hewling family and treated his two grandsons, William and Benjamin, like his own sons. In the summer of 1685, both grandsons took up arms in support of the Duke of Monmouth's attempt to defend the "Good Old Cause" and remove James II (r.1685-1688), a professed Roman Catholic, from the English throne.[16] After the defeat of Monmouth's make-shift army at Sedgemoor in 1685, William and Benjamin sought to escape by sea, but their attempt at escape was foiled by contrary winds. Forced to return to England, they were captured and imprisoned. Kiffin and the brothers' sister Hannah exhausted every avenue to gain their release. Kiffin even offered the large sum of £3,000

---

[14] *Ibid.,* 48.

[15] *Ibid.,* 49, 162.

[16] For a discussion of these events and their impact on Baptists, see Christopher Hill, *A Tinker and a Poor Man: John Bunyan and His Church, 1628-1688* (New York: Alfred A. Knopf, 1989), 310-322.

in exchange for his grandsons' freedom. Not even this offer, though, moved Judge George Jeffreys (1648-1689) to grant clemency. Instead, William, age 19, and Benjamin, age 22, were executed in September of 1685.[17] Kiffin later recalled that "it was a great comfort to me, and still is, to observe what testimony they left behind them of that blessed interest they had in the Lord Jesus and holy confidence of their eternal happiness."[18] Once again, Kiffin found solace in the hope of his faith.

William Kiffin did not restrict his activities to business, church and home life. He took an active interest in the affairs of city and state. Although he abhorred the seamier side of politics, Kiffin understood the value of court connections and, as we have already seen in the Aylesbury case, he used his political influence to help his fellow Baptists. On the national level he served once as an MP for Middlesex in the parliament of 1656. On the local level Kiffin held a couple of important positions. In 1671, he became a master of the Leathersellers' Company. Although this was not primarily a political position, Kiffin's membership in the guild and his active role in its leadership gave him access to important information that served to keep him in touch with current political and economic policy. In 1687 Kiffin was appointed Alderman of the Ward of Cheap in the City of London, a Justice of the Peace and a member of the Lieutenancy. Because these appointments were made by James II, Kiffin took up his positions reluctantly. Still, in his nine months of service as an Alderman, Kiffin distinguished himself as a provider for those in need. He sought to alleviate the suffering of orphans, and on one occasion he provided help for poor French Protestants in their worship.[19] In short, William Kiffin was an active, though sometimes reluctant, participant in the political affairs of his day.

On December 29, 1701, at the age of 85, after a long, eventful and fruitful life, William Kiffin died peacefully in his bed. His loss to the

---

[17] For the best secondary accounts of the Hewling tragedy, see White, "William Kiffin," 102, and Ramsbottom, *Stranger Than Fiction*, 56-62.

[18] This quotation appears in Ramsbottom, *Stranger Than Fiction*, 61.

[19] For an overview of Kiffin's political life, see Richard L. Greaves and Robert Zaller, eds., *Biographical Dictionary of British Radicals in the Seventeenth Century* (Brighton, Sussex: The Harvester Press, 1983), II, 155-156.

Particular Baptist cause and community that he had served for over sixty years was keenly felt. Records concerning his funeral are few. He was buried in the famous Nonconformist cemetery in Bunhill Fields, London.[20] His legacy survived in those who carried on in the Particular Baptist faith that William Kiffin had worked so tirelessly to establish.

Kiffin's thought on baptism

Kiffin's teaching and perspectives on the Christian life had a profound impact within the Particular Baptist community and beyond. On a number of important theological and practical issues Kiffin represented the Particular Baptist position with fervour, consistency, and sincerity. In the face of attacks from outsiders and opposition from within his own denomination, Kiffin stood firm in his heartfelt conviction that in all things one should maintain a strict conformity to the teaching of the Scriptures.

The first significant doctrinal disputation in which Kiffin had an active part took place in Southwark, London, on October 17, 1642. On this occasion, Kiffin and three other Baptists confronted Daniel Featley (1582-1645), a member of the Westminster Assembly of Divines, on the question of infant baptism.[21] In the course of the debate, Kiffin clearly laid out what would become the basic tenets of the Particular Baptist position on baptism. First, Kiffin maintained that the Scriptures explicitly taught believers' baptism.[22] Second, he flatly rejected pædobaptism. To Featley he declared, "I except against your administration of Baptisme, it is not rightly administered in your Church; for you baptise Children and that is not agreeable to God's Word."[23]

---

[20] Ramsbottom, *Stranger Than Fiction*, 93-100.

[21] For a brief biographical sketch of Featley, see William S. Barker, *Puritan Profiles: 54 Influential Puritans at the time when the Westminster Confession of Faith was written* (Fearn, Ross-shire: Christian Focus Publications, 1996), 47-51.

[22] Daniel Featley, *The Dippers dipt: or, the Anabaptists duck'd and plung'd over head and ears, at a Disputation in Southwark* (London, 1645), 3.

[23] *Ibid.*, 5.

Last, Kiffin argued that only immersion constituted the biblical mode of baptism. "The way and manner of dispensing this Ordinance," Kiffin told Featley, "the Scripture holds out to be dipping or plunging the whole body under water."[24]

These key positions taken by Kiffin in defense of the Particular Baptist view of baptism would later be enshrined in the *First London Confession of Faith* (1644), which would serve as the doctrinal standard for Particular Baptist advance from the late 1640s to the mid 1670s. For example, in Article 39, which Kiffin co-authored, it was stated that "Baptism is an ordinance of the New Testament, given by Christ, to be dispensed only upon persons professing faith, or that are disciples, or taught, who upon a profession of faith, ought to be baptized."[25] Similarly, in his tract of 1681 entitled *A Sober Discourse of the Right to Church Communion*, Kiffin defended the notion that a biblical order existed and should be maintained. He stressed that no person should be baptized without first giving a "visible profession of faith."[26] Through such expressions of his beliefs concerning baptism Kiffin helped to articulate and clarify the Particular Baptist position on this vital issue.

Communion and church membership

While his statements on baptism were significant, Kiffin's views on communion and church membership were equally influential. In a dispute with John Bunyan (1628-1688), the famous tinker turned pastor and writer, that lasted over eight years, Kiffin argued that the Scriptures clearly taught that "none ought to be partakers of the Lord's Supper, but such as have been Baptized."[27] Communion was to be restricted to those who had experienced regeneration and baptism. Furthermore, Kiffin insisted that only those who had been baptized as believers should be

---

[24] *Ibid.*, 182.
[25] William L. Lumpkin, *Baptist Confessions of Faith* (Valley Forge: Judson Press, 1969), 167.
[26] *A Sober Discourse of the Right to Church Communion* (London, 1681), 151.
[27] *Ibid.*, preface.

allowed into the membership of a local Particular Baptist church.[28] In contrast, Bunyan took a more open approach and allowed those who simply professed faith in Christ access to both the Lord's table and church membership.[29] The debate between Kiffin and Bunyan helped to divide and then fix Baptists into the closed and open communion camps.

Kiffin's dispute with Bunyan also illustrated a literal hermeneutical approach to the Scriptures and an emphasis on maintaining the purity of the faith that characterized Particular Baptists throughout the British Isles during the seventeenth century. The London Baptist pastor preferred a straightforward interpretation and application of the Scriptures. In his view it was essential that strict conformity to the teaching of Christ regarding the ordinances be maintained so that "order" in worship may not be "turned into Anarchy."[30] "It is commendable," Kiffin noted in his *Sober Discourse*, "to keep the ordinances of Christ pure as they were delivered, because it prevents the creeping in of the Inventions of Men in the Worship of God."[31] Thus, for Kiffin it was incumbent upon the Christian to walk circumspectly in strict accordance with the Scriptures.

Kiffin's Calvinism

Central to Kiffin's teaching and perspective on the Christian life were the doctrines of election and God's sovereignty. In common with his fellow Particular Baptists, Kiffin held to John Calvin's teaching that a predestined elect were chosen for salvation before the world began. In the *Second London Confession of Faith* (1677/1689), which Kiffin signed on behalf of his Devonshire Square church, particular redemption was clearly described:

---

[28] For an recent discussion of Kiffin's view on both of these subjects, see Michael A. G. Haykin, *Kiffin, Knollys and Keach: Rediscovering Our English Baptist Heritage* (Leeds: Reformation Today Trust, 1996), 49-51.

[29] For a summary of Bunyan's views in this regard, see Hill, *A Tinker and A Poor Man*, 292-295.

[30] Kiffin, *Sober Discourse*, 21-22.

[31] *Ibid.*, 48.

Those of mankind that are predestinated to life, God, before the foundation of the world was laid, according to his eternal and immutable purpose, and the secret Councel and good pleasure of his will, hath chosen in Christ unto everlasting glory, out of his meer free grace and love; without any other thing in the creature as a condition or cause moving him thereunto.[32]

For Kiffin, salvation was by the will of an Almighty God.

Similarly, as one who was chosen by God for salvation, Kiffin taught that God had a sovereign and divine purpose for his life and the lives of his fellow Baptists. At the end of his memoirs, for instance, Kiffin underscored this belief in God's providence:

I leave these several providences and mercies behind me, that you may consider on them. I have tasted of the goodness of God, and his favour towards me from my youth; it being now sixty years since it pleased the Lord to give me a taste of his rich grace and mercy in Jesus Christ. Although my unprofitableness under these mercies and providences that hath attended me, hath been very great, they are not to be looked upon as products of chance; as many do serve experiences and deliverences, which they receive from God in the course of their lives: but the fruits of the care and goodness which God is pleased to shew to his poor people. While in this world there is not any design hatched against them for their ruin, but they are rescued from it by the special care and providence of God. I may say, by experience, if the Lord had not been my help, many a time I had been swallowed up quick.[33]

As this statement well indicates, Kiffin believed that the tragedies and triumphs of life were ordained of God to fulfil his divine purpose and plan.

---

[32] *Second London Confession of Faith* 3.5 (Lumpkin, *Baptist Confessions of Faith*, 254-255).
[33] Orme, *Remarkable Passages*, 89.

Kiffin's significance

While Kiffin wrote about his perspective on the supreme authority of the Scriptures, the vital importance of believer's baptism and its relationship to communion and membership in the local church, and the complete sovereignty of God in the affairs of life, there were many other subjects on which he preferred to remain silent or allow his actions to speak for him. For example, on the question of church discipline and how it should be practised Kiffin says little. The available church records make it clear that in the Devonshire Square Church strict discipline was maintained, and members were disciplined for a broad range of offenses. Similarly, although he was an ardent advocate for religious toleration, Kiffin did not directly spell out his views in print that would have served as instruction for succeeding generations of Baptists. These silences are frustrating for the historian, but understandable in light of the pressures of ministry and business with which Kiffin had to wrestle.

Despite the fact that Kiffin wrote far less than many of his contemporaries, his contribution to the Particular Baptist cause was substantial. As one of the founders of the Particular Baptist denomination, William Kiffin has left an indelible mark on Baptist history. It was Kiffin, who, along with others, first encouraged Baptists of like mind to join together in association and to express their beliefs in a confession of faith.

In addition to his role as a founding father of the denomination, Kiffin demonstrated leadership as a shepherd to the Baptist flock, both his own congregation and the wider Particular Baptist constituency. His words concerning baptism, communion and church membership were formative and became the basis of much subsequent Baptist teaching on these subjects. Kiffin was also a man of principle and integrity. In him Baptists saw one who was steadfastly committed to what he believed the Scriptures taught.

Kiffin also excelled in the worlds of business and politics. His rise from "rags to riches" and his superior business acumen afforded him opportunities that Nonconformists in his day rarely enjoyed. With his wealth and political connections William Kiffin could have easily succumbed to the temptation to become carnal and uncaring. In fact, he used the freedom that his wealth provided to serve others. Moreover, Kiffin employed his political connections and offices to come to the aid of Baptists in trouble and to alleviate the suffering of the poor and disadvantaged. He was a man connected to both country and community.

Perhaps Kiffin's greatest contribution to the furtherance of the Baptist cause lay in his devout character. His willingness to contend for the truth, suffer persecution, endure hardship and use his resources and gifts for the expansion of Christ's kingdom made him a model that others would respect and emulate. Many Baptists would agree with the sentiments expressed by the Baptist historian and pastor Joseph Ivimey (1773-1834): "I consider Mr. Kiffin to have been one of the most extraordinary persons that the denomination has produced, both as to the consistency and correctness of his principles and the eminence of his worldly and religious character."[34] This statement reveals the true legacy of William Kiffin. In his lifetime he experienced both deep sorrow and material success; he made his mistakes, yet, even friends and foes alike could never question his commitment to discipleship and the development of godly character. In William Kiffin the Particular Baptists had a man who worked tirelessly for their advance. As a leader in the fight for religious toleration, staunch opponent to false teaching and a true guardian of the faith entrusted to him, William Kiffin distinguished himself as one of the most notable among early British Baptists.

Further reading

William Orme, ed., *Remarkable Passages in the Life of William Kiffin: Written by Himself, and Edited from the Original Manuscript, with Notes and Additions* (London: Burton and Smith, 1823) is undoubtedly the best single source on Kiffin's life. It includes an introduction by Orme, Kiffin's own memoirs and useful notes. Joseph Ivimey, *The Life of William Kiffin* (London, 1833) intersperses Kiffin's memoirs with history provided by the author. Although it is not as readable as Orme, this source is essential reading for anyone interested in Kiffin.

---

[34] *The Life of William Kiffin* (London, 1833), xi.

Necessary reading for any scholarly examination of Kiffin's life is Barrie R. White, "William Kiffin—Baptist Pioneer and Citizen of London", *Baptist History and Heritage*, 2, No. 2, (July 1967), 91-103, 126. Michael A.G. Haykin, *Kiffin, Knollys and Keach: Rediscovering Our English Baptist Heritage* (Leeds: Reformation Today Trust, 1996) offers his reader a brief but scholarly overview of Kiffin's life. This is one of the most recent and important contributions to the study of Kiffin.

A highly readable and highly informative account of Kiffin's life and ministry is available in B. A. Ramsbottom, *Stranger Than Fiction: The Life of William Kiffin* (Harpenden, Hertfordshire: Gospel Standard Trust Publications, 1989). Unfortunately, the absence of documentation and an index limit the utility of this book.

R. White sculp

John Bunnyon.

JOHN BUNYAN (1628-1688)

Allen Smith

John Bunyan was born in very humble circumstances in Elstow about a mile from Bedford. Little is known of his family and early life. Most of the knowledge we have of Bunyan's early life is, in fact, gleaned from his writings, in particular, *Grace Abounding to the Chief of Sinners* (1666) and *The Doctrine of the Law and Grace Unfolded* (1659).

His father was a tinker, that is, a mender of old pots and pans, and John followed in this trade. In deeding his worldly belongings to his wife in 1685, he refers to himself as a "Brazier"[1] and apparently he worked at this trade throughout his life. His education was limited to the earliest grades, probably in a school endowed to promote education of the poor in and around Bedford.[2] He describes his education in *Grace Abounding to the Chief of Sinners* thus: "Notwithstanding the meanness and inconsiderableness of my parents, it pleased God to put it into their hearts to put me to school, to learn both to read and write; the which I also attained, according to the rate of other poor men's children; though, to my shame I confess, I did soon lose that little I learned, and that even almost utterly, and that long before the Lord did work his gracious work of conversion upon my soul."[3]

There is no record that Bunyan's parents contributed in any way to his spiritual understanding or moral training. In referring to a rebuke for the vileness of his swearing he said, "I wished with all my heart that I

---

[1] George Offor, "Memoir of John Bunyan" [*The Works of John Bunyan*, ed. George Offor (1863 ed.; repr. Edinburgh: The Banner of Truth Trust, 1991), I, cxxi].

[2] *Ibid.* (*Works*, I, iii).

[3] *Grace Abounding to the Chief of Sinners* §3 (*Works*, I, 6).

might be a little child again, that my father might learn me to speak without this wicked way of swearing:...for...I am so accustomed to it, that it is but in vain for me to think of a reformation."[4] When he wrote *Christian Behaviour* (1663), he covered the various family relationships and in concluding "Duties of Children to Parents" he says, "O! how happy would it be, if God should use a child to beget his father to the faith!...The Lord, if it be his will, convert our poor parents, that they, with us, may be the children of God."[5] This may well have been the cry of Bunyan's heart for his own father's conversion and it could indicate that his parents did not know the Lord. His mother died when he was 16 years of age and his sister Mary followed a month later.

Bunyan's military experience

Following the death of his mother and sister in 1644, Bunyan entered the Parliamentary Army. He served until some time after June, 1647. Old muster rolls of "Officers and souldiers" show Bunyan quartered at Newport Pagnell in June, 1644, and his name appears on a muster of soldiers ready for disbanding on June 17, 1647.[6] In some early writings on Bunyan's life there are questions as to whether he served under the Royalist or the Cromwellian Army. The historical record is conclusive that he served with the latter.

However, the reasons given for Bunyan being in the Royalist Army provide some insight into Bunyan's life and military experience. One reason given for his being a Royalist is that John Gifford (d.1655),[7] who is believed to have baptized Bunyan and did become his pastor, was a major in the army of Charles I. Gifford was involved in an insurrection

---

[4] *Ibid.* §27 (*Works*, I, 9).

[5] *Works*, II, 564.

[6] Frank Mott Harrison, *John Bunyan: A Story of His Life* (Repr. Edinburgh: The Banner of Truth Trust, 1964), 9.

[7] For an account of Gifford's conversion and ministry in Bedford, see H. G. Tibbutt, ed., *The Minutes of the First Independent Church (now Bunyan Meeting) at Bedford 1656-1766* (Bedfordshire Historical Record Society, 1976), 15-21.

in the County of Kent, arrested and sentenced to death. He escaped from prison and fled to Bedford where he was involved in the persecution of the "godly persons with great fierceness." But he was converted and in 1650 organized the Bedford Church, which played a major part in Bunyan's conversion and Christian experience.

A second reason given for Bunyan being a Royalist is that he was not a Christian at this time and the Parliamentary Army under Oliver Cromwell was made up of a strongly religious constituency. According to one report, when Cromwell saw the condition of the Parliamentary army after the first battle, he said, "I will remedy that. I will raise men who will have the fear of God before their eyes, and who will bring some conscience to what they do; and I promise you they shall not be beaten." It was not long before Cromwell's own moral integrity and spiritual character manifested itself in the army, and especially so soon as he was surrounded with persons motivated by the identical faith. To be sure, all who were in Cromwell's "Ironsides" were not believers, but the courage and challenge of the leaders must have had a great influence on the others. Cromwell himself invited known men of faith to address the soldiers. When they were encamped near Cambridge, for example, Richard Baxter (1615-1691), a Puritan divine who was a Royalist in his sympathies, was invited to be a chaplain, but he declined. He later expressed regret about his decision, saying, "these very men,...were the men that afterwards headed much of the army, and some of them were the forwardest in all our changes; which made me wish that I had gone among them."[8]

Bunyan writes little of his military life. He mentions someone taking his place at sentinel duty on one occasion and being fatally wounded in the head. At another time he fell into a "creek of the sea" and nearly drowned. It may be that the spiritual influence in Cromwell's army did have some effect on him. He was noted for his swearing, but it was said of the troops "no one swears but he pays his twelve pence."[9] Although he never mentions them, there were two printed items distributed to all

---

[8] J. H. Merle D'Aubigné, *The Protector: A Vindication* (Harrisonburg, Virginia: Sprinkle Publications, 1983), 62.

[9] *Ibid.*, 62.

the soldiers in the Parliamentary Army which would have been available
to Bunyan. They were *The Souldiers Pocket Bible* (extracts from the
Geneva Bible) and *The Souldiers Catechism*, which was "composed for
the Parliament's Army: Written for the encouragement and instruction of
all that have taken up Armes in this Cause of God and His people;
especially the common Souldiers."[10] The influence of these volumes on
Bunyan may have been limited by the extent of his reading ability. He
does indicate that much of his education was gone by the time of his
conversion.

Finally, since many of the Baptists were participants in the
Parliamentary Army, surely their testimony would have had some effect
on Bunyan.[11] Cromwell often asserted that the composition of his army
was very different from that of ordinary armies. His army was largely
made up of pious freeholders and farmers, men who had ventured their
lives for religious liberty.[12] And when we take a close look at Bunyan's
life it would seem that some of these men did set an example for him.

Conversion

It is readily evident that Bunyan was an object of sovereign, efficacious
grace. He describes the tender years of his youth as having "few
equals…for cursing, swearing, lying, and blaspheming the holy name of
God."[13] Yet, in these days frightening dreams made him conscious of his
sin and the reality of the day of judgment and the torments of hell. But,
he notes in *Grace Abounding*, as he grew older these thoughts that
distressed his soul when "nine or ten years old" were pushed aside.
"Until marriage I was the very ringleader of all the youth that kept me
company, into all manner of vice and ungodliness." The thought of

---

[10] Harrison, *John Bunyan*, 11-12.
[11] Robert G. Torbet [*A History of the Baptists* (3rd ed.; Valley Forge, Penn-sylvania: The Judson Press, 1963), 44] has argued that the associational or-ganizations in the Army later played a major role in the organizing of Par-ticular Baptist Churches into regional Baptist associations.
[12] D'Aubigné, *Protector*, 89.
[13] *Grace Abounding to the Chief of Sinners* §4 (*Works*, I, 6).

religion was "grevious" to him and the words of "Christian piety would be as it were a prison for me...yet, even then...hearing one to swear that was reckoned for a religious man, it had so great a stroke upon my spirit, that it made my heart to ache."[14] We see here the implementation of the truth of Romans 2:14-15 in his life—"The Gentiles...show the works of the law written in their hearts, their conscience also bearing witness."

Within about a year of his discharge from the Army he married a woman whose first name is not known. He says of their entering the marriage state: "This woman and I, came together as poor as poor might be, not having so much household stuff as a dish or spoon betwixt us both, yet this she had for her part, *The Plain Man's Pathway to Heaven*, and the *Practice of Piety*, which her father had left her when he died."[15] He would write that his mercy was "to light upon a wife whose father was godly." He became interested in religion but initially only the externals were of concern to him.

The event that first caused him to consider religious matters seriously came about as he was standing "at a neighbor's shop window cursing and swearing and playing the madman." The woman of the house protested, "That I was the ungodliest fellow for swearing that ever she heard in all her life."[16] From this point on he forsook his swearing and began reading the Bible. He became quite knowledgeable and had great respect for religious leaders. The general populace began to consider him a rather religious man but he was without a saving knowledge of Christ. "I was now a brisk talker also myself in the matters of religion, but now I may say, I heard, but I understood not."[17]

In Bedford one day working at his trade as a tinker this interest in religious talk led to a major change in his life. The "providence of God" brought him into the hearing of some poor women who were discussing the things of the Lord. Up until this time he had no understanding of

---

[14] *Ibid.* §10-11 (*Works*, I, 7).
[15] *Ibid.* §15 (*Works*, I, 7). The two books mentioned by Bunyan are both by Puritan authors.
[16] *Ibid.* §26 (*Works*, I, 9).
[17] *Ibid.* §37 (*Works*, I, 10).

gospel truth. In fact, although he was religious, the reality of the forgiveness of sin in Christ was unknown to him.

The women were discussing the things of the Lord and testified of the workings of Christ in their hearts. To Bunyan these were words "far above, out of my reach; for their talk was about a new birth, the work of God on their hearts." He was greatly affected by their words and said "their talk went with me; and my heart would tarry with them."

Thus began a long struggle as he read the Scriptures and conferred with others regarding the things of Christ. He came under the influence of the Ranters, an Antinomian group, but he was delivered through the study of God's Word. In his own words: "The Bible was precious to me in those days." But, although he now saw the reality of who Christ was, he still did not have full assurance in his heart as to his relationship with the Lord. He studied the doctrines of grace to discern whether he was one of the elect of God. Bunyan struggled alone in these matters—he states, "I had in this matter broken my mind to no man"—and these struggles were preparing him for the many testings and trials he would be called to endure as a Christian.

Through his struggles, the poor people from Bedford continued to influence his thoughts. He had no questions as to their spirituality. After months of discussion and Scripture study on his own he says, "I began to break my mind to those poor people in Bedford, and to tell them my condition." They told their pastor, John Gifford, who was now pastoring Saint John's Church in Bedford, under the new rules of the Commonwealth. Gifford talked with him about his spiritual condition and had him present when he was discussing spiritual matters with others. Pastor Gifford was persuaded that Bunyan was a believer and encouraged him in the Lord. But being brought into the presence of and discussions with "Holy" John Gifford and the saints at Bedford stirred up further consciousness of his depraved nature. For some time Bunyan struggled with doubts and lack of assurance, but as he attended the preaching of the Word, he became more and more aware of the preciousness of Christ. He wrote of Gifford:

> This man made it much his business to deliver the people of God from all those false and unsound rests that, by nature, we are prone

to take and make to our souls... Wherefore I found my soul, through grace, very apt to drink in this doctrine, and to incline to pray to God that, in nothing that pertained to God's glory and my own eternal happiness, he would suffer me to be without the confirmation thereof from heaven...for now I saw clearly there was a great difference between that faith that is feigned, and according to man's wisdom, and of that which comes by a man's being born thereto of God."[18]

Thus, he became thoroughly established in salvation by the grace of God. He saw his only hope was through faith in the shed blood of Christ, that faith being produced in the heart by the grace of God.

Baptism and early Christian experience

Bunyan was baptized upon his profession of faith in a creek near the river Ouse in 1653. His immersion was a conscious choice on his part. Gifford's church did not require any particular form of baptism. They permitted "every individual freedom of judgment as to water baptism; receiving all those who decidedly appeared to have put on Christ, and had been received by him."[19]

The year Bunyan was baptized and became a member of the church at Bedford was notable in another way. This was the year Oliver Cromwell became Lord Protector. Cromwell was as noted for his leadership in the affairs of state, as Bunyan was known as a gospel writer and preacher. Indeed, in his lifetime Bunyan preached to some of England's greatest preachers and politicians. On some of these occasions he preached to members of Cromwell's family and also to the great theologian John Owen.[20] When Charles II once asked the learned Owen how one of his "great erudition could sit to hear an illiterate tinker prate," the Puritan divine replied, "May it please your Majesty, if I

---

[18] *Ibid.* §117-118 (*Works*, I, 20).
[19] Offor, "Memoir" (*Works*, I, xxxi).
[20] Harrison, *John Bunyan*, 180.

could possess that tinker's abilities for preaching, I would most gladly relinquish all my learning."[21]

When Bunyan saw the marvelous doctrine of salvation by grace alone he felt a compulsion to present the message of salvation in Christ to others. He felt a distinct call to pastoral ministry. In his own words: "methought I heard such a word in my heart as this—I have set thee down on purpose, for I have something more than ordinary for thee to do; which made me the more marvel, saying, What, my Lord, such a poor wretch as I?"[22] The Dissenters usually had three requisites for preaching: ability, inclination, and opportunity. Bunyan's ministry manifested all three. Speaking of the fruit of his ministry, he could say, "the tears of those whom God did awaken by my preaching would be both solace and encouragement to me...These things, therefore, were as another argument unto me that God had called me to...this work." He observed that when he had a work to do God gave him a desire to preach at a certain place along with a burden for certain souls, and they would be "given in as fruits of my ministry."[23] For five years, from 1655 to 1660, he preached the gospel throughout the countryside and in the villages around Bedford. It was also in the 1650s that he launched into his writing ministry. It would be sixteen years later, in 1671, that he would be set apart as the pastor of the Bedford Church. In between lay twelve years of imprisonment.

Imprisonment

Soon after the restoration of the monarchy in 1660, Bunyan was arrested. His crime was preaching the gospel without license of the Established Church.

His first wife had died in 1655 and left him with a number of small children. He remarried shortly after and his second wife, Elizabeth, proved a providential blessing to him. He was imprisoned in 1660 and

---

[21] Offor, "Memoir" (*Works*, I, cviii).
[22] *The Doctrine of the Law and Grace Unfolded* (*Works*, I, 549).
[23] Offor, "Memoir" (*Works*, I, xlii); *Grace Abounding to the Chief of Sinners* §287 (*Works*, I, 42-43).

she was bold in appearing before the Assizes to plead in his behalf.[24] Bunyan's imprisonment meant his family was alone. He was especially concerned for his blind daughter, Mary. In order to support his family he crocheted laces while he was in prison, and the family sold these to buy bare necessities. Through the sympathy of his jailer, there were many occasions when he was permitted to be out of prison to fellowship with the members of the church and visits from his family were also permitted. He also had an extensive ministry to other prisoners, of whom many were fellow Christians. Although they were not the only ones, the Baptists were some of the most persecuted at this time.

Bunyan is claimed by both Baptists and Congregationalists. He listed himself as a Congregationalist when he applied for licenses under the Act of Indulgence of 1672.[25] Although Bunyan himself was baptized by immersion, neither he nor the church at Bedford required baptism of any form as a prerequisite for membership. This had been the practice of Gifford and the following pastor, John Burton (d.1660), and Bunyan followed them without alteration. This position not only caused controversy in the church at Bedford, but Particular Baptists like William Kiffin who advocated closed communion found themselves in controversy with Bunyan over this issue.[26] The church was counted among the Baptists during the days of Bunyan, but it eventually became a bona fide Paedobaptist Church.

Some controversies

Bunyan was a prolific writer. During his lifetime he wrote more than 60 publications. His first, *Some Gospel-truths Opened*, was published in 1656. A year later he wrote a sequel entitled *A Vindication of... Some Gospel-Truths Opened*. These first two of Bunyan's works were primarily a defense of the basic doctrines of the Christian life, especially

---

[24] *A Relation of the Imprisonment of Mr. John Bunyan (Works*, I, 60-61).

[25] A. C. Underwood, *A History of the English Baptists* (London: The Carey Kingsgate Press Ltd., 1956), 104.

[26] Thomas Armitage, *A History of the Baptists* (1887 ed.; repr. Minneapolis: James and Klock Christian Publishing Co., 1977), 2: 518-526.

those dealing with the person and work of Christ. He exposes the error of the Quakers and their doctrine of the inner light. On May 23, 1656, Bunyan had met with and debated a number of Quakers. Edward Burrough (1634-1663), a leading Quaker, wrote a reply to the questions Bunyan had asked of the Quakers present and posed some questions of Bunyan in return. The second work is the reply of Bunyan to Burrough and his questions.[27] This was the first of three major controversies in Bunyan's life.

The second controversy revolved around the doctrine of justification. Edward Fowler (1632-1714), Vicar of Northill, Bedfordshire, and later the Bishop of Gloucester, had written *The Design of Christianity* (1671), in which he argued that the work of Jesus Christ as Saviour was to place man in a similar position to that of Adam before the fall. "Christ's work," Fowler affirmed, "was to establish only an inward real righteousness. ...There can be no pretence for a man, to think that faith should be the condition or instrument of justification." Essentially Fowler's position denied the imputed righteousness of Christ. Righteousness, in his way of thinking, was granted on the basis of repentance by the sinner. In his words, "men are not capable of God's pardoning grace, till they have truly repented them of all their sins."[28]

Bunyan responded by writing *A Defence of the Doctrine of Justification, by Faith* (1672). This work seeks to proclaim the Reformers' doctrine of justification and contend for imputed righteousness as the basis of justification as opposed to Fowler's inward "real righteousness." In doing so, Bunyan identified himself with a strict Calvinism, and opposed not only Arminianism but also the Moderate Calvinism of a Richard Baxter. Baxter held that Christ, by his active obedience, had qualified himself to be the Saviour of the world and by his passive obedience had obtained salvation for all who believed. Although Bunyan never identified himself with the particular names of the theological systems he made it clear that he believed that Christ had made a full and efficient satisfaction for his elect.

---

[27] *Some Gospel-truths Opened* (*Works*, II, 175); *A Vindication of... Some Gospel-Truths Opened* (*Works*, II, 205-206).

[28] *A Defence of the Doctrine of Justification, by Faith* (*Works*, II, 280).

His death for us, was so virtuous, that in the space of three days and three nights, it reconciled to God in the body of his flesh as a common person, all, and every one of God's elect. Christ…presented himself to the justice of the law, as a common person; standing in the stead, place, and room of all that he undertook for; He gave 'his life a ransom for many.' Mat. 20.28.[29]

The third area of controversy was the communion issue. The Bedford Church minutes indicate that "the principle upon which they thus entered into fellowship one with another and upon which they did afterwards receive those that were added to their body and fellowship was faith in Christ and holines of life, without respect to this or that circumstance or opinion in outward and circumstantiall things."[30] The reason for this position was so as to avoid "disputings and occasion to janglings and unprofitable questions," among which the issue of believer's baptism was placed. But the Bedford congregation would not be able to avoid this issue. It came to the fore as a result of the ministry of Benjamin Coxe in Bedfordshire.[31]

Coxe, a graduate of Oxford University, became a Baptist in the early 1640s. From the mid-1640s onwards he was a central figure in the London Particular Baptist community and a firm advocate of closed communion. At the same time he was involved in ministry in Bedford. It is not known how long Coxe's ministry continued in Bedford, but it may well be the case that a nucleus from Coxe's ministry became a part of the church that John Gifford pastored in the early 1650s. If so, they would have contended for baptism as a prerequisite to the communion table.

John Burton followed Gifford as pastor and continued the practice of open communion. Bunyan was called to the pastorate of this church in 1672 and he maintained the practice of Gifford and Burton. He soon

---

[29] *The Saints' Knowledge of Christ's Love: The Unsearchable Riches of Christ (Works*, II, 20).

[30] Tibbutt, ed., *Bunyan Meeting*, 17.

[31] On Coxe, see W. T. Whitley, "Benjamin Cox", *Transactions of the Baptist Historical Society*, 6, No.1 (1918), 50-59.

found himself, though, in open conflict with the Particular Baptists of London. His principal opponents were William Kiffin, Henry Denne (fl.1644-1661), Thomas Paul and Henry D'Anvers (d.1687). In 1672 Bunyan published his *Confession of My Faith and A Reason of My Practice in Worship*, in which he declared his position that baptism was "no prerequisite to the Lord's table." Over the next couple of years, his Particular Baptist opponents responded to Bunyan's position. The strongest response came from Kiffin and was entitled *Sober Discourse of Right to Church Communion* (1681).[32] Although this was a heated controversy, the Particular Baptists clearly considered Bunyan one of their own, except for his adverse view on baptism and church communion. Bunyan had strong convictions regarding the matter and refused to grant letters to those churches who did not practice open communion.[33] After Kiffin published his *Sober Discourse of Right to Church Communion*, Bunyan made no further responses in the controversy.

Major theological contributions

His most notable work, *Pilgrim's Progress*, was published in 1678. *Grace Abounding to the Chief of Sinners*, published in 1666, is autobiographical, written while in prison and is a testimony of God's grace working in his life. His most profound theological work is *The Doctrine of Law and Grace Unfolded*, published in 1659. In theological circles, this work has been his most widely-read. In it he sets forth the Puritan concept of the covenant of grace. He did not follow every aspect of covenantal theology. For instance, he distinguished between the covenant of works and the covenant of grace more than other Puritans generally did.

This point of view is seen in another theological issue to which Bunyan made a major contribution. In 1685, he published *Questions about the Nature and Perpetuity of the Seventh-Day Sabbath*. This

---

[32] This 1681 edition of this work was republished in 1996 by The Baptist Standard Bearer, Inc. of Paris, Arkansas.

[33] Armitage, *History*, 2:524.

work is a response to the Seventh-Day Baptists who were Reformed in their view of salvation, but who also believed it was essential to observe the Sabbath on the seventh day. Here Bunyan also differed with the general Puritan view. Puritan Sabbatarianism contended that the Sabbath was a creation ordinance, while Bunyan argued that it was ceremonial and first instituted in Exodus 16 "as a peculiar observance to distinguish the Jews from all other nations... 'I gave them my Sabbaths to be a sign between me and them.' Ezk. 20.12."[34] Walter J. Chantry, a twentieth-century Reformed Baptist pastor and author, has seen a dichotomy in Bunyan's view on the Sabbath. According to Chantry,

> John Bunyan wrote against seventh-day Christians, giving much attention to what he considered the ceremonial element in the fourth commandment. ...Some of the same propositions used to assault the seventh-day Sabbath would (if allowed to stand) bear equal weight against any Sabbath whatever.[35]

Bunyan did, however, believe that there was a moral duty for the saints to observe the first day of the week as the "Christian Sabbath."

Bunyan preached to multitudes, both rich and poor, and through the many years of trials and imprisonments he remained faithful to the gospel of grace. He knew by vivid personal experience what it meant to be saved by grace. He was a warm and bold preacher who had a heart to serve not only his Lord but considered himself a servant to the saints. His last days display this dedication to the cause of Christ.

In the final year of his life, he published six volumes and left twelve in manuscript ready for publication.[36] After making a journey of mercy to Reading to reconcile a father and son, he continued on to London where he had some speaking engagements. He was making the trip by horseback and got caught in a heavy downpour of rain which left him

---

[34] *Works*, II, 360.

[35] *God's Righteous Kingdom* (Edinburgh: The Banner of Truth Trust, 1981), 138.

[36] Offor, "Memoir" (*Works*, I, cxiii).

wet and cold. He was taken with a fever and after ten days of illness in the home of a friend, he entered the "Celestial City" in August of 1688. On September 3 his body was buried in Bunhill Fields, where many other Dissenting ministers are buried.

Further reading

I first read one of Bunyan's writings while serving in the military. *Grace Abounding to the Chief of Sinners* was in the literature rack at the base chapel. This was shortly after my own conversion and although I did not realize it at the time, it would lay a foundation for years of marveling at the amazing grace of God toward sinners. One particular manuscript that Bunyan left unpublished at the time of his death was *The Saints' Knowledge of Christ's Love*. If you sit down and read this work in a quiet place, you can get a real sense of what Bunyan's preaching must have been like.

Up until recently the standard edition of Bunyan's works was *The Works of John Bunyan*, ed. George Offor (1863 ed.; repr. Edinburgh: The Banner of Truth Trust, 1991), 3 volumes. Offor includes an introduction to each of the treatises, with a biographical sketch of Bunyan's life, times and contemporaries. In the last few years, Oxford University Press has been issuing critical editions of all of Bunyan's works in a series entitled *Miscellaneous Works*.

John Brown, *John Bunyan (1628-1688): His Life, Times, and Work*, ed. and revised Frank Mott Harrison (London: The Hulbert Publishing Co., 1928) is a standard reference work on Bunyan. Roger Sharrock *John Bunyan* (London: Macmillan & Co. Ltd., 1968) has an excellent bibliography of works on Bunyan and his times. The more recent book by Gordon Wakefield, *Bunyan the Christian* (London: Harper Collins, 1992), is an excellent study of Bunyan the man and his spirituality.

Richard L. Greaves, *John Bunyan* (Grand Rapids: Wm. B. Eerdmans Publishing Co., 1969) is a volume in the *Courtenay Studies in Reformation Theology* series, and is a valuable study of Bunyan's theology. For a briefer overview of Bunyan as a theologian, see Harry L. Poe, "John Bunyan" in Timothy George and David S. Dockery, eds., *Baptist Theologians* (Nashville: Broadman Press, 1990), 26-48.

THE
Pilgrim's Progreſs
FROM
THIS WORLD,
TO
That which is to come:

Delivered under the Similitude of a

DREAM

Wherein is Diſcovered,
The manner of his ſetting out,
His Dangerous Journey; And ſafe
Arrival at the Deſired Countrey.

I have uſed Similitudes, Hoſ. 12. 10.

By *John Bunyan.*

Licenſed and Entred accoʒding to Oʒder.

LONDON,
Printed for *Nath. Ponder* at the *Peacock*
in the *Poultrey* near *Cornhil,* 1678.

BENJAMIN KEACH.

BENJAMIN KEACH (1640-1704)

Tom J. Nettles

"**H**is capacious soul soon aspired after higher things."[1] So continued Benjamin Keach all his life. He seemed never convinced that he had exhausted all truth, or even his own capacity for understanding as much truth as possible. Pressing, challenging, correcting, debating, examining, interpreting, Keach bumped and bristled his way through life, leaving everything around him much different than it was when he discovered it.

He was born February 29, 1640, and died July 18, 1704, having lived through what may well have been the most revolutionary period in English life. Both church and state had made radical adjustments and, largely owing to the energy of Keach, Particular Baptists had become a definitive force in the development of English Dissent.

Converted at fifteen, his personal study of the Bible led him to deny the validity of infant baptism and unite with a Baptist church. He was

---

[1] Thomas Crosby, *The History of the English Baptists* (London, 1738-1740), 4:269. Crosby has discussion of Keach in two major sections of this four-volume history: an account of some of the sufferings of Keach is contained in 2:185-209, and a biographical section is in 4:268-314. He felt justified in giving this much attention to Keach because he, Crosby, had "been blessed with the happiness of a good wife, the youngest off-spring of the reverend gentleman whose memory is hereby revived" (4:268). Crosby, who sold these books from his home, sold also his pedagogical talents from there. At the end of volume 1, he advertised a school which he called a "Mathematical School." There he taught arithmetic, algebra, geometry, trigonometry, the use of globes and charts, and "The Italian Method of Book-Keeping," and promised that in a month's time a person would be "made capable to give the Amount of any Quantity, at any Price."

baptized by John Russell, a General Baptist pastor, and by age eighteen had shown such zeal and skill that the church set him apart to the work of the ministry. In 1660, Keach married Jane Grove, a woman worthy of the glory that persecution and suffering bring. In addition to bearing five children, she bore the brunt of the days of persecution that her husband faced. In all of this she did not complain or tempt Keach to mollify his position for the sake of peace, but counted "it an honour done them both, in that they were called to *suffer* for the sake of Christ."[2]

Early in his ministry Keach preached without molestation, but with the restoration of Charles II (r.1660-1685) to the throne and the rise to power of Lord Clarendon, life for dissenters became difficult. In Buckinghamshire, some of the commissioners vied with each other for the position of greatest zeal in the prosecution of non-conformists. In 1664, Keach, under siege for being a preacher in a dissenting congregation, was almost killed when troopers threatened to trample him with their horses. Being rescued from that, he nevertheless was thrown into a torturous confinement.

Neither discouraged nor intimidated by his mistreatment, later that same year Keach published *The Child's Instructor; or, a new and easie Primmer*. In this was affirmed such "damnable positions, contrary to the book of Common Prayer, and the Liturgy of the Church of England" as these: believers' baptism, regenerate church membership, the millennial reign of Christ on earth, the spirituality of the call to the ministry, that human learning could not replace being gifted by God "in order to the making of a true minister," and that the use of persuasion and entreaty was superior to compulsion and force.[3] In asserting these positions,

---

[2] Crosby, *History*, 4:274. Crosby also records: "She was of an heavenly conversation, her discourse was savoury, and for the most part about divine things, seeking the spiritual good of those, with whom she conversed, and so succesful was she herein, that some have acknowledged, that their conversion to God, was thro' the conversation they had with her." Keach memorialized her in a book published in the year of her death, 1670, entitled *A Pillar Set Up*.

[3] This position was a clear distinctive of Baptist life and remains one of its boldest and most salutary contributions to modern religio/political theory.

Keach had written "seditiously, wickedly, and maliciously" and was a "seditious, heretical, and schismatical person, evilly and maliciously disposed, and disaffected to his Majesty's government, and the government of the *Church of England.*"[4] Jail, stocks, and book burning under his nose seemed mild punishment for such dangerous crimes.

While Keach's ministry was marked by courage and esteemed as profitable for "comfort and edification," his doctrinal position concerning the extent of the atonement and the freedom of the will soon would undergo change. William Cathcart states, "the reading of the Scriptures and the conversation of those who knew the will of God more perfectly relieved him from both errors."[5] A move to London provided contact with the Particular Baptists, opportunity for study, and brought about his adoption of the Calvinist stance of the Particular Baptists. David Bogue and James Bennett in noting this theological shift remark: "The result was a renunciation of his former opinions, and the embracing of the calvinistic system, for which, as he advanced in years, he became peculiarly strenuous, and as peculiarly severe against those whom he conceived to believe his own former creed." They then add, in reaction to his characteristic intensity, "Had he shewn less of this

---

Keach continued to argue for this freedom until the end of his life. In his exposition of the New Testament parables entitled *Gospel Mysteries Unveil'd* (London, 1704)—repr. Grand Rapids: Kregel Publications, 1974 as *Exposition of the Parables in the Bible*—Keach comments on the phrase "Compel them to come in" (Luke 14:23): "There hath long been contention amongst Christians and learned men, what our Saviour meaneth by his compulsion; some would from hence infer that outward force and violence is hereby intended, even to pull them in by head and shoulders, or drive them by whips and cudgels, or by penal laws, or by fire and faggot to frighten them; which certainly is far from the sense of the text, for the will of man admits of no violence or external force, by the civil magistrates; so that outward compulsion, hath no colour of foundation from hence; for neither Christ or his apostles ever used any such way, to make men Christians, or to receive the truth" (*Parables*, 546).

[4] Crosby, *History*, 2:193, 189.

[5] *The Baptist Encyclopedia* (Philadelphia: Louis H. Everts, 1881), 637-638.

severity, it would have been as honourable to himself, and no less beneficial to the cause of Christ."[6]

"Severity" misconstrues the driving energy behind the famous Baptist's interminable confrontations. The desired outcome of his writings was not principally that he might be shown right and his opponents wrong, but that God's people would enjoy all the blessings of the covenant of grace in purity. His clear, graphic, animated, and lively defenses of the doctrines of grace urge the saints to find their complete joy and security in the eternal purpose of God as effected in the

---

[6] *History of Dissenters* (London, 1808-1812), 2:265. The time of this change is not stated explicitly by Crosby or any of the historians which follow him. Probably, subsequent to his selection as pastor of the small congregation at Southwark in 1668 [typeset wrongly in Crosby, *History*, 4:272 as 1688 and strangely followed by Joseph Ivimey, *A History of the English Baptists* (London: B. J. Holdsworth, 1823) III, 409] he made this discovery. Jim Carnes concludes: "As a result of his marriage and new friends, Keach became a Particular Baptist in 1672, and led many of his members to assist him in organizing a new church" ["The Famous Mr. Keach: Benjamin Keach and His Influence on Congregational Singing in Seventeenth Century England" (Unpublished M. A. Thesis, North Texas State University, 1984), 41]. Carnes surmises that the influence of the "new friends," Hanserd Knollys and William Kiffin, sealed the shift from General Baptist to Particular Baptist. Michael Haykin, *Kiffin, Knollys, and Keach* (Leeds: Reformation Today Trust, 1996), 86, agrees with this conclusion: "However, the fact that Knollys officiated at the marriage of Keach to Susannah Partridge certainly leads one to believe that this influential figure played a role in Keach's coming over to the Calvinistic Baptists." J. Barry Vaughn proceeds with great caution in discussing this change leaving the greatest possible latitude in the absence of specific evidence: "Sometime between 1655 (the date of his baptism) and 1672 (the year Keach's church moved to Horsleydown in Southwark), Keach made the transition from General Baptist to Particular Baptist" ["Benjamin Keach" in Timothy George and David Dockery, eds., *Baptist Theologians* (Nashville: Broadman Press, 1990), 52]. Vaughn includes the documentation from the church register for Knollys's performance of the wedding: "Benjamin Keach and Susannah Partridge his wife were maried [*sic*] the two and twentyeth [*sic*] of April by Mr.han: knowles."

invincible work of Christ for "'tis a great, a full, and compleat Salvation that is contained in this Covenant."[7] His ecclesiological works aim at establishing the church as the joyful unblemished bride preparing to meet her husband, the Lord Jesus Christ. The church should reflect the glory of God in its ordinances, officers, worship, and discipline.[8] Each

---

[7] *The Everlasting Covenant, A Sweet Cordial for a Drooping Soul* (London: H. Barnard, 1693), 35.

[8] This chapter will not have space to discuss his ecclesiology. Characteristically, Keach was at the forefront of discussion and controversy about the church and its ordinances. He interacted in print and in public with different views of baptism, expounding the Baptist view of believer's baptism in opposition to those who held infant baptism. He discussed both the Reformed view and the Anglican view. Titles on this issue include *Pedobaptism disproved* (1691), *The Rector Rectified and Corrected or Infant Baptist Unlawful* (1692), *The Ax Laid to the Root, or One Blow More at the Foundation of Infant Baptism and Church Membership* (1693). He advocated, in distinction from a national body or state church, the autonomy of churches and the necessity of internal ongoing discipline. On that issue he published *The Glory of a True Church, and its Discipline display'd* (1697). He was in the forefront of arguing for the use of hymns in worship as a part of the ordained worship of God. On that account he wrote and published *The Breach Repaired in God's Worship; or Singing of Psalms, Hymns, and Spiritual Songs proved to be an Ordinance of Jesus Christ* (1691); *The Banquetting-House, or a Feast of Fat Things* (1692); *Spiritual Songs, Being the Marrow of the Scripture in Songs of Praise to Almighty God; from the Old and New Covenant* (1700) and others. He also contended for the legitimacy of a ministry fully supported by offerings from the church [*The Gospel Minister's Maintenance Vindicated* (1689)] and the laying on of hands as a Gospel ordinance [*Laying-on-of-Hands upon Baptized Believers, as such, Proved an Ordinance of Christ* (1698)]. He clearly stated his strong convictions not only about sustaining the preacher but about ministerial qualifications, and style, content, and importance of preaching. In the preface to *The Display of Glorious Grace* (London, 1698) Keach wrote, "As I Preach not to please Mens Ears, so but little regard ought to be had to the Scoffing Reflections of such Men, who contemn everything of this kind, unless it consists of a Fancy-ta[l]king Modelation of empty *Rhetorick*, or a high *Florid Stile*...I am not for Airy and *Florid Orations* in the ministration of the Work

writing not only swells with the energy of one who is pressing out the borders of his knowledge through personal experience and understanding, but is designed to convince the reader of the importance of right views on each respective subject. His preaching must have churned with the same intensity and interest, for the congregation grew significantly throughout his life. Thomas Crosby notes that "God was pleased to give such success to his ministry that he quickly increased to a credible number; and they had frequently occasion, to enlarge the place of their assembling, so that at length it became a place large enough for the accommodation of near a *thousand people.*"[9] His writings on salvation, therefore, embody all the force and clarity of his life.

Salvation

For Keach, the wisdom of God in the planning and procurement of salvation elicited ceaseless wonder. Holy angels longed to look into it and are amazed to behold it. In all of its proportions, God's grace in salvation displays the glory of God in manifold ways and involves a multi-faceted manifestation in the world. A brief discussion of the major elements of this merciful act of God constitutes the bulk of this chapter.

---

of God, but for that plain way of preaching used by the Holy Apostles, and our Worthy *Modern Divines* [Puritans]. Besides, could I so Preach or Write, as is the Flesh-pleasing, Ear tickling *a-la-mode* of the times, of such who study Words more than Matter, it would be utterly dislik'd by all such *Pious Christians*, for whose sake, and at whose Importunity these Sermons are published" (iii). He also had confrontations with Sabbatarians in his church who rejected the divine appointment of the Lord's day as replacement for the Jewish Sabbath. He debated with the Quakers, and even had a daughter who became a Quaker whom he sought to convert even on his death bed. He debated with Matthew Caffyn [Caffin] over the eternal and essential deity of Christ. Crosby says, "Preaching the Gospel was the very pleasure of his soul, and his heart was so engaged in the work of the ministry, that from the time of his first appearing in public, to the end of his day, his life was one continued scene of labour and toil" (*History*, 4:304).

[9] Crosby, *History*, 4:273.

Covenant

In the mind of Keach, as well as that of the Apostle Paul, salvation originated in the "grace that was given us in Christ Jesus before the world began" (2 Timothy 1:9).[10] This pre-mundane provision for salvation, called the Covenant of Redemption (also according to Keach the covenant of grace or the covenant of peace), arose from the wisdom and grace of the Triune God. When God considered humanity, he viewed its fallen and miserable state standing desperately in need of reconciling grace. He instituted every aspect of the redemptive scheme both in matter and means and determined its efficacy for a select group, called the elect. Others would be left to follow the implications of their own rebellion and spiritual death resulting in condemnation. The temporal manifestation of this covenant is in the incarnation and work of Christ,

---

[10] Keach discusses the covenant in many places. A clear statement of its origin follows. "II. *Proposition,* That this *Covenant of Peace* was entered into between the Father and the Son before the World began. Hence the Apostle saith, (aluding [*sic*] to this Covenant) *God hath saved us, and called us with an holy calling, not according to our Works, but according to his own purpose and Grace which was given us in Christ Jesus before the World began.* Moreover, Our Lord Jesus saith, that *he was set up from everlasting, from the beginning, or ever the Earth was.* That is ordained, substituted and anointed to be the great Representative and Covenanting-Head in behalf of all the Elect of GOD" (*Display of Glorious Grace,* 10). The words of 2 Timothy 1:9 are cited several times by Keach in support of his development of the covenant: e.g., *ibid.,* 21, 29, 33. See also his *Everlasting Covenant,* Introduction, 8, 20. In the latter, proving that the covenant of redemption and the covenant of grace are the same covenant, Keach writes, "so that the Covenant of Grace it appears, was made by the Holy God, in the Person of the Father, with us in the Person of the Son; mind the Text, *Who hath saved us, and called us with an holy Calling, not according to our Works, but according to his own Purpose and Grace, which was given to us in Christ Jesus, before the World began,* 2 Tim.I.9." On page 32 of the same work he re-emphasizes: "Thus Christ, and his Seed, are but one Party in the Covenant of Grace, as it was primarily made between the Father and Son, who was set up from everlasting, as our Head, And thus, in Christ, Grace was gave to us before the World began, as the Apostle saith, 2 *Tim.I.9.Who hath saved us...*"

the calling and justification of the sinner, and in the complex of factors that provides assurance of sonship to those who embrace Christ's work.

The Covenant and all its accompanying blessings is the driving force in and gives coherence to Keach's entire theological scheme. It provides, therefore, strategic supportive strands in Keach's web of interpretation. The central concern of the eternal covenant of peace ("The whole economy of man's redemption, and all the transactions of the Almighty from the beginning of the world, in and by Jesus Christ," that is, "those covenant transactions between the Father and the Son, about our salvation before the world began") was to "magnify God's glorious grace"[11] in the recovery of "all God's Elect from Sin, Wrath and Misery."[12] It reveals clearly, therefore, of necessity the Triune nature of God.

Trinity

God's operations in the scheme of salvation bears an analogous relationship to the eternal ontological relationship within the Triune God so that in "this Covenant there is a clear Revelation or Manifestation of the Three Persons in the Deity, and their Glory doth equally and joyntly shine forth."[13] Though revealed only darkly under the Old Covenant, the Covenant of Grace gives a "full Declaration of their distinct Personality."

The Father ontologically "by eternal Generation" begets the Son and by covenant sends the Son as mediator; the Son begotten of the Father eternally took to himself by covenant the position of being, on earth, the

---

[11] *Parables*, 744.

[12] *Everlasting Covenant*, 32. Keach's infralapsarian view of the covenant is clear in the way he develops this eternal arrangement. The "Elect, tho not then in Being, yet are here considered as fallen, wretched and forlorn Creatures." When the Son fulfills his terms of the covenant to glorify the Father by honoring all of his attributes in perfect obedience to the Law, he may say, "Thy demands are done, therefore let me have my Reward, and let mine Elect *be made one in us*" (32).

[13] *Ibid.*, 24.

brightness of the Father's glory, weaving the robe of righteousness to honor the body and human nature prepared for him by the Father, and "shed his Blood to make our Peace with God the Father"; the Spirit eternally proceeds "from the Father and the Son" and in the covenant brings to fruition the gracious decrees of the Father and works of the Son for *"The work, and Office of the Spirit,* in this Covenant, *is to quicken* all that the Father hath given to Christ." He convinces the world of sin, righteousness and judgment, renews, regenerates, restores the image of God, sanctifies, gives new and holy affections for God, works faith in us, puts the robe of righteousness on us, sheds the love of God abroad in our hearts. All of these things are analogous to his procession from the Father and the Son in the eternal dynamic display of love and holiness. He convinces us that "Christ's Righteousness is able to justifie and save us" because Christ's righteousness "carryed him to the Father" and the same "will bring us thither."[14]

In his exposition of the Parable of the Lost Sheep, Keach summarized his understanding of the working of the Trinity for the salvation of the elect.

> Brethren, each person of the blessed Trinity has their special and peculiar work in the salvation of sinners: the Father loves the sinner, elects the sinner, finds out a ransom, a Saviour, and Surety for the sinner, and entered into a covenant with him from eternity, upheld him in doing all his work, and accepted of his undertaking for them... And Jesus Christ hath his work also, who hath wrought out a complete righteousness for all them whom he covenanted with the Father, to bring home them he died for on the tree... Moreover, the Holy Ghost hath his proper and peculiar work, which is to renew, quicken, call and regenerate, and effectually to sanctify all those the Father elected, and the Son redeemed, or died for, eternally to save from wrath and hell... As the Father rejoiced to see the Son glorifying of him, which was the grand design of the

---

[14] *Ibid.,* 24-27.

Son in all he did, so Christ and believers rejoice to see the Holy Ghost glorifying of the Son.[15]

Person and offices of Christ

The historically orthodox understanding of the person of Christ supported Keach's treatment of reconciliation and justification. "Christ must be God and Man," Keach said, "if he be a fit Mediator betwixt God and Man." All of the blessings of salvation flow from this mystery of godliness. "We had never been able to have drawn near to God, nor have been mystically united to God, had not there been such an Hypostatical Union of our Nature to the Divine Nature in Christ's Person; for that was the Spring, I say, and Foundation of our Union."[16] This union of the second person of the Trinity with human nature in one person met every concern of God and every need of man so that "Christ is every way qualified to be Mediator of the Covenant."[17]

Christ's threefold office of prophet, priest, and king has particular salvific reference to the elect. The God/Man acting as priest "hath satisfied justice by a condign Price" and has merited "Grace and Glory for all God's Elect." On that basis, as a priest "he intercedes now in Heaven, that all those for whom he died may be called, and have the Merits of his Blood applied to their Souls."[18]

The particularity of Christ's death has direct implications for the spread of the gospel in the whole world. On the one hand, if Christ has died for all without exception, then God's providence is remiss in allowing most of those for whom he died never to hear the gospel. In fact, God's character might be questioned; for if Christ died "to satisfie Divine Justice for every individual Person, then he would be unjust in not sending the gospel to them all." On the other hand, election and Christ's covenantal priestly work render universal preaching necessary, for "where any Elect Sinners are, or dwell, thither the Proclamation

---

[15] *Parables*, 367-368.
[16] *Display of Glorious Grace*, 44.
[17] *Ibid.*, 39.
[18] *Ibid.*, 40, 67.

shall, and must go, to bring them all into the Bonds of the Covenant."[19]
Keach's view of particular atonement thus secures the certain efficacy of
Christ's death, the immutability of God's justice and veracity, and the
necessity of preaching the gospel in the whole world.

As king, he subdues our enemies for us,[20] gives us laws, statutes, and
ordinances, governs his church, and subdues "all the Elect unto
himself."

> I mean, to work Grace in them, and to change their Hearts, and
> vanquish the Power of Sin, and *Satan*, for this is and must be done
> by that Almighty Power which he exerts by his Spirit in their
> Souls, and so takes possession of them as King and Supream
> Ruler, whom as a Priest he purchased by his Blood.[21]

The exertion of almighty power comes because sinners are "dead in Sin,
and stand in as much need to be quickened by Jesus Christ, or to have a
Principle of Divine Life infused into them...as Lazarus had to be
quickened and raised again." All the conversion some professing
Christians have had is an external reformation consequent on the
exercise of natural powers. This has no effect, however, of changing the
heart, restoring the image of God, or forming Christ in them. In the work
of redemption not only is a price paid whereby Christ appeased the

---

[19] *Ibid.*, 167-168. This introduces an issue to be treated later. Rather than
making the preaching of the gospel restricted and discouraging its
proclamation in all the world, thus introducing some of the errors of Hyper-
Calvinism, Keach's view explained why, in the providence of God, some
nations in fact were without the gospel. Just as insistently, however, he argues
that the use of means will extend to every place where God has his elect, that
is, in all the world. He thus holds forth both the hope and the necessity of
extending the preaching of the gospel to all nations.

[20] Already subdued are sin, the world, the devils, and death. Soon to fall,
from Keach's perspective, were the "Mahometan Power" and Roman
Catholicism, which he calls "the *Beast*, and *Mystery Babylon*, which is now
at the very Door" (*ibid.*, 70-71). Cp. the views of Knollys on Roman
Catholicism, above pages 57-58.

[21] *Display of Glorious Grace*, 70-71.

wrath of God by satisfying the justice of God, but by "Power and blessed Conquest...those evil and vicious habits" are removed. No one may be said to be redeemed by Christ "until he is redeemed from his Sins, or delivered from that Enmity that naturally is in his Heart against God, or that sacred image of God be again restored in him."[22]

As a prophet Christ reveals the "Will, Purpose, counsel, and Design of God unto his Chosen." He gives the "knowledge of Salvation to his People," for none can "savingly know this, but as Christ reveals it by his Spirit, as the great Prophet and Teacher of the Church."[23] This work of the Spirit in subjection to the prophetic ministry of Christ gives not only saving knowledge of the Gospel, but assurance of the infallible certainty and truthfulness of the Bible.

Keach, evoking the arguments of both John Owen and John Calvin (1509-1564) in establishing this point, said that "it is absolutely necessary, to the stability and assurance of our faith, in order to eternal life, to have the internal testimony of the Holy Spirit upon our hearts, or the effectual operations thereof." By this gracious work, the sincere Christian, who "has no skill to defend the truth by force of arguments" against subtle and sophisticated "artificers" who point to the obscurities and apparent difficulties of Scripture to "insinuate objections against it," may so experience the power and grandeur of Scripture, so taste, feel, and see its divinely originated character that he will stand "firm as a rock," with his faith greatly confirmed against any such onslaught.[24]

---

[22] *The Counterfeit Christian; or the Danger of Hypocrisy* (London, 1691), 27-28. Keach emphasized the sobering reality that the power of natural conscience together with the preaching of the word, the rod of affliction, and different kinds of assistance and help may create a church member, preacher, or one, who in the eyes of men, is of blameless life. Yet that person may not be changed in heart "or regenerated by the effectual and special Operations of Christ's Spirit, nor have Union with Christ" (29).

[23] *Ibid.*, 72-73.

[24] *Preaching from the Types and Metaphors of the Bible* (Grand Rapids: Kregel Publications, 1972), xxvii. This work was formerly published in London in 1855 under the title *Tropologia; A Key to Open Scripture Metaphors, together with Types of the Old Testament.*

Justification

Because Keach agreed with the sixteenth-century reformers[25] on the key position of justification by faith alone in God's covenantal arrangement for salvation, Keach devoted several major works to that theme: *The Marrow of Justification* (1692), *The Everlasting Covenant* (1693, a funeral sermon for the Particular Baptist pastor Henry Forty), *A Golden Mine opened; or, the Glory of God's rich Grace displayed* (1694), *Jacob's Ladder Improved (Christ Alone the way to heaven)* (1698), *A medium betwixt two Extremes* (1698), and *The Display of Glorious Grace; or the Covenant of Peace opened* (1698). The theme is abundantly present also in the two major expository works on the parables and on the types and metaphors in the Bible. The style of presentation is expository, pastoral and polemical.

Keach defended the doctrine of justification so ardently for two reasons: one, it gives glory to the perfections of Christ and exalts him; two, sinners may have comfort in no other way. For example, in the

---

[25] Keach regularly refers to his harmony with the rest of "Protestantism" on this doctrine and recognizes the indebtedness of the Christian world, under God, to the faithfulness of Martin Luther (1483-1546) and Calvin. He also sees himself in harmony with Puritanism at large on this doctrine, though he had no fear to confront them on their views of baptism and other issues of ecclesiology: "The Righteousness, and Benefits of Christ's Righteousness, is made ours, when we relye, or trust to God's free Promise as the immediate and sole Cause of Pardon and Life, (as all true Protestants formerly affirmed)...Let such be exhorted, to lay to heart and repent, who darken the Doctrine of God's Free-grace, and eclipse the glory of the Everlasting Covenant, that turn it into a Law of conditional Obedience... why should that glorious Doctrine of Justification, that shone forth in the days of *Martin Luther*, and has been the Ground of so many godly Christian's Hope; nay, Martyrs, now be struck at?" (*Everlasting Covenant*, 29, 42); "By the *Baxterian Party* I expect to be called an *Antinomian*, for that hath been their Artifice of late, to expose the *True Ancient Protestant Doctrine* about *Justification*" (*Display of Glorious Grace*, v); "God leaves out our names, and puts in Christ's Name, that the Debt, Satisfaction, and Curse might fall upon him alone. See Dr. *Goodwin*" (*ibid.*, 103).

parable of the Lost Son Keach compares the "best robe" to the "garment or robe of justification." Such justification is none other than "the righteousness of Christ, which is put upon, or imputed to them that believe in Jesus to their justification before God."

Particularly in light of Roman Catholic views and the Neonomianism of Richard Baxter, Keach wrote insistently about this active obedience of Christ as the matter of the sinner's justification. "Some say it is only called the righteousness of God" because he accepts "our faith, repentance, and sincere obedience" as righteousness. It is enough, say they, that Christ has merited for us God's acceptance of "our inherent righteousness and good works." Is this the Gospel? It is nothing but "a piece of new popery," Keach would say.

Rather, sinners must have a righteousness that is "wrought out by him who is perfect God in our nature." It is not, as Baxter and Rome think, that Christ's death is the meritorious cause of, or opportunity for, our justification. "Christ's righteousness, i.e., his active and passive obedience," Keach insisted, "is the matter of justification, or the material cause; and as it is imputed to us, also the formal cause thereof."[26]

The nature of the case would permit no other sort of mediator nor provisions for salvation of any other kind. "The whole Work of making Peace is solely committed to our Lord Jesus Christ, not to see others do it." Every part of the work is done by Christ himself, including "what is necessary to be done *for us, in us, and by us also.*"

This fullness of provision, though a sovereign decision, was not merely an arbitrary arrangement. Keach affirmed God's infinite freedom and dismissed the idea that there was "a necessity laid either upon the Father or the Son to enter into this Covenant of Peace for us." But once by "Free and Sovereign Grace" the determination to save is present, then the "necessity for Christ to be the Mediator and Surety of it" follows. Another way of peace may exist that is hidden in eternity and in the infinite mind of God. But, based on the revelation given us, we cannot conceive of it. God's honor, law, justice, truth, all demand this way. "No

---

[26] *Parables,* 400. The many allusions to justification Keach gives in his *Display of Glorious Grace* were strategically repetitive, his purpose being "chiefly to refute the New prevailing Errours about Justification."

pardon, no Peace could be procured by Men nor Angels, nor as an absolute or simple Act of Mercy, without the Impeachment of God's *Justice, Truth,* and *Holiness,* &c. therefore it could not be so done at all." [27] Only such a justification will establish the eternal covenant as well-ordered and sure.

The view that justification is a mixture of Christ's meritorious work with our inherent holiness and evangelical obedience depends on a general atonement. Christ, according to the necessities of this view, was the "Head of all Mankind in dying, and all, as so considered, have Union with him." Many of those, however, for whom he died "shall never be saved by his Life" because they do not answer the "Condition of Faith and sincere Obedience." From this perspective, Christ's work as priest is more extensive than its final application by the Spirit, for "Faith must be wrought out by the Creature through the help of the Spirit."[28]

But a scheme of justification built on general atonement and conditional covenant violates the nature of God and the perfection of Christ's mediatorial work. Keach cites Romans 5:10 as proof that Christ's death procures with certainty all the other aspects of salvation. The same may be inferred from Romans 8:32. If God has given us his Son in death and we have been reconciled by that death, then how much more will we be assured of all the benefits of his obedient life and resurrection life.

---

[27] *Display of Glorious Grace,* 34-36, *passim.* Another compelling reason for seeing this way of salvation as necessary because it is analogous to God's nature and not simply an arbitrary means is in Keach's discussion of the love of the Father for the Son. "To say God might have entered into a Covenant of Peace for us any other way than by the Mediator Jesus Christ, or through his Death and Atonement would...reflect upon his Love to his own dear Son: For why should the Son of God be made a Curse for us, or suffer the cursed Death of the Cross, to make our Peace, if Peace could be made any other way, without the least injury to the Justice, Law, or Holiness of God, &c. No doubt, my Brethren, but that the Son of God had been spared, if he had foresaw that our Peace might have been made some other way" (*ibid.,* 36-37).

[28] *Everlasting Covenant,* 39.

Were not all the Elect, or all Christ dyed for, vertually (as in our Head) reconciled to God by the Death of Christ? and doth not the Apostle assure us that we shall much more be saved by Christ's Life, if he reconciled us to God by his death? was not the Gift of Christ in his death for us a greater gift than the gift of the Spirit to us? Did not we all rise from the dead with Christ, vertually when he was raised? And doth not that give us Assurance that we shall be actually quickened and raised? First from a death in sin, respecting our souls; and also be all raised to Eternal Life and Glory, at the last day respecting our Bodies.[29]

This view honors God in "exactly suiting with and answering the pure nature of God." His justice "cannot find one flaw in it." His truth discovers not "the least exception against it, in respect of the threats of God against Adam for his disobedience." Even so excellent an attribute as the holiness of God "beholdeth not the least stain, spot of sin, or blemish in it." In addition to that, it exactly answers "that righteousness which the law of God requireth of us to our justification before God, i.e., a sinless righteousness."[30]

Justification by the imputed righteousness of Christ not only honors every attribute of God but is the only ground of hope for the sinner both here and hereafter. Every comfort required by the soul in distress may be met in the perfection of Christ's work, the "best robe." It is "our only title to heaven, and that which frees and delivereth us from the pangs of

---

[29] *Ibid.*, 39-40. Earlier (*ibid.*, 35-36) Keach makes this same point and shows how integral efficacious atonement is to his understanding of the covenant and all its provisions including justification. Our sinful condition, including both condemnation and corruption, the resulting necessity of salvation by grace, the perfection of the wisdom of the Tri-une God, and the unique qualifications of Jesus Christ as mediator all conspire to make impossible a salvation conditioned on human response. Human response is certainly within the covenant, but as a fruit, not a root, as an effect, not a cause—a condition only in the sense that the characteristic always will be present in the elect, not in the sense that either the inception or completion of salvation is contingent on it.

[30] *Parables,* 400.

hell." Would any man dare come to his death bed clinging to his own righteousness, obedience, or good works? All who would trust such emptiness would find themselves in a deplorable state for "it is the righteousness, the death, and merits of Christ that give believers ease, comfort, and hope at the hour of death, and will give boldness in the day of judgment."

In addition, when distress assaults the soul, when accusation or oppression come from without or within, nothing else will support the sinking soul. When sin presses the conscience, when the law shoots bitter arrows of its curse, when Satan unloads his fiery darts, or when "death looks grim upon the soul," only the righteousness of Christ suffices as our "plea against them all, and yields a believer sweet help and succour."

> Jesus Christ made an end of sin, as to its guilt and condemning power, and hath satisfied both law and justice, and vanquished the evil, and taken away the sting of death; so that justice is on our side, and pleads for us, as well as mercy, and death hereby is become a blessing, and no part of the curse to such who have this robe upon them.[31]

Not only is the sinner's comfort at stake, but his very salvation, in this view of justification. Any attempt to mix in works, whether it be "home-spun righteousness," a trust in our faith as righteousness, or the confidence in inherent righteousness that comes from the internal working of the Spirit, is an attempt to go about to establish one's own righteousness. Such trust is hypocritical confidence and results in condemnation, for it is "not through our personal Righteousness, though joined or coupled with Christ's Merits, that we are justified, but through the personal Righteousness of Christ alone, and the Merits of his Blood received by Faith." Not receiving this doctrine is unbelief, for what is unbelief but an "actual or vertual denial of the Truth of the Gospel,

---

[31] *Ibid.*, 401.

when Men do not assent to the Doctrine of it, by an act of the Understanding?"[32]

Richard Baxter's separation of the covenant of grace from the covenant of redemption also separated Christ's work from the matter of our justification. This reality agitated Keach to ardency in his discussion of the covenant in its relation to justification. "Some men would have us believe," Keach says, "that the Covenant of Grace in the latitude of it, is but that merciful conditional Covenant of Faith, and Gospel Holiness." God enters this covenant with us, according to Baxter, and "we shall be Justified and Saved" if "we perform the covenant to the end...in sincere Obedience."[33] The results of this Baxterian construction were disastrous and dangerous to the souls of men. "We are not under Grace, but under a Law that will keep us in Doubts and Bondage as long as we live." But even worse, "if we have no other Righteousness than this, which is either within us, or wrought by us, we shall certainly drop down into Hell when we come to die."[34]

Assurance and evangelism

Given that the covenant is well-ordered and sure, that God's elect are known to him from before the foundation of the world, that the provisions Christ has made are sufficient for every aspect of salvation and effectual in applying it, and that all of God's elect certainly will come to salvation and no more than God's elect will come, two practical questions arise. One, how may one seek salvation under such circumstances and how may one be assured that his faith is the faith of God's elect? Two, should the gospel be preached to the unconverted with a view to calling them to salvation?

---

[32] *Counterfeit Christian*, 20, 35, 41. In this work Keach strongly emphasizes the doctrines of justification and regeneration as antidotes to hypocrisy. Hypocrites of various sorts either have false perceptions or faulty experiences of the nature of Christ's work outside of us, on the one hand, and in us, on the other.

[33] *Everlasting Covenant*, 17.

[34] *Ibid.*, 18.

Assurance and its evidences

On the issue of seeking salvation and assurance Keach developed a balanced system of objective truth and self-examination. The three-fold cord of the certain efficacy of Christ's work, personal evidences of a changed heart, and the internal witness of the Spirit make possible one's confidence in being a child of grace.

The objective certainty of salvation for a certain number of persons need not discourage any person from finding assurance. Paul considers God's sovereignty as the foundation of all true hope. If any would lay a charge against God's elect, the defense may be summarized in the simple affirmation that "It is God who justifies." If the specter of God's just wrath threatening condemnation gives distress to the soul, one must remember, "It is Christ who died, Yea who is risen again."[35]

Keach presents the Everlasting Covenant as the "Hope, Desire, Salvation, and Consolation of every true Believer." It was devised by the infinite wisdom of God. In fact, it is the "Top Glory of all his Transactions" for the sake of sinners from all eternity. It exalts all the attributes of God and abases man. It provides a full and complete salvation, leaving no part of it in doubt or contingent on helpless humanity. It is tested and proved and has never failed any—"O what black, what guilty, what filthy, and what bloody sinners," Keach cries out, "have been saved by the Grace of, and Blood of the Covenant." It gives us God himself and Christ himself as our portion and thus is suited to any state of guilt, despair, affliction, trial, calamity, fear, doubt, and "Spiritual Dissertions, whatsoever."[36]

If any aspect of justification depended on the work of man, then no assurance would be possible. Rather than discouraging assurance, therefore, the covenant encourages it. As the *Second London Confession of Faith* says: "This certainty is not a bare conjectural and probable

---

[35] See Romans 8:32ff., where Paul argues strongly for the infallible efficacy of God's electing purpose as fully consummated in Christ's death, resurrection, and ascension. This then serves as constituting God's favor and love in the face of all opposition, adversity, and turmoil.

[36] *Everlasting Covenant*, 34-37.

persuasion, grounded upon a fallible hope; but an infallible assurance of faith, founded on the Blood and Righteousness of Christ, revealed in the Gospel."[37] God's absolute determination to save a certain number of sinners based on the infinitely worthy work of Christ must be the presupposition of any doctrine of assurance which has internal biblical consistency. Any point along the chain of justification that rests on the holiness, righteousness, will, determination or perseverance of the sinner becomes the broken link that spoils assurance, and, according to Keach, spoils justification.

> *No Cordial* like what this Covenant hath provided for us, to bear up and revive our drooping Spirits; and whoever you are, that under your Fears, Doubtings, Temptations or Despondings, that seek Relief any where else, will but deceive your own poor and deluded Souls... will not *Satan* shew you notwithstanding all your sincerity you have in your Hearts, great Hypocrisie?... And though you have done much good, will not your Consciences tell you, you might have done more? you gave a *Shilling* may be to this poor, and that poor and distressed Object, when may be you ought to have given a *Pound*. O Sirs! your Relief lies in Christ, and in the Covenant of Grace, in Christ's perfect and compleat Righteousness in his Death, or you have none, nor never will...
>
> O Soul! here's thy Relief, even in the Blood of this Covenant in Christ's Death; under all thy Fears, and Temptations of *Satan*, and under the sad Accusations of thy own Conscience... If thou wants Righteousness and Strength, say, Christ is thy Righteousness... Thus there is Relief in this Covenant for poor doubting and desponding Souls in all their Troubles and Temptations.[38]

---

[37] *Second London Confession of Faith* 18.2 [in William L. Lumpkin, *Baptist Confessions of Faith* (Valley Forge: Judson Press, 1969), 274]. Keach's treatment of assurance conforms to this delineation and contains also the other nuances that are in the other three paragraphs of this chapter on assurance. For a full text of the *Confession*, see Lumpkin, *Baptist Confessions*, 242-295.

[38] *Everlasting Covenant*, 37-38.

Having assurance founded on the certainty of justification allows greater latitude in the investigation of the nature of saving faith. If one were dependent on an internal work for justification, then both the honor of God as manifest in his immutable justice and the comfort of sinners striving to enter in at the narrow gate would suffer loss. God would admit less than perfect obedience to his law as sufficient for life. But the truth of the matter is that "God could not in point of Justice, considering his Infinite Holiness, Rectitude of his Nature, and the Sanction of his Law, abate any thing; no not one Farthing of the whole Debt, but must have full Satisfaction."[39]

Moreover, the sinner would never know if his obedience were at a sufficient level of acceptance, for God's law and Christ's righteous life are far above him. In point of fact, the sinner "must forego or give up all his own Righteousness as good for nothing; nay to account it as Dung in point of justification at God's Bar" or compared to Christ's righteousness. Instead of seeking justification by his own righteousness or by his own "Faith and sincere Obedience," he is "utterly to renounce it, and to submit to the Righteousness of God."[40] Freed of any delusion of personal righteousness, even if perceived in relative terms, the criteria for hope emerge from a discernible body of evidences. Given Christ's obedience as the foundation of life, God's honor and justice remains uncompromised and the sinner's quest for assurance has hope for success.

The second strand in the cord of assurance is observation of distinctive evidences of a work of the Spirit. One does not have justifying faith without sanctification, for "faith...hath a two-fold office." Consistent with all the mental and spiritual concepts preparative to justification, in sanctification faith, "in respect of its own blessed inward virtue and quality... also purges the soul, and sanctifieth the whole man." Keach states it strongly in his exposition of the parable of the Marriage Supper.

---

[39] *Display of Glorious Grace*, 58.
[40] *Ibid.*, 59-60.

[W]here justification is, there is also sanctification; a man is not sanctified that is not justified, nor are any actually justified that are not sanctified; though it is true, "God justified the ungodly,["] i.e., They are ungodly just at the time when God first justified them, they are not holy and sanctified persons before they are justified, because it is the righteousness of Christ alone that is the matter of our justification before God, which no man hath imputed unto him until he believes in Jesus Christ; but though they are all ungodly ones, just at the time when God justified them, i.e., he finds them ungodly, when he comes to pass the act of free justification upon them; yet God doth not leave them unsanctified by the Spirit.[41]

The Christian, therefore, is "not to work for Life, but from Life." If one is justified, then assuredly faith has been wrought in his heart by the Holy Spirit, a "Principle of Life wrought in the Soul" which causes one to "live a Holy Life and renounce all Sin and Iniquity from a Principle of Faith." The Christian sees sin as "so hateful unto God, and so abominable in his Sight" that out of love to Christ he desires to "do all things whatsoever he commandeth him."[42] With this motivation of love, the law, though impossible to keep so as to be justified by it, is the guide to sanctification, for "as a perfect Rule of Righteousness" and "being so unchangeable a Law," we grow in our desire to keep that which "obligeth us to perpetual Obedience."[43] This sanctification is not optional, but an intrinsic and inevitable part of the provisions of the Covenant of Redemption and bound up in its eternal wisdom. "Christ never leaves his Elect, until he hath brought them to these Terms."[44]

With such glorious privileges at stake and such a clear delineation between those who shall inherit them and those who shall not ("He that believeth not is condemned already"), Keach exhorts sinners to "labour and strive to receive Jesus Christ," and believers to "labour after a

---

[41] *Parables*, 547-548. The quote which begins with "God" does not have the close quotes in the original.

[42] *Display of Glorious Grace*, 60.

[43] *Ibid.*, 103.

[44] *Ibid.*, 61.

strong Faith in Christ" for the measure of their peace will be according to the degree and measure of their faith. He then urges everyone to make trial and "examine themselves, whether they have Peace with God, or not." Following are the "Rules" by which one may know whether he or she is in covenant.

First, the true believer will be at war with sin, have sin cast out of his love and affections, loathe it, hate it because it is hateful to God and has caused Christ so much pain. There will be an "unreconcilable opposition" in the believer against all sin. Second, the believer will "mourn for sin, because it caused such cursed Enmity" evoking rebellion against God. Third, Keach asks, *"Are you reconciled to the Ways of God,* even to the strictest Acts and Duties of Holiness? Do you love the Word of God because of its Purity?"

Fourth, The believer will love the people of God, pray for them, avoid bitterness, reproachful language, and censorious reflections. " 'Tis to be feared, that such are not at Peace with God, that are not at Peace with all the Children of God." Fifth, a believer will mourn for the salvation of those he loves that are yet unreconciled to God. Sixth, the believer will "Love, Esteem, and highly Respect and Honour the Ambassadors of Peace" and loathe to hear them maligned and slandered. Seventh, do you seek to live at peace with your own conscience, with your family, and with the church? Finally, do you "long for the Peace of Jerusalem and pray for the time God will "give his People Intire and Universal Peace."[45]

The last two pages of the *Counterfeit Christian,* following a list of twelve questions for self-examination, summarize the characteristics of the true Christian. Keach did not want to leave the impression that his doctrine of justification abandoned the field of obedience to the Neonomian Baxterians. Obedience mattered just as much to Keach. It

---

[45] *Ibid.,* 299-300. Keach urged this kind of examination quite often. In *A Golden Mine opened; or, the Glory of God's rich Grace displayed* (London, 1694), he listed five tests of true faith all directed toward the person of Christ (499). He also labored to distinguish between true faith and false faith as seen in his exposition of the parable of the unclean spirit in Matthew 12. Further, see note 47 below.

was an indispensable element in his understanding of the scheme of salvation. His construction had no tendency "to take us off of Holy Duties and Obedience." But as he emphasized often, obedience was from life, not for life. He thus identified sources in the true Christian from which obedience flowed.

Since obedience flows from a principle of spiritual life, or saving grace, the Christian's actions are neither self-righteousness nor dead works. In doing acts of obedience from a principle of faith, he seeks no acceptance with God from his actions, but he sees himself justified and accepted only in Jesus Christ. He acts also from a principle of love to Christ and consequently is for the "hardest part of Religion, as well as for the easiest part of it." His love causes him constantly to attend "upon the means of Salvation, as well as to expect salvation itself." Last, his end, or purpose, is the honor and glory of God. The true Christian, therefore, desires "to live to God on Earth, as well as to live with God in Heaven."[46]

---

[46] *Counterfeit Christian*, 55-56. Keach warns his hearers against presumption and lists twelve subjects, some of which are repeated in other examination lists, to prompt serious spiritual introspection. Question 3, for eample, queries, "Are you willing to suffer and part with all that you have, rather than sin against God? Do you see more evil in the least Sin, than in the greatest Suffering?" Question 9 probes, "Do you more pry into you own Faults, than into the Miscarriages of others? Are you universal in your Obedience? And do you obey Christ's Word, his Commands, because you love him?" After proposing these twelve items, Keach assists the reader in personal resolution of the questions the considerations may have stirred up. "Consider of these few Questions, and do not doubt but that your Hearts are sincere, when you can give a comfortable Answer to them, though it be with some fear and doubts that still may arise in you. A true Christian is ready to mistake his Portion, and take that to be his, that belongs to an Hypocrite; as an Hypocrite on the other hand, mistakes that which belongs to him, and applies that to himself, which is the Portion of sincere Christians: but Grace is like a small Seed at first, that cannot be soon espied in the House, *i.e.* the Heart, especially when there is much Smoak and Darkness yet remaining." Keach then gives the for clearly distinctive marks of a "godly Man, or he that is a true Christian" summarized in the text above. The righteousness manifest

These tests, though the details of the lists differ at some points from document to document, reflect the phrase in the *Second London Confession*, "the inward evidence of those graces of the Spirit unto which promises are made."[47] They show Keach's writings and preaching as in vital unity with that great body of Puritan divinity which mastered the art of pastoral theology. At its core, Puritan thought (and Particular Baptist thought) scrutinized and unveiled the biblical teaching on the organic relationship between the objective and external in the work of Christ and the subjective, experiential, and internal by the work of the Spirit. In uniting the Elect with Christ to receive all the graces of his redemptive work, the Spirit also forms Christ in them in the new birth and sanctification. As Keach contended, "The Covenant of Grace is sure, and all the Blessings thereof, because the Execution of Christ's last Will and Testament, is put into the Hands of the Holy Spirit; he is the great Executioner of this Covenant."[48] The examination assumes, therefore, both the objectivity of redemption and the certainty of internal graces. These graces operate immediately but discernibly and in accord with truth. This leads to the third rope in the cord of assurance.

The *Second London Confession* calls this third element "the testimony of the Spirit of adoption, witnessing with our Spirits that we are the children of God."[49] Keach shows his familiarity with the *Confession* and his use of its proofs when he quotes Romans 8:16-17 in support of this element of assurance. Verbal and conceptual similarities mark his statement, "The Holy Spirit witnesses by it self, by an inward and secret Persuasion or Suggestion, that God is our Father, and we his Children, and also by the Testimony of his Graces and powerful Operations, tho' not in the like Degree and Clearness to all Believers."[50]

---

by the true Christian, though not for justification, exceeds that of the Scribes and Pharisees.

[47] *Second London Confession* 18.2 (Lumpkin, *Baptist Confessions*, 274).

[48] *Everlasting Covenant*, 33.

[49] *Second London Confession* 18.2 (Lumpkin, *Baptist Confessions*, 274).

[50] *Everlasting Covenant*, 34. The text actually reads "by an inward an secretd." The typesetter evidently placed the word "secret" before the "d" of the previous word, which was supposed to be "and."

J. Barry Vaughn, in quoting this sentence from Keach, says, "The danger of Keach's doctrine of assurance is that assurance could come to be nothing but a feeling."[51] That warning is pertinent should one isolate the "inward...Suggestion, that God is our Father." That kind of isolation, however, would be inconsistent with the fullness of Keach's doctrine of assurance as well as his warnings that confidence in the absence of evidence is delusion. Keach clearly wanted to maintain a real internal work of the Spirit in which assurance goes beyond a mere rational demonstration to the natural faculties. Along with that, he would be careful to protect the consistency of that internal witness with the "Testimony of his Graces and powerful Operations."

Evangelism

A second practical issue begging for attention in light of Keach's consistent Calvinism is evangelism. Given the immutability of the eternal covenant, which includes eternal unconditional election, effectual calling, and limited atonement, is there a place for evangelism? Barry Vaughn surmises that "Keach's high Calvinist soteriology did contribute to the development of hyper-Calvinism in the succeeding generation." He believes that Keach was "close to the hyper-Calvinists in his attitude toward foreign missions," and his atttitude much like that of the Hyper-Calvinists who opposed Carey.[52]

---

[51] Vaughn, "Benjamin Keach" in George and Dockery, eds., *Baptist Theologians*, 60.

[52] *Ibid.*, 60-61. The reference to William Carey is anachronistic since Carey and the beginning of the modern missionary movement is over ninety years away from the publication of *Gospel Mysterie Unveil'd*. One can only judge according to Keach's attitude toward the duty to evangelize in principle. I will demonstrate that he is clearly with Carey on the "obligations of Christians to use means for the conversion of the heathen." It is interesting to note also that Joseph Ivimey, one of the keenest observers of the origins and tendencies of the Hyper-Calvinist controversy aligned his sympathies with Keach in opposition to the Hypers. I do not agree with all of Ivimey's methods or conclusions, but his view on Keach's relationship to the leading issues of the controversy is noteworthy in light of Vaughn's observation.

Vaughn's judgment is based on a passage in *Gospel Mysteries Unveil'd* in which Keach describes God's sovereign distribution of gospel preaching as an evidence of the specific and effectual purpose of Christ's death. Keach wrote that God might have sent the "whole Lump of fallen Mankind to Hell." Why is the gospel in England and not in India? Why does England have light and many nations are under the darkness of Popery, Paganism, or Mahometanism? "If Christ died for all, why is not the Gospel preached to all?" Keach's succinct reply is that the "Gospel he doth not give to all, nor his Spirit, Faith, and other Gifts that are necessary to Salvation, to many thousands in the world; therefore he did not give his Son to die to save them all."[53]

"Although [the writer] venerates the piety of the eminent men by whom this error was introduced and propagated, he has felt it his duty to expose the baneful tendency of their principles. He is happy to think, on this subject, with those useful and distinguished ministers, the Stennetts and the Wallins, a Keach, a Piggott, and a Gifford; and he feels persuaded, had their manner of preaching been universal, the churches would not have suffered the decline which evidently appears to have taken place in numbers and zeal, towards the close of the reign of George II" (Ivimey, *History*, III, xi).

[53] *Parables*, 362. Vaughn quotes the same passage from Book II, 75-76 of the 1701 multi-volume edition of *Gospel Mysteries Unveil'd*. The quote comes from Keach's treatment of the "The Lost Sheep" in which Keach gives an unrelenting, extended, detailed, and insistent interpretation of God's utter sovereignty in the salvation of sinners. We must be picked up by Christ and carried home to God on his shoulders alone.

Keach also takes direct action against the leading tenet of Arminianism as he sees it, "that there is a power in the will of man, to incline him either to choose or refuse, to yield or resist, to embrace Christ and the operations of the Spirit, or reject him and all those operations" (*Parables*, 362). As Keach saw it, the Arminian places the "efficacy of grace, and of the death of Christ, and success of the gospel" on the will of man. "The will determines the whole success, whether it shall be effectual, or ineffectual." In the matter of doxology, therefore, the Arminian may praise God and Jesus Christ that a way is provided whereby we might be saved, but "that we are saved we may thank ourselves, and glory in our wisdom, care and diligence" (*ibid.*, 363). This defeats the whole scriptural theme of salvation by grace alone as well as the specific intent of the parable, according to Keach.

In this passage, as in other places on this same issue, Keach argues from the greater to the lesser. Since the Father gave up his Son to die, how much more will he provide the circumstances whereby a person redeemed by that death might hear the gospel. If he gave his Son to die, how much more will he give the Spirit to make the preached message effectual. But since he has not done these two latter in most places, it stands to reason that he has not given his Son to die for all. In this argument for limited atonement, Keach does not advocate that preachers be selective in those to whom they preach or that they not encourage sinners to seek Christ and strive earnestly to close with him and place faith in him.

In fact, Vaughn overlooks Keach's strong application of the theology of this parable in the second part of his exposition. Among the friends and neighbors who rejoice at the finding of the sheep are ministers and members of the church. When sinners are found "poor ministers succeed in their great work, as instruments in the hand of God." Nothing could be a greater encouragement or strengthen their hand and hearts more than to see one who was "condemned to die, lying in a deep dungeon, or in a horrible pit, now set at liberty." The task and calling of the minister as an ambassador is "to persuade sinners to receive and embrace the Lord Jesus." The truths of Christ's seeking and finding all of his people should stir up ministers "to do their utmost in order to the conversion of sinners." They should not be weary, nor faint, nor be discouraged even when reproached by men and Satan for "God has appointed preaching as his great ordinance, for the...conversion of lost sinners."[54]

And though the minister has no power either of virtue or persuasion to change a heart and bring a sinner home, but only Christ alone by his Spirit can do that, nevertheless, ministers "are to do what they can, they are to invite them, press, them, entreat and persuade them to come."[55] A faithful ministry "will do what the Lord commands them to do" with the confidence that "in God's heart is room enough for millions of souls; and in God's house there is not only bread enough, and to spare, but

---

[54] *Ibid.*, 368-370.
[55] *Ibid.*, 546.

room enough also."[56] A minister of Christ, in order "to accomplish his Ambassy, and to bring the King's Enemies to accept of Peace," must pray, entreat, and "beseech Sinners to be reconciled to God." In fact, like the apostle who cried tears over the lost, "Faithful Ministers art willing to spend their Lives to win Souls to Christ, yea, to die upon the spot to save one poor Sinner."

> Our Great Master thought not his Blood too dear to make our Peace, and shall Ministers think their Strength, their Lives, their Blood too much, that so they might see the Travel of Christ's Soul; I mean, Sinners reconciled unto God, or Christ's Blood by Faith sprinkled on their Hearts: Many like the Minister's Dignity, but few like their Work and Duty. My Brethren, it is a great Trust that is committed to them.[57]

Urgency in calling sinners to trust Christ, persuading them to comply with terms that are "easie," beseeching them to accept of "offered"[58]

---

[56] *Ibid.*, 546.

[57] *Display of Glorious Grace*, 141-142.

[58] How Keach would have responded to the controversy that began about 1707 over the use of the word "offer" when speaking of the gospel of God's grace, one may only speculate. Congregationalist Joseph Hussey (1660-1726) argued that grace was not offered and the minister only could describe the "operations" of God's grace. Without arguing strengths and weaknesses of Hussey's position, and recognizing that Keach is an anachronism to the controversy, it may still be conceded that Keach did not shrink from using the word "offer" frequently and knowledgeably in his presentation of the Gospel: "This proclamation offers Free Pardon of all Sins, both past, present, and to come, to all that believe in Jesus Christ" (*Display of Glorious Grace*, 168); "All are condemned in the first Adam, and their Condemnation will be aggravated upon them, because they reject the Offers of Peace, or the Mediation of Jesus Christ, and believe not in him; and indeed all Men would do this was not Infinite Love shewed, and Power put forth towards some according to God's Eternal Purpose in Election" (*ibid.*, 610); "Shall Christ and all Covenant Mercies be offered to you? a Feast of fat Things provided for you, and will you make light of this Offer and gracious tender of Salvation"

grace all seen as the "Duty" of the gospel minister neither constitutes Hyper-Calvinism nor prepares the way for it.

Persuasion, clearly and consistently advocated and regularly practiced by Keach as a task of the gospel minister, stands outside the normal boundaries of Hyper-Calvinism. At the close of this same exposition Keach calls to the unconverted, "Sinners...then labour to return to God! attend upon the word, cry to him to help you to believe."[59] At another place, the preacher exhorts, "Sinners, Will not you accept of Peace?" Then in a series of exhortations, questions, and motives "to stir you up thus to do" Keach seeks to lay hold of the sinner for Christ. Shall such a mediator die to make peace and any sinner refuse the peace that he has made? When the terms are so easy (believe, trust, sue out pardon through his blood), and the stakes so high (a woeful condition awaits any who seeks salvation in another way), and the savior so competent (great sinners, abominable sinners, profane sinners are saved by him), how could any refuse to trust and accept him?[60] For sinners who lie condemned by the covenant of works, that Christ has obliged himself to work all our works "in us, as well as for us" is good news. To them Keach calls, "O sue out your pardon, by taking hold of Christ."[61]

(*Everlasting Covenant*, 42); "We say the will of a natural man, may and doth resist the common emotions of the Spirit, and offers of grace; but that special grace which God puts forth upon the soul with an intent according to his own eternal purpose to bring it home to himself, and effectually to call or regenerate, they cannot, shall not resist" (*Parables*, 362); "Though the Jews were first to have salvation offered unto them, yet the grace of God is extended further, even to the Gentiles also" (*ibid.*, 546). These uses of "offer" could be multiplied. However, one should notice also that Keach believed rejection of the gospel aggravated one's condemnation, a teaching contrary to Hyper-Calvinism, which rejects the obligation of the unregenerate to repent and believe the gospel since they have no power to do so. What one has no power to do, they argue, he has no obligation to do.

[59] *Parables*, 370.

[60] *Display of Glorious Grace*, 65-66.

[61] *Ibid.*, 106.

Evangelism for Keach involved also theological integrity and church purity. Those who taught baptismal regeneration, or even covenantal blessings connected with infant baptism, Keach feared were deceiving people with false hope. "O the danger of the pernicious Doctrine!" he lamented. There may be many who "flatter themselves with the Hopes of Heaven from this false Foundation, thinking they sucked in the true Faith, and true Religion, with their Mother's Milk, and were made Christians" when a priest scattered water on their faces when but babes. Those same people "never doubt of their Salvation" but are "Enemies to the Life and Power of Godliness" and have been made Christians in a way "which Christ and his Apostles never taught."[62]

Others may share in a proper view of baptism but are careless in admitting members to the church. They conduct many into membership from whom little evidence is present of the new birth. Pastors must learn that " 'tis not a great Church, but a holy and good Church Christ loves." Some churches would be stronger and better if "many were severed from them." For pride and covetousness, however, many preachers are busy to "bring Men into visible Profession, and make them Members of Churches" rather than to preach in such a way as to "shew them the necessity of Regeneration, Faith, or a changed Heart."[63]

Keach's earnestness and intensity both for evangelism and church purity, and for pastoral zeal and pastoral discretion unfolds in pathetic timbre and poetic rhythm in a part of his closing reproofs.

We too often see when People are got into Churches, they conclude all is well; and when Conversion is preached, they do not think it concerns them, but others who are openly prophane: and thus they come to be blinded, may be to their own Destruction; and if their Blood do not lie at some of your Doors, it will be well. I am afraid some nowadays like the Pharisees, may be said to compass Sea and

---

[62] *Counterfeit Christian*, 51, 52.
[63] *Ibid.*, 54.

Land to make Proselytes, but when made, are two fold more the Children of Hell than before, as our Saviour intimates.[64]

Conclusion

If Keach served in contemporary Baptist life as a "Baptist Bishop," and were to issue a series of episcopal admonitions, what might we expect him to say? He would look with disbelief and wonder at the abundant opportunities for formal training that modern-day Baptists have. He would know of many faithful contemporaries that could have been challenged and made more productive in this context. He probably also would be a bit perplexed that such bountiful opportunity often yields scant results both in theological seriousness and practical ministry.

He would likely comment on our preaching. As he did in his own day, he would criticize much as unworthy of the majesty of its purpose. "There is too little of it." he might say, "because you seem to have no confidence in its glory." Should we explain that other activities give variety and keep the interest of the people, he might respond, "I am sure the devil has no greater delight than to know that preachers consort with his purpose of elevating the world above the Word. As long as anything appears more agreeable and palatable than the feast of grace set forth in Scripture, you forfeit the ordained means of grace and threaten to fill the church with mere professors and not true Christians."

Another institution over which Bishop Keach demonstrates an energetic and optimistic curiosity is the large number of mission boards and agencies that the heirs of British Dissenters have established. We are happy he seems so pleased with this development. "The expansiveness of your missions makes me marvel at God's providence," is his first remark. Surely he could have just as easily congratulated us on how superior our vision is about world evangelization. "From reflecting on the nature of the Covenant of Peace, I expected that eventually this would happen. More ministers should seize upon this opportunity for spreading the gospel in all the world. It is something that God himself has determined by sending his Son to die for people from

---

[64] *Ibid.*, 54

every nation and tongue and tribe. He will not be robbed of the fruit of the travail of his soul." Since his travels have not taken him to any of the mission fields, he asks, "Do these missionaries believe that the Covenant of Peace is their embassy?" Happily, we think there are some, even a growing number, but the large majority would not understand or evangelize according to his view of the covenant. He seems pleased with the zeal, but reticent about the message. He holds his tongue, however, and appears to be formulating an analysis for later discussion.

His silence gives us the opportunity to point to several large evangelical movements of different sorts as well as a growing attention to biblical authority. We point to piles of publicity and literature proving the health of contemporary Baptist life from our participation in these. "The affirmation of the divine origin of Scripture and its resultant inerrancy represents a faithful stewardship on your part. I also affirmed and defended this." He pauses thoughtfully. "From what I have heard," he continues deliberately while clasping his hands together and putting both index fingers to his lips, "these movements have generated little serious biblical exposition; the exposition I have heard is normally truncated from the rest of Scripture and contains little that is recognizable as historic Reformation, Puritan, Particular Baptist doctrine. The doctrine I have heard has been so Arminian, man-centered, free-willish that one could never learn what grace is from them."

We look incredulous that that this revered Baptist forefather could be so critical. "You shouldn't be surprised at this," he continues. "You have forfeited coherence for eclecticism. Though you have made many gains in scholarship and biblical studies and have a facade of evangelical unity, you have lost confidence that the Bible has an organizing theme. For me (and frankly for everyone) the Covenant of redemption holds Scripture together. If you understood the centrality of the covenant, you would have greater unction in your preaching and a powerful ally in your interpretive method. Also you would be clearer about the points of unity and difference in your evangelical groups and could provide antidotes to the malignant effects of such uncritical groupyism." The strange combination of amusement at his word coinage, impatience at his narrowness and bafflement at his convicting perspicacity renders us unable to generate a question before he adds, "And you must recapture

the importance of the Doctrine of Grace. God has established the honor
of himself, each of the three persons of the Trinity, on the sovereignty of
his mercy and grace. You are afraid that these doctrines will retard
evangelism because you have failed to grasp that they *are* evangelism."

We begin to regain our composure because now he is on our turf.
Evangelism is something we know. Why, our methods have improved so
much since he was a pastor that he can be quiet and learn from us.
"Look at the size of our churches and the number of our baptisms," we
boast. "Certainly this is one of our major successes." Looking strangely
somber and unintimidated, the bishop interrupts. "No, this probably is
your major failure. The danger of hypocrisy is great even under the most
searching preaching and spiritual example. Remember Simon Magus,
Judas, Diotrephes, and Hymenaeus. Your churches have so streamlined
and trivialized the process of preparation that virtually any profession is
received as genuine with little or no evidence of gospel knowledge,
brokenness for sin, or fleeing to Christ. The sorrow and division in many
churches is the direct result of your so-called success in evangelism.
Large numbers of those on your church rolls and many who attend
regularly would be disciplined in my day for persistent ungodliness,
grumbling, gossip, worldliness, and divisiveness. They are sick and do
not know; wounded but see no need of a physician. *It is a dangerous
thing to make a profession of religion, without true regeneration first
being wrought in the soul; it is better not to have any professions, than
to have such as are contrived and not sincere."*

A speech about his judgmental spirit is beginning to take shape in our
minds. He continues, however, unabated and, strangely, not haughtily,
but with tears forming in his eyes. "Not only do I detect carelessness
about regeneration, there is little extended teaching about the doctrine of
justification by faith. This is not merely a controversial point owing to
the overtures now being made by the papists or to the biblical theology
of my countryman E. P. Sanders, but an evangelistic issue. I have heard
much insistence on the sinner's part of responding, but little about how
God has made certain through Christ's blood and righteousness that his
elect people will be saved. How God can be just and yet justify the
ungodly is the mystery into which angels long to look. How angels can
long to look into it and yet the church give so little attention to it

distresses me. For all these truths I labored long and with much suffering in my life. Against the powers of the established church and the cult of powerful and popular personality I sought to guard and establish the truth. I have cast my legacy to you and long that it not be lost on an ungrateful and shallow people."

We are glad the visit is short, for we have begun to feel the "severity" of this Baptist polemicist. He goes, and we are relieved, but his absence is replaced by the voice of one who knew him well and saw both the "vivacity of his temper" and the "goodness and tenderness of his nature."

> He, with unwearied diligence, did discharge the duties of his pastoral office, preaching both in season and out of season... How would he bear the infirmities of his weak brethren! That such as would not be wrought upon by the strength of reason, might be melted by his condescension and good-nature.... He shewed an unwearied endeavour to recover the decayed power of religion, for he lived what he preached, and it pleased God so to succeed his endeavours in the Gospel, that I doubt not, but there are some yet living that may call him father, whom he hath begotten through the Gospel.[65]

And suddenly our resentment melts, and we are not so glad that he is gone.

Further reading

The chief primary source for the life of Keach comes from his son-in-law, the early Baptist historian Thomas Crosby. See his *The History of the English Baptists* (London, 1738-1740), 2:185-209; 4:268-314. For more recent accounts of his life and thought, see Hugh Martin, *Benjamin Keach (1640-1704): Pioneer of Congregational Hymn Singing* (London: Independent Press Ltd., 1961); Kenneth Dix, *Benjamin Keach and a monument to liberty* (Dunstable, Bedfordshire: The Fauconberg

---

[65] Crosby, *History*, 4:304-305.

Press, 1985); James Barry Vaughn, "Public Worship and Practical Theology in the Work of Benjamin Keach (1640-1704)" (Unpublished Ph. D. Thesis, University of St. Andrews, 1989); *idem*, "Benjamin Keach" in Timothy George and David Dockery, eds., *Baptist Theologians* (Nashville: Broadman Press, 1990), 49-76; Michael A. G. Haykin, *Kiffin, Knollys, and Keach—Rediscovering our English Baptist heritage* (Leeds: Reformation Today Trust, 1996), 83-97. For a brief sketch of his life, see R. L. Greaves, "Keach (or Keeche), Benjamin" in his and Robert Zaller, eds., *Biographical Dictionary of British Radicals in the Seventeenth Century* (Brighton, Sussex: The Harvester Press, 1983), II, 150-151.

There is a significant amount of literature on Keach's place in the history of English hymnody. See especially Hugh Martin, "The Baptist Contribution to Early English Hymnody", *The Baptist Quarterly*, 19 (1961-1962), 195-208; David W. Music, "The Hymns of Benjamin Keach: An Introductory Study:, *The Hymn*, (July 1983), 147-152; James Patrick Carnes, "The Famous Mr. Keach: Benjamin Keach and His Influence on Congregational Singing in Seventeenth Century England" (Unpublished M. A. Thesis, North Texas State University, 1984); Alan Clifford, "Benjamin Keach and Nonconformist Hymnology" in *Spiritual Worship* (London: Westminster Conference, 1985), 69-93; Donald C. Brown, "To Sing or Not to Sing: Seventeenth Century English Baptists and Congregational Song" in *Handbook to The Baptist Hymnal* (Nashville, Tennessee: Convention Press, 1992), 55-64.

THE
Breach Repaired
in God's Worſhip:
O R,
Singing of PSALMS, HYMNS,
and Spiritual Songs, proved to be
an Holy Ordinance of JESUS CHRIST.
With an Anſwer to all Objeĉtions.

AS ALSO,
An Examination of Mr. ISAAC MARLOW's
two Papers, one called, *A Diſcourſe
againſt Singing,* &c. the other *An
Appendix.* Wherein his Arguments and
Cavils are deteĉted and refuted.

By BENJAMIN KEACH, Preacher of
God's Word, and Paſtor of the Church
of Chriſt meeting on *Horſelydown,
Southwark.*

Job 6. 25. *How forcible are right words! but what
doth your arguing reprove ?*
Iſa. 52. 8. *Thy Watchmen ſhall lift up the Voice, with
the Voice together ſhall they ſing.*

London, Printed for the Author, and ſold by *John
Hancock* in Caſtle-Alley on the Weſt ſide of the
Royal-Exchange, and by the Author at his Houſe
near *Horſelydown* in *Southwark.* 1691.

THE REV.^D SAM.^L STENNETT, D.D.

Published as the Act directs by W.^mButton.Jany 29.1796.

THE STENNETTS

B. A. Ramsbottom

When Benjamin Keach lay dying in London, he sent for his friend Joseph Stennett (1663-1713)—one of the remarkable Stennett family. When Joseph Stennett came, Keach said to him, "I want you to preach my memorial sermon," and Stennett asked, "What shall I speak about?" Keach said, "I want you to preach my memorial sermon on this text [and you can see just how typical it was of Benjamin Keach]: "I know whom I have believed, and am persuaded that He is able to keep that which I have committed unto Him against that day" II Timothy 1:12. As it happened in God's providence, when Keach died Joseph Stennett was ill, but some time later he did preach the memorial sermon on that text, though he never would agree to many entreaties to have that sermon printed.

Who, then, were the Stennetts? The Stennetts were a very remarkable Particular Baptist family. There were four generations of eminent ministers, their witness to the truth extending over a period of about a hundred and fifty years. They were all gracious, very learned, well known, influential in the country. They were all faithful to the doctrines of grace, commonly called Calvinism. A most remarkable witness, a most remarkable family!

Now, my intention is to take you one by one through the four generations of the Stennetts: the great-grandfather, the grandfather, the father, and then the son.

Edward Stennett (d.1691)

First of all then, Edward Stennett; he being the father of the Joseph Stennett who preached Keach's memorial sermon.

Edward Stennett had been a chaplain in the Parliamentary army during the Civil War, and because he took the side of Parliament against the King, his relations separated from him. This meant that though a talented man, he was left without any means of support; so he took up medicine. Remarkably, he not only became a doctor, but a doctor both famous and prosperous; so much so that when he settled in Wallingford, Berkshire, he made his home in the castle there. And inside that castle he had a Particular Baptist congregation to whom he preached. Think of it: a Particular Baptist pastor living in a castle, a Particular Baptist church and congregation meeting in a castle! And because it was a castle, there was a wonderful advantage. This castle had once been a royal residence, and because of that it was exempt from search. Now Edward Stennett was preaching to his Particular Baptist congregation in days when there was no toleration, when the Particular Baptists were not permitted to meet. But this congregation was free to worship because no search warrant could be taken out to enter the castle to see what was taking place.

During this time Edward Stennett was favored of God with a very remarkable deliverance. Close to the castle in Wallingford lived a gentleman who was a Justice of the Peace. He was a very strong upholder of the Established Church and bitterly hated Edward Stennett and his ministry, even though Stennett had showed him the greatest of kindness and been a great help to him as a doctor. Nevertheless, because of his hatred to the truth, this Justice of the Peace determined to overthrow Stennett and his ministry, and as there could be no search of the castle, he devised a very wicked plan. He gathered a few people together and the plot was that the case should be taken to Newbury Assizes where they would all swear on oath that they had been present in the castle when a Nonconformist service had taken place—so that Edward Stennett would be arrested and imprisoned. So great was their hatred of the truth, they were willing to descend to perjury. Even the local vicar joined this little group.

Soon the time came when Edward Stennett was summoned to appear before the Assizes at Newbury. Now this was the remarkable deliverance. Just before the appointed day the Justice of the Peace's son, who was at Oxford, disappeared with a traveling actress, and the Justice had to go after him and so was not available on the day. The vicar suddenly died. Another who was going to be a perjured witness was taken seriously ill so that he could not attend (and later died). A fourth fell down and broke his leg so that he was unable to travel there. Eventually, out of the seven or eight, there was only one left, Edward Stennett's gardener, and he was so overcome with shame to think of what he was doing that he refused to appear. So when Edward Stennett eventually appeared at Newbury Assizes, there was not a single person there to witness against him.

An interesting thing about Edward Stennett (and all the four generations of Stennetts) was that they were all Seventh-Day Baptists. They believed the doctrines of grace, they practiced believer's baptism, but they kept Saturday as the Sabbath. Of course, being gracious men, walking in the fear of God, they also kept Sunday so that they would not cause any difficulty or concern for their brethren.

In those days there were a number of Seventh-Day Baptist congregations. Generally speaking they died out in Great Britain many years ago, though up until recently there was still one congregation of Seventh-Day Baptists in London, though meeting in a private house.

About the year 1686 Edward Stennett came up to London to preach to a wealthy Particular Baptist congregation that met in Pinners' Hall. Very interesting are these old Particular Baptist meetings in London. Many of them met in the old halls that belonged to the various trade guilds. This was the Pinners' Hall. It had once been an Augustinian monastery and was a vast building with six galleries; here a Particular Baptist church worshiped. It would appear that Edward Stennett still lived down at Wallingford, and traveled up to London from time to time to preach.

The testimony of Edward Stennett's contemporaries is that he was a very worthy man. It is recorded of him that he knew what it was both to be severely persecuted and also to be imprisoned for Jesus' sake. When he died the epitaph for him and his wife was written by his son Joseph and appeared upon their grave:

Here lies an holy and a happy pair;
As once in grace, they now in glory share.
They dared to suffer, but they feared to sin,

And meekly bore the cross the crown to win:
So lived, as not to be afraid to die;
So died, as heirs of immortality.

Joseph Stennett (1663-1713)

We now come to Edward Stennett's son, the second of this remarkable family. This was the member of the family who was specially connected with Benjamin Keach.

Because of his father's position and influence, Joseph had an excellent education at the Grammar School at Wallingford, and in his very early days was called by God's grace. At the age of 22 Joseph moved up to London, where, first of all, he made his living as a schoolmaster (or private tutor) and became connected with his father's congregation in Pinners' Hall. At the age of 25 he married a French Huguenot lady. This was three years after the Huguenots were expelled from France by the Revocation of the Edict of Nantes (1685) by Louis XIV, when many of them fled to Great Britain. At the age of 27 he succeeded his father, becoming the pastor at Pinners' Hall. His ordination service was taken by the venerable Hansard Knollys, one of the 'founders' of the Particular Baptist denomination in England.

The days of Joseph Stennett's pastorate at Pinners' Hall were days of great spiritual prosperity. Joseph Stennett, as a Seventh-Day Baptist being free on the Lord's day, also preached each Lord's day to a well-known congregation of Baptists meeting at the Barbican in London. However, after some years, he was suspended from this office at the Barbican, the reason being given that he was "far too Calvinistic."

Now, what of the man? He was very highly esteemed, earnest, godly, a fluent preacher. He was also a man of eminent literary ability, speaking French, Italian, Hebrew, and various Oriental languages. He published a translation of Plato. Also he was a writer on religious subjects. He wrote on baptism, opposing the claims of those who contended for infant baptism. He also wrote controversial works, defending the truth against the Roman Catholics, against the Unitarians, and against the Quakers. Because of his abilities it was said that he could have had the most exalted positions in the Church of England. There was great pressure on him to cease his Nonconformity and to conform to the Church of England, and many honors were promised him. Yet in later years Joseph Stennett said this was not even a temptation to him! He never even considered it.

Joseph Stennett's influence was great. Amongst his Christian friends he was continually sought for advice. In the political world he was often consulted by the great Whig lords in Parliament. On the other hand, the Tory party tried to win him over to their side, feeling that if they had him, they would gain the support of most of the English Dissenters. In fact a number of the well-known political pamphlets of the day ("squibs," as they were known) are reputed to have been written by Joseph Stennett.

It was during Joseph Stennett's ministry in London that England gained one of its most famous victories at the battle of Blenheim in 1704 under the great Duke of Marlborough. On that occasion Joseph Stennett preached a thanksgiving sermon in which he compared the French soldiers falling into the River Danube to Pharaoh's troops being swallowed up in the Red Sea. Very remarkably Queen Anne (r.1702-1714) was so pleased to receive a copy of this sermon that she sent a grant of money to Joseph Stennett; remarkably, because she was always a rigid opponent of all those who dissented from the Church of England.

Joseph Stennett was also a hymn-writer of quality; in fact, he was the earliest Baptist hymn-writer whose hymns ever appeared in hymn-books and were in common use. Most of the hymns he wrote were on Baptism and the Lord's Supper. His friend and associate Nahum Tate (1652-1715), the poet laureate (he was the author of "While shepherds watched"), described his contemporary Joseph Stennett as being a "good poet." While the great Isaac Watts (1674-1748) was not ashamed to confess that he borrowed some of his lines from Stennett's hymns, saying that he greatly admired the beautiful language.

Humanly speaking, Joseph Stennett's hymns are the reason why hymn-singing did not sink into oblivion. Let me explain. At first there was no hymn-singing. Then Benjamin Keach introduced hymn-singing into his congregation and at first there was tremendous controversy about the congregational singing of hymns. Sad to say, Keach's own hymns were of rather a poor quality of poetry. Just one example:

The antiquity of scripture show
That they are most divine,
For no writings did the world know
As soon as they did shine.

That was typical of Keach's hymns. They were sound doctrinally, but most unpoetical. And so really they did not take on, and there was the danger that hymns would just fall into disrepute.

Then Joseph Stennett appeared, and some of his hymns are very beautiful. Strangely, none of Joseph Stennett's hymns seem to be sung today, but the old Particular Baptists (using John Rippon's *Selection of Hymns*) sang many of them. Here is just one verse of one of Joseph Stennett's hymns, the opening verse of one of his hymns on the Lord's Supper:

Lord, at Thy table I behold
The wonders of Thy grace:
But most of all admire that I
Should find a welcome place.

At the age of 49 Joseph Stennett's health broke down. He came into Buckinghamshire to live with one of his daughters, and there he died. Concerning Joseph Stennett's end, the Baptist historian Thomas Crosby recalls that those who were present spoke of the pleasant smile on his countenance. He signified in a calm manner a firm and well-grounded hope of a blessed condition in an eternal world. One of his friends asked him, being so weak in body, how did he feel in his soul? His answer was: "I rejoice in the God of my salvation, who is my Strength, and my God." So died Joseph Stennett in the year 1713.

Joseph Stennett the younger (1692-1758)

Now, the third of this interesting family was another Joseph Stennett, if you will, Joseph Stennett, Jr., or, as he was known later, Dr. Joseph Stennett.

Joseph Stennett the younger was at first a Particular Baptist minister at Abergavenny, and then at Exeter. Then in 1737 he became the Particular Baptist pastor of a congregation meeting in Little Wild Street, London. This was a church which always met on Sunday, though Joseph Stennett the younger, like all his family, still kept the Saturday strictly as the Sabbath. His ordination service was taken by the renowned John Gill.

Joseph Stennett the younger was noted as being one of the most eloquent preachers of his day. Also, he was a true patriot. A most interesting event is recorded of his ministry in the year 1745, the year of the rising of Charles Edward Stuart (1720-1788), popularly known as Bonnie Prince Charlie, when he sought to win back the British throne to the Stuart house. Bonnie Prince Charlie gathered an army in Scotland and began to march south, seeking to reach London and to overthrow the Protestant house of Hanover. As history tells us, eventually he was turned back when he reached the city of Derby; but there were awful fears that there might be the re-establishment of Roman Catholicism in England and the loss of Protestant privileges. We read of Philip Doddridge (1702-1751) in Northampton helping to gather together men to fight, and the British Dissenters generally were seized with feelings of great patriotism.

It was at this time Joseph Stennett the younger preached a remarkable sermon, during which great enthusiasm was felt by his congregation. So strangely were their hearts moved that many of the gentlemen in the congregation rose from their seats during the sermon, drew their swords from their scabbards, waved them above their heads and cried out aloud that they would die holding allegiance to the Protestant faith and to the house of Hanover. Perhaps, then, it is not too surprising to find that Joseph Stennett the younger was well known by the King, George II (r.1727-1760), and esteemed by him. He was very friendly with various of the most eminent persons in England in his day.

Joseph Stennett's fame and learning being heard of in Scotland, the University of Edinburgh granted him the degree of Doctor of Divinity, this being recommended by their Chancellor, the Duke of Cumberland. In those days no Dissenter had the privilege of entering either of the Universities of Cambridge or Oxford.

In 1758, this eloquent preacher died. This was his dying testimony: "It is my great comfort, in view of eternity, that I have been led in these changeable, sad times steadily and constantly to maintain those doctrines, which I find are able to support me at such a season as this. I always thought the great design of the gospel was to lay the creature in the dust, and exalt the great Redeemer."

So died Joseph Stennett the younger. His funeral sermon was preached by John Gill from the text: "For me to live is Christ, and to die is gain" (Philippians 1:21).

Samuel Stennett (1727-95)

This brings us to the fourth generation, the fourth in this remarkable family, Joseph Stennett, Jr.'s son, Samuel Stennett. His is the name that is most familiar because of his hymns, which are still sung.

Samuel Stennett, great-grandson of the original Edward, was called by grace early in life and was baptized by his father. In one of his hymns (Rippon's *Selection* 437) he gives his testimony of how the Lord called him by grace. In that hymn he says this (among other things):

Darkness, and pain, and grief,
Oppressed my gloomy mind;
I looked around me for relief,
But no relief could find.

At length to God I cried;
He heard my plaintive sigh;
He heard, and instantly he sent
Salvation from on high.

My drooping head he raised;
My bleeding wounds He healed;
Pardoned my sins, and with a smile
The gracious pardon sealed.

At the age of 21 Samuel Stennett was appointed assistant pastor to his father, this being a practice that was quite common in the eighteenth century. Then, ten years later, upon his father's death he succeeded him as sole pastor. The nineteenth-century Baptist historian J. M. Cramp says: "Few men have risen so high in general esteem." He was esteemed both as a preacher and a writer, and for his learning, his kindness, his wisdom, his zeal and his holy life.

In Stennett's congregation at Little Wild Street could be seen one of the well-known figures of the eighteenth century, John Howard (1726-1790), the prison reformer. Whenever John Howard was in London he worshiped with Stennett, though his membership stood with the Independent church at Bedford. When John Howard died, Stennett preached and published a sermon on the text: "He went about doing good" (Acts 10:38). Howard testified of how much he missed Stennett's ministry when he was absent—and often he was absent, traveling not only through Britain but throughout Europe gathering together information to help him in his campaign for the improvement of prison conditions. He wrote a letter to Samuel Stennett from Smyrna on 11 August, 1786, which included this:

> With unabated pleasure I have attended your ministry. No man ever entered more into my religious sentiments, or more happily expressed them. O sir, how many Sabbaths have I ardently longed to spend in Wild Street! If at sea, I keep retired in my cabin. It is you that preach [meaning that he was reading Stennett's printed sermons], and I bless God that I attend with renewed pleasure. God in Christ is my Rock, the portion of my soul. I have little more to add, but accept my renewed thanks. I bless God for your ministry.

Samuel Stennett is described as a man of great refinement and polished manners, so that he moved very easily in high society and thus warmly recommended the cause of the Nonconformists and religious freedom amongst the nobility. Like his father, he too was given a Doctorate in Divinity, this time from the University of Aberdeen. Again, like his honored grandfather, he could have had many honors in the Church of England but he continually refused them.

Today Samuel Stennett is best known as a hymn-writer. Many of his hymns appeared in John Rippon's *Selection of Hymns*. John Julian, in his standard work on hymnology, *A Dictionary of Hymnology* (1891), said that at that time there were twenty-eight of Samuel Stennett's hymns in current use. We think of hymns like:

"How charming is the place!"

"How soft the words my Savior speaks!"

"Let avarice from shore to shore,
    Her favorite God pursue."

"What wisdom, majesty and grace
    Through all the gospel shine!"

"Where two or three with sweet accord."

"My Captain sounds the alarm of war."

"Come, every gracious heart
    That loves the Savior's name."

This last one seems to be perhaps the best known; you find it in most hymn-books, though with a slight variety in the first line.

In the last days of his life Samuel Stennett lost his wife, and from that time he lost interest in everything here below. Yet his preaching became more fervent. The two last sermons he ever preached were marked by a very peculiar and special savor of Christ, as the dying man spoke very sweetly of Jesus as his great High Priest, "touched with the feeling of our infirmities." This had followed a sleepless night when he had been awake, feeling very ill, and yet led to feel the sympathy of the Lord Jesus. He spoke of this as one of the happiest nights of all his life.

His last days were days of much blessing. On his death-bed, in great weakness, he was given vinegar with which to gargle. He replied, "In His thirst, they gave Him vinegar to drink. O, when I reflect on the sufferings of Christ, I am ready to say, 'What have I been thinking of all my life?' What He did and suffered are now my only support." Also he feelingly repeated a verse from one of his own hymns:

Father, at Thy call I come,
In Thy bosom there is room

For a guilty soul to hide,
Pressed with grief on every side.

Among his last utterances was: "Christ is to me the chiefest among ten thousand, and the altogether lovely." So died Samuel Stennett in 1795.

A touching little story is told concerning a verse of one of Samuel Stennett's hymns in more recent times. On one occasion a well-known minister was staying at a home where the bedroom was in poor condition, and there was even a hole in the roof. Now that night was very wet, and throughout the night the rain could be heard falling in the bedroom where the minister was sleeping; yet that particular night he was wonderfully favored in his soul. The next morning, when his host apologized for the state of the room and especially the leak in the roof, the minister, feeling the blessing of the Lord in his soul, very graciously replied in the language of Samuel Stennett:

Not the fair palaces
To which the great resort,
Are once to be compared with this,
Where Jesus holds His court.

So we give thanks to God for the Stennetts, especially because of their faithful witness to the truth. They never deviated, they never compromised. Some of them were called to suffer, some of them had the greatest allurements to draw them aside, but they never deviated from the truth.

Their witness stretches over a period of a hundred and fifty years: first, the Civil War; then Commonwealth times, the times of the Puritans; then days of persecution; then times of toleration; then the Age of Reason, in which there was awful spiritual decline in Great Britain; finally the Evangelical Revival, and afterwards. Their witness stretched over all those times—a period of a hundred and fifty years. Learned, refined, honorable, above everything else godly, they were faithful to the truth as in Jesus. They never deviated, they never compromised.

John Gill, D.D.

W.H. Collingridge, City Press, Long Lane, London.

JOHN GILL (1697-1771)[1]

Robert W. Oliver

When Dr. John Gill died on October 14, 1771, a young Anglican clergyman, Augustus Montague Toplady (1740-1778), requested that he might take the graveside service in Bunhill Fields. John Rippon (1750-1836), Gill's successor at Carter Lane, tells us that "this respect was suitably acknowledged, but Dr Gill was conscientiously a Dissenter, though he might in his youth have been sent to one of the universities had he and his parents approved of it."[2] Thus it was that Toplady's request was politely declined and two Particular Baptist pastors, Benjamin Wallin (1711-1782) and Samuel Stennett were responsible for the services of the day.

However flattering the support of such a prominent Anglican Calvinist may have been, Gill's family and friends knew that there were important issues at stake. Some sixty-three years earlier Edward and Elizabeth Gill, John's parents had taken a significant stand for Dissent in the Midland town of Kettering. Mr. and Mrs. Gill were founding members of the Particular Baptist church in Kettering. They had joined the Baptist church shortly before the birth of John. It soon became clear to them

---

[1] This chapter was originally presented as a talk to The Strict Baptist Historical Society on March 15, 1996. Portions of this chapter have also appeared as "John Gill (1697-1771): His Life and Ministry" in Michael A. G. Haykin, ed., *The Life and Thought of John Gill (1697-1771): A Tercentennial Appreciation* (Leiden/New York/Koln: E. J. Brill, 1997), 6-50, *passim.* Used by permission.
[2] *A Brief Memoir of the Life and Writings of the Late Rev. John Gill, D. D.* (1810 ed.; repr. Harrisonburg, Virginia: Gano Books, 1992), 135-136.

that John was a boy of above average intelligence and so, it must have
been a great delight when they secured a place for him at Kettering
Grammar School. His rapid progress justified his position. He showed a
bent for the classical languages which were the staple of grammar
school education at the time. But it was not long before the family suffered a grievous disappointment.

The master of the Grammar School enforced a rule which required all
pupils, Dissenters as well as Anglicans, to attend the parish church daily
at the hours of prayer. It was in the reign of Queen Anne when pressures
were being brought to bear on Dissenters and already some of their
ambitious men were beginning to compromise their principles. The Gills
had no doubt as to what they ought to do. Although it meant terminating
his formal education when he was only eleven years old they withdrew
John from the school. Various attempts were made to secure further
schooling but these proved fruitless and so John had to start work in his
father's wool merchant's business. There is no evidence that John Gill
ever resented the sacrifice made at this time.

John Gill—Orthodox Dissenter

Dissent was facing threats to its continued existence at the beginning of
the eighteenth century, not least were those which threatened to destroy
its orthodoxy. To define Orthodox Dissent I propose to turn to a small
but elegantly-written volume, *Essays in Orthodox Dissent* by Bernard
Lord Manning, sometime Fellow of Jesus College Cambridge. Manning
was also a Dissenter, although not a Baptist. In 1939 he wrote,
"Orthodox Dissent is the name which distinguished those Dissenters
who resisted Arian and Socinian tendencies in the eighteenth and nineteenth centuries. It still usefully distinguishes us who are proud to be
their descendants."[3] Manning continued: "Orthodox Dissent is the Dissent which has its foundation not in political opinions, but on the Word
and the Sacraments."[4] Gill would have wished to substitute the noun
ordinances for sacraments and definitely would have rejected Manning's

---

[3] *Essays in Orthodox Dissent* (London: Independent Press Ltd., 1941), 6.
[4] *Ibid.*, 7.

definition of baptism, but he surely would have approved the essence of the definition.

The main facts about John Gill's life are these. Born in Kettering on November 23, 1697, John was converted when he was twelve years old as he listened to the preaching of his pastor William Wallis (d.1711). He was not however baptised until he was nineteen years old. He was reluctant to make a premature confession of faith. However, almost immediately after his baptism he began to preach. Some three years later he received a call to the pastorate of Benjamin Keach's old church at Horselydown in Southwark, London. Sadly this call occasioned a church split and although Gill's supporters were the majority they moved out to a rented meeting house as their opponents had secured the lease of the meeting house in Goat Yard. By the middle of 1720 the rival group had ended their lease of the Goat Yard premises and Gill and his friends were able to return to their old home.

At Goat Yard they continued until 1757 when they built a new meeting house in Carter Lane, still in Southwark, and there Gill ministered until shortly before his death in 1771. Many years earlier Gill's abilities as a student and his proficiency in the oriental languages had been recognised by the University of Aberdeen which conferred upon him a doctorate in divinity in 1747.

Dissenters under pressure

The Toleration Act of 1689 was never intended to be a generous recognition of universal freedom of worship. Certainly it was not an invitation to Dissenters to evangelise freely. Orthodox Dissenters who subscribed to the doctrinal articles of the Church of England were to be allowed to worship unhindered in their registered meeting houses but their public worship was not to extend beyond these places.

These facts need to be noted before we condemn the Dissenters too sternly for their somewhat limited evangelism. Later George Whitefield and John Wesley as ministers of the established Church of England enjoyed much greater liberty within the law and were less likely to be molested when they went beyond it, as they often did. The penal legislation designed to keep Dissenters away from places of power and influence remained on the Statute Book. The Corporation Act required all who aspired to high office in local or national affairs to produce evidence that they had received the sacrament of the Lord's Supper according to the rites of the Church of England sometime in the previous twelve months. The Toleration Act divided the nation socially. Dissenters had to take the status of second-class citizens, a lot which, as we have seen, the Gill family was ready to accept. The ensuing division of England into Church and Chapel lasted long after the repeal of the legislation hostile to Dissent. As late as 1928 Bernard Manning could write, "Whilst the Parish Church and the golf links are both socially sound on a Sunday morning, Ebenezer and Sion are still not only not quite nice but distinctly the wrong thing."[5]

In the early eighteenth century Dissent showed some signs of faltering. The stalwarts who had given such clear and costly leadership during the penal years were passing from the stage. Bishop Gilbert Burnet (1643-1715) told Edmund Calamy that Dissent would die out in their generation. There were indications that this could be a true prophecy. Some Dissenters were prepared to receive the communion in an Anglican church occasionally. For the sake of office they were prepared to compromise just enough to prise open the restrictions of the Corporation Act, a practice known as occasional conformity. Baptists strongly disapproved of the practice and usually disciplined members who attempted it. There were many Presbyterians, Independents and Anglicans who disapproved of what they considered to be the mercenary exploitation of a sacrament. The writer, Daniel Defoe (c.1661-1731) described it as "playing peep-bo[6] with the Almighty."

The challenge of Arianism

Dissent was threatened, however, by an evil more insidious than political and social discrimination. Christianity itself was being threatened by Unitarianism in both its Arian and Socinian forms. This dangerous heresy was threatening all the Protestant denominations. It appeared first in

---

[5] *Ibid.*, 88
[6] I.e. bo-peep.

the Church of England but was to do its greatest damage among Dissenters. The old Presbyterian and General Baptist denominations were almost entirely destroyed by it. The threat came from a direction least expected.

The philosopher, John Locke (1632-1704), sometime a student of John Owen at Oxford, had entered a strong plea for toleration in a small but powerful work entitled *A Letter concerning Toleration*. Locke had long ceased to be an evangelical, but he could see the folly of compulsion in matters of religion. His thinking helped to push the politicians in the direction of religious toleration. However he urged men to test revelation by reason and not to accept the teachings of such Christian stalwarts as Athanasius (*c*.297-373) or Calvin (1509-1564) blindly. By the second decade of the eighteenth century it is clear that Locke's *Letter concerning Toleration* was being used in a new way. Christians were moving beyond a readiness to tolerate heretics outside the church to a reluctance to discipline them within its bounds.

The Salters' Hall Synod

Events in Exeter provoked a crisis. A Presbyterian minister said that he believed "the Son and the Holy Ghost to be divine persons but subordinate to the Father." After an unsuccessful attempt to resolve the problem locally, the Exeter ministers appealed to their colleagues in London. These in turn invited their Baptist and Independent colleagues to join them in discussing the issue at a meeting that became known as the Salters' Hall Synod on 19 and 24 February 1719.

The meeting was confused. Instead of majoring on the theological question of Christ's divinity, the assembled ministers debated whether it was right to demand subscription to a creed anyway. A vote was taken: the result was 57 to 53 against subscription. The doctrine of our Lord's divinity never had proper consideration. A further meeting was held at Salters Hall on 3 March and on this occasion the defeated minority did subscribe to an orthodox statement on the Trinity. In the end the Exeter ministers demanded subscription and expelled the Arian ministers, but a confused signal had been given at Salters' Hall.

Meanwhile the London ministers were divided into subscribers and non-subscribers. Not all non-subscribers were Unitarians, but some certainly were, and others were moving in that direction. Weakening of doctrine is seldom restricted to a single issue. An anonymous writer in 1732 described what was happening. He pointed out that Arminianism was leading on to Arianism and Socinianism.

> It is very often first manifested in their attacking the divine decrees by applauding the doctrine of universal redemption as a sentiment that is full of benevolence; from thence they appear fond of pleading the cause of the heathens, and of the possibility of salvation merely by the light of nature in a sincere improvement of the powers and faculties of men; and by degrees these charitable sentiments produce a small opinion of revelation, and of the necessity of it in order to salvation... No wonder they became hereupon sceptics and amongst other truths the doctrine of the Trinity is with them a matter of jest and ridicule.[7]

The Salters' Hall Synod took place some three months before John Gill first came to preach in London at the influential Particular Baptist church at Horselydown, Southwark. This visit in April and May 1719 led to a call, followed by ordination and induction almost a year later. The call to Gill divided the church and there were many months of anxiety for the twenty-two year old preacher. While affairs at Horselydown must have filled his mind he cannot have been unaware of the wider excitement which Salters' Hall had generated. Dissent was facing a crisis. The needs of the times were to force him into a position of leadership.

---

[7] "A View of the Dissenting Intrest in London of the Presbyterian and Independent Denominations from the year 1695 to the 25 of December 1731" (Unpublished manuscript in Dr Williams's Library, London, MS. 38.18, pages 82-83). Quoted by permission.

The emergence of a leader

John Gill's early years in London were not easy. He had to face determined opposition to his settlement as a pastor in Southwark. After this
trouble had been passed, he found himself at odds with Thomas Crosby,
the man who had been his strongest supporter. His wife Elizabeth suffered an extended period of ill health. It is no surprise to discover that by
1723 he too was seriously ill. But from about 1724, when Gill was
twenty-six years old, a period of recovery began. He was now supported
by a loyal church. Perhaps the strains of those early years matured him
spiritually and enriched his preaching. It was at this time that he began
the series of sermons which formed the basis of one of his best loved
works, *An Exposition of the Book of Solomon's Song* (1728).

He published a number of occasional sermons before he found himself forced into controversy. In 1727 and 1728 he published two small
books defending baptism by immersion and strict communion. These
were *The Ancient Mode of Baptism by Immersion* and *A Defence of the
Ancient Mode of Baptism by Immersion.* Both were written in response
to two anonymous attacks on the Baptist position. Although anonymous
it was known in Northamptonshire that the author was Matthias
Maurice (1684-1738), pastor of a prosperous Independent church at
Rothwell, which was only a few miles from Kettering, where Gill had
been brought up, converted and baptized. In fact, the Kettering Baptists
considered that Maurice was launching an attack on them. It was not
surprising that they turned to Gill for help. British Baptist historian
Barrie White has described this as "an arid debate," but concedes that
Gill's books made him "more widely known among the Baptists."[8]

A more substantial work to appear in 1728 was *The Prophecies of
the Old Testament respecting the Messiah.* This was a contribution to
the debate against the Deists. Deism was a form of religious rationalism
which appealed to the sophisticated at this time. The Deists denied special revelation and the doctrine of providence. They believed in a Creator
who had brought the world into being and then left it to its own devices.

---

[8] "John Gill in London, 1719-1729: A Biographical Fragment", *The Baptist Quarterly,* 22 (1967-1968), 86.

Gill entered the lists against Anthony Collins (1676-1729), one of their prominent writers. Gill appears to have been stung by a comment "that no *Calvinist* could write in this controversy to any advantage."[9] He responds to the Deists by showing how the coming of Christ fulfilled prophecies given throughout the Old Testament period.

By 1728 Gill was demonstrating his tremendous capacity for hard work. In the same year he published his *Exposition of the Book of Solomon's Song*. The writer of his earliest life says that this "served very much to make Mr Gill known, and to recommend him to the esteem of spiritual persons."[10] He was now coming to the attention of people outside his denomination. He had taken a public stand against the barren speculations of Deism and also by his work on the Song of Solomon showed himself to be an exponent of experiential Christianity.

An indication of Gill's increasing acceptance was the establishment of the Great Eastcheap Lecture. This was set up in 1729 by a group from various denominations. It arranged for Gill to give a weekly Wednesday evening lecture at Great Eastcheap meeting house in the City of London. Gill continued this engagement from 1729 to 1756. Many of his written works were first delivered as lectures at Great Eastcheap. They included his treatises on *The Trinity, Justification,* the first two parts of *The Cause of God and Truth* as well as continuous expositions of several books of the Bible which later were included in his commentaries. Attendances were good throughout the 27 years of this lecture. Gill only terminated this engagement because he felt that he should give more attention to needs of his own church and also he needed to give more time to writing.

Widespread challenges to orthodoxy led a wealthy London merchant, William Coward, to take the initiative in establishing a lectureship through the winter and spring of 1730 and 1731. Nine ministers spoke on the great doctrines of Christianity at the Independent meeting house in Lime Street. Seven of the lecturers were Independents and two were

---

[9] *A Summary of the Life, Writings and Character of the Late Reverend and Learned John Gill, D.D.* (London: George Keith, 1773) [in John Gill, *A Collection of Sermons and Tracts* (London: Geogre Keith, 1773), I, xvii].

[10] *Ibid.* (*Collection of Sermons and Tracts,* I, xvii).

Baptists. One of the latter was John Gill who gave two lectures on "The Resurrection of the Dead." The entire series of lectures was published in 1732. The published lectures led to a controversy between Gill and Abraham Taylor on eternal justification.

The doctrine of the Trinity

Opposition to the doctrine of the Trinity presented the most serious challenge to Dissent in the first half of the eighteenth century. Leaders such as Isaac Watts and Philip Doddridge do not seem to have appreciated the seriousness of the attack. John Gill used the opportunity of his Great Eastcheap Lectures to defend the orthodox teaching. This series was published in 1731 as *A Treatise on the Doctrine of the Trinity*. Later John Rippon explained that this work was occasioned by the spread of Sabellianism among some of the Baptist churches. Sabellianism, named after Sabellius, a third-century heretic, is a form of Unitarianism. It teaches that the Father, the Son and the Holy Spirit are not distinct persons, but rather separate roles which the One God has taken on at different stages in the economy of salvation.

Rippon did not identify the teachers of Sabellianism in Gill's day, but the figures from the Salters' Hall debate, eleven years earlier indicate a measure of confusion on the doctrine of the Trinity. At that meeting 14 Particular Baptists and only one General Baptist had subscribed to the orthodox doctrine, whereas 14 General Baptists had refused to subscribe as had 2 Particular Baptists. These figures must be treated with care as some of the objectors were opposed to subscription to what they considered to be a man-made statement of faith. What we can note is that the overwhelming majority of London Particular Baptist ministers were willing to make a subscription to orthodoxy and most General Baptists refused. It was a time of theological flux, when a number of men were moving from orthodoxy and Gill felt it necessary to nail his colours to the mast.

From the convictions he enunciated in the early years of his ministry Gill did not move. One of the last pieces that he wrote was a tract, *A Dissertation Concerning the Eternal Sonship of Christ* (1768). At that time he wrote:

My treatise on the Trinity was written near *forty years ago*, and when I was a young man. And had I now departed from some words and phrases, I then used, it need not, after such a distance in time be wondered at. But so far from it, that upon a late revisal of the piece, I see no reason to retract anything I have written, either as to sense or expressions; save only, in a passage or two of Scripture, which *then* did not stand so clear in my mind as proofs of the eternal generation of the Son of God.[11]

Rippon explained that it was Gill's concern about the Trinitarian controversy, which he "had narrowly watched," that moved him to write the *Dissertation concerning the Eternal Sonship.* Gill wrote:

It is easy to observe, that the distinction of Persons in the Deity depends upon the generation of the Son. Take away that which would destroy the relationship between the first and second Persons, and the distinction drops.[12]

Interestingly Gill does not attempt a scriptural defence of the doctrine of the eternal Sonship in the *Treatise.* Probably this was because he was at work on such a defence in his *Complete Body of Doctrinal and Practical Divinity* (1769-1770), which was published over the next two years. What he does is review the history of the doctrine from the Early Church to his own day and thereby show that orthodox Trinitarians have always believed it.

Prior to this the doctrine of the eternal Sonship had become an issue in Gill's own church. In July 1768 Isaac Harmon, one of the members, was excluded by a unanimous vote of the church for having "declared he had long been at enmity with the doctrine of the Eternal Sonship of Christ by generation of the Father." John Allen, pastor of the Petticoat Lane Particular Baptist Church, defended Harmon, saying that he had been excommunicated, "purely to please his [Gill's] froward will." It

---

[11] Rippon, *Memoir*, 37.

[12] *A Complete Body of Doctrinal and Practical Divinity* (1839 ed.; repr. Paris, Arkansas: The Baptist Standrad Bearer, 1989), 142.

was at this point that Gill persuaded the church to strengthen the teaching of its *Declaration of Faith* on the doctrine of the eternal Sonship.[13]

Gill was succeeded as pastor at Carter Lane by John Rippon, who bore testimony to Gill's faithfulness.

> The Doctor not only watched over his *people,* "with great affection, fidelity, and love;" but he also watched his *pulpit* also. He would not, if he knew it, admit any one to preach for him, who was either cold-hearted to the doctrine of the Trinity; or who *denied* the divine filiation of the Son of God; or who *objected* to conclude his prayers with the usual *doxology* to Father, Son, and Holy Spirit, as three equal Persons in the one Jehovah. Sabellians, Arians, and Socinians, he considered as real enemies of the cross of Christ. They *dared* not ask him to preach, nor *could* he in conscience, permit them to officiate for him. He conceived that, by this uniformity of conduct, he adorned the pastoral office.[14]

The person of Christ

John Gill's defence of the eternal Sonship relates to the doctrine of the Trinity. Rejection of the doctrine of the eternal Sonship is not necessarily a rejection of the divinity of Christ. Some years earlier, however, Gill had had occasion to turn his attention to the doctrine of Christ's divinity. In 1736 a Particular Baptist church was formed in Birmingham. In the following year this small group of Christians opened a meeting house in Cannon Street. In later years Cannon Street Chapel in Birmingham was to occupy an honored place in Particular Baptist life. Its beginnings were, however, a struggle.

The building of the Meeting House proved to be a signal for an outburst of ridicule against this young church. An anonymous pamphlet appeared entitled *A Dialogue between a Baptist and a Churchman.* The

---

[13] R. Philip Roberts, *Continuity and Change: London Calvinistic Baptists and The Evangelical Revival 1760-1820* (Wheaton, Illinois: Richard Owen Roberts, 1989), 180.

[14] Rippon, *Memoir*, 127-128.

Birmingham Baptists depended on visiting preachers who were scorned as "very ridiculous and antic," but the real offence seems to have been that the meeting house was opened for reviving "old Calvinistical doctrines and spreading Antinomian and other errors in Birmingham."

The Baptists of Birmingham appealed to John Gill for help. The pamphlet seemed to be written by an Anglican, but the local people were well aware that its real author was a Dissenter, Samuel Bourn, Jr. (1689-1754), who held pastorates at the New Meeting in Birmingham and at Coseley, Staffordshire. Gill charged Bourn with insincerity because he appeared to be posing as an Anglican, but this imposture provided Gill with the opportunity to compare Bourn's teaching with both the *Thirty-nine Articles* and the *Westminster Shorter Catechism*. Bourn was in fact a Presbyterian who had abandoned the orthodox doctrine of Christ at the time of the Salters' Hall controversy. According to the *Dictionary of National Biography*, "Bourn had a warm temper and was not averse to controversy" and he also "had a great name for heterodoxy."[15]

He launched two attacks on the Baptists of Birmingham, to both of which Gill replied in *An Answer to the Birmingham Dialogue-Writer*, Parts I and II. In these Gill made a vigorous statement of the orthodox teaching on the divinity of Christ over against the Arian views of Bourn. Bourn attacked the doctrines of the divinity of Christ, election, original sin, efficacious grace, imputed righteousness and the saints' perseverance as well as believers' baptism. Gill pointed out that apart from the last doctrine the teaching of the Baptists was consistent with that of the Reformers and also the official teaching of the Church of England. He described these as,

> doctrines which no church, community, or set of men under any denomination, have reason to be ashamed of; and it is the glory of the *Particular Baptists,* what is greatly to their honour, that they are so zealously affected to those truths, and to the utmost of their

---

[15] Alexander Gordon, "Bourn, Samuel, the younger", *The Compact Edition of the Dictionary of National Biography* (London: Oxford University Press, 1975), I, 193.

abilities defend them, in an age, when there are so many apostates from the faith once delivered to the saints.[16]

Gill's reply gave him the opportunity to range through a wide field of Christian doctrine. Although there are points where he developed certain peculiarities he was able to demonstrate a great measure of unity with the truths held by the Reformed tradition for some two hundred years.

Principles of Dissent

John Gill maintained close friendships with at least two of the Anglican leaders of the Evangelical Awakening, Augustus Montague Toplady and James Hervey (1714-1758) of Weston Favell. These two Anglican clergymen were prepared to break through the considerable barrier which separated Church and Dissent to maintain fellowship with him. After Gill's death Toplady wrote a beautiful tribute to his friend, which was included in the introduction to the 1773 edition of Gill's *Sermons and Tracts*.[17] The friendship was reciprocated on a personal level by Gill, who was ready to acknowledge his areas of agreement with Calvinistic Anglicans, although he knew that the gulf between Anglicanism and Dissent was too deep to be bridged without a far-reaching change in the separated parties.

Personal friendships never blunted John Gill's convictions. The heritage of Dissent was too precious to be compromised. Moreover, his Baptist beliefs frequently brought him into collision with Anglicans. Such a challenge led to his writing *The Dissenters' Reasons for Separating from the Church of England* in 1751.[18] This was in response to an attack by a Welsh clergyman. Anglicans frequently hurled the charge of schism against Dissenters. In the seventeenth century John Owen had had to rebut the same accusation. The Welsh clergyman revived the charge in the middle of the eighteenth century and directed his anger particularly against those whom he described as "rebaptizers." Old tales

---

[16] *Collection of Sermons and Tracts*, II, 108.
[17] *Ibid.*, I, xxxiii-xxxv.
[18] *Ibid.*, II, 371-381.

about continental Anabaptists were resurrected with horror stories about events in Munster in the sixteenth century. If atrocities were to be discussed, though, Gill could point to a persecuting spirit in the Church of England in the previous century and continued, "yet it is not even now quite clear of persecution, witness the Test and Corporation-acts by which many free-born Englishmen are deprived of their native rights."[19]

There were, however, bigger issues involved in the debate between Anglican and Dissenter. Gill could not find the marks of a true church in the Church of England. True doctrine was seldom preached, the "ordinances of Baptism and the Lord's supper are not duly administered in it, according to the Word of God,"[20] and even Anglicans in their formularies acknowledged the lack of discipline. These defects pointed to the real nature of the problem. There was a fundamental flaw in the formation of the Church of England.

> We like it never the better for its being constituted by men: a Church of Christ ought to be constituted as those we read of in the *Acts of the Apostles,* and not established by *Acts of Parliament*; as the articles, worship and discipline of the church of *England* be; a *parliamentary* church we do not understand; Christ's *kingdom* or church *is not of this world*; it is not established on worldly maxims, nor supported by worldly power and policy.[21]

In a later work, *Infant-Baptism, A Part and Pillar of Popery* (1766), Gill returned to the subject of national churches. He saw infant baptism as a rite which drew together institutions which should be separate. He wrote of infant baptism, "it is the basis of national churches and worldly establishments; that which unites the church and the world and keeps them together."[22] Of the Church of England he wrote, "it is by the baptism of infants it is supplied with members, and is supported and main-

---

[19] *Ibid.*, II, 381.
[20] *Ibid.*, II, 373.
[21] *Ibid.*, II, 371.
[22] *Ibid.*, II, 522.

tained; so that it may be truly said, that infant baptism is the basis and foundation of a national church."[23]

The baptismal controversy

The tract, *Infant Baptism, A Part and Pillar of Popery*, shows that Gill's Baptist and Dissenting convictions were closely allied. He wrote at least fourteen pieces on the subject of baptism from treatises to tracts and a published sermon. In addition, he faced the issue in other writings. Sometimes he faced able opponents such as Jonathan Dickinson (1688-1747) of New Jersey. At other times he found himself in controversy with abusive arguers like the Birmingham dialogue writer. It was not a debate that Gill relished, perhaps because he found himself at odds with those whose doctrinal position in other respects he accepted. In 1765 he wrote that he was "unwilling to renew the controversy about baptism unnecessarily; and being determined to write only in self-defence when attacked."[24]

These words were written in the preface to a sermon given at the baptism of Robert Carmichael (d.1774), a Scottish minister who had adopted Baptist principles and who came to London to be baptised by Gill. Gill decided to print this sermon because of misleading accounts that had been published in two letters to a newspaper. Gill complained that he had been accused of "railing against my brethren, and the whole christian world." He continued, "it is hard we cannot practise what we believe, and speak in vindication of our practice, without being abused, vilified and insulted in a public newspaper."[25]

Gill may have been reluctant to involve himself in the baptismal controversy. Nevertheless he proved an able champion for believer's baptism by immersion and his extensive writings on the subject were welcomed by his brethren who often found themselves having to defend their distinctive position.

---

[23] *Ibid.*, II, 522.
[24] *Ibid.*, II, 497.
[25] *Ibid.*, II, 497.

The significance of John Gill

It is doubtful if John Gill saw himself primarily as a controversialist. He was a preacher and teacher whose first responsibility was to his church and congregation in Southwark and after that to a wider group of like-minded churches. However, his usefulness spread beyond his own denomination to the point where even Anglicans like Toplady were prepared to bear testimony to his stature. We have been concerned in this sketch of Gill's life and thought primarily with Gill's occasional writings, many of which are quite short but not unimportant. We need to remind ourselves that they were produced in the midst of continued pressure of preparation for the pulpit and the adaptation of many of his sermons for publication as part of his larger works. Spurgeon wrote of Gill: "He was always at work; it is difficult to know when he slept, for he wrote 10,000 folio pages of theology."[26] It is important to be aware of these larger works which contributed so much to his reputation as a theologian.

Between 1735 and 1738 he published *The Cause of God and Truth* in four volumes. This is a major defence of the five points of Calvinism. It is a significant contribution to the Arminian controversy. It was written in response to a work by Daniel Whitby who had died in 1726. Whitby was an Anglican clergyman, who by the time of his death had embraced Unitarianism. He had hoped it would be possible to unite Anglicanism and Dissent on a broad Latitudinarian basis. The Latitudinarians attached little importance to matters of dogma although they were generally sympathetic to Arminianism and were the creators of the Anglican ethos of the eighteenth century. At a time when many Dissenters were weakening in their doctrinal convictions Gill expressed his resolution in *The Cause of God and Truth*. The work retains its usefulness although there are places where Gill bursts the limits of sound exegesis to sustain a Hyper-Calvinist position.

Gill's greatest work was his *Exposition of the Old and New Testaments*. The New Testament began to appear in folio volumes in 1745.

---

[26] *Commenting and Commentaries* (London: Passmore & Alabaster, 1876), 9.

The last volume of the Old Testament was completed in 1766. With the completion of this work Gill became the first person to complete a verse-by-verse commentary on the whole of Scripture in the English language. This was followed by his *Body of Doctrinal and Practical Divinity*, a systematic theology which was finished in 1770.

In this chapter I have deliberately avoided addressing in depth the question as to whether John Gill was a Hyper-Calvinist, because I believe that preoccupation with this issue has promoted a tendency to overlook his important contribution to Orthodox Dissent and the Particular Baptist community. Recent reference to the question makes it impossible to ignore this completely. That he stood in the Calvinist tradition there can be no doubt. There remains the question as to whether he went beyond the Calvinism of the Genevan Reformer and also beyond that of the Puritans and the Particular Baptist fathers of the previous century.

There can be no doubt that Gill denied the free offer of the gospel which the historic confessions of the seventeenth century proclaimed and that he made his position clear on more than one occasion.[27] Equally there can be no doubt that he taught the doctrine of eternal justification which was condemned by the confessions of the seventeenth century.[28]

Modern attempts to argue that Gill was not a Hyper-Calvinist have not been convincing. In part confusion seems to have arisen because of dependence upon the interpretations of W. T. Whitely and A. C. Underwood, neither of whom were sympathetic towards Calvinism and neither of whom is a safe guide in the interpretation of John Gill. A further cause of confusion arises from the popular view that Hyper-Calvinists are never concerned for the salvation of sinners. There are many examples of Hyper-Calvinists who have had a deep concern for the salvation

---

[27] *An Answer to the Birmingham Dialogue-Writer* (*Collection of Sermons and Tracts*, II, 118-119); "Recommendatory Preface to the Hymns of Richard Davis", printed in G. T. Streather, *Memorials of the Independent Chapel at Rothwell* (Rothwell: Rothwell United Reformed Church, 1994), 64; *The Doctrine of Predestination Stated, and Set in the Scripture Light* (1752) [in his *Sermons and Tracts* (London: W. Hardcastle, 1814-1815), III, 118].

[28] *Body of Doctrinal and Practical Divinity*, 203.

of the lost. Gill was one such and examples can be produced of him ex-
pressing a concern for such and pressing those who were awakened to
seek salvation. His Hyper-Calvinism appears in the absence of direct
exhortations and appeals to the unconverted to turn from their sin in repentance and to cast themselves upon Christ. It is at this point that I am
compelled to part company with John Gill.

Gill was a great figure in the life of the eighteenth-century Particular
Baptists, but great figures sometimes contribute significantly for both
good and ill. As C. H. Spurgeon was to write in the nineteenth century:
"Gill is the Coryphaeus of hyper-Calvinism, but if his followers never
went beyond their master, they would not go very far astray."[29]

Conclusion

To reject John Gill's Hyper-Calvinism does not mean that we have to
denigrate him or ignore his place in history. I am convinced that his
positive contribution to eighteenth-century Dissent and the Particular
Baptist community has too often been ignored.

Several years ago I wrote that "Gill has undoubtedly had a bad
press."[30] I wrote those words in a review of Tom Nettles' outstanding
book, *By His Grace and for His Glory*. Dr. Nettles dealt very sympa-
thetically with Gill and helped to call our attention to this significant
eighteenth-century figure. Regretfully I felt compelled to disagree with
his assessment of Gill's Hyper-Calvinism. I believe that Gill's Hyper-
Calvinism did great damage at the time and even more in the hands of
lesser men.

Gill, however, was not a single issue man. He was a man of outstanding industry and above all outstanding for godliness. As a champion for
orthodox Christology he should receive our gratitude. It is easy to overlook the reality of the threat to orthodoxy in the eighteenth century. We
may sometimes suppose that it was the Great Awakening which recovered the ground for orthodoxy. The Awakening undoubtedly played a

---

[29] *Commenting and Commentaries*, 9.
[30] " 'By His Grace and for His Glory' ", *The Banner of Truth*, 284 (May
1987), 32.

major part, but it did not preserve the old Presbyterians and General Baptists from a collapse into heterodoxy. Neither did all of the converts of the Awakening remain true to biblical teaching on the Trinity and the person of Christ. The tragic case of Robert Robinson (1735-1790) may be an isolated one, but he was a Particular Baptist pastor who had professed conversion under the ministry of George Whitefield, but who seems to have sunk into the swamp of Sabellianism.

The Apostle Paul at Corinth "was determined not to know anything...save Jesus Christ and him crucified" (1 Corianthians 2:2). That surely was the resolve of John Gill and in the areas I have discussed we surely have to accept Dr. Nettles' conclusion, "Perhaps rather than imputing blame upon Gill for the leanness of the times, he should be credited with preserving gospel purity, which eventuated in the efforts to use means for the conversion of the heathen."[31]

I began with a definition borrowed from Bernard Manning. I would like to put myself in debt to him once more in conclusion. He paid tribute to those Congregationalists who were contemporary with John Gill. I would like to employ his eloquence to describe the Particular Baptists.

In an age of spiritual depression these forefathers of ours walked and did not faint. When their numbers dwindled, when their political influence had disappeared, when many of their congregations were dying out, the faithful remnant, maintaining the ministry of the Word and Sacraments, won a victory more illustrious than the victories of Naseby and Marston Moor and Worcester, more enduring than the victories in the nineteenth-century ballot boxes. They showed once for all that ecclesiastical liberty and orthodox doctrine were not incompatible. They asserted triumphantly in the most unfavourable circumstances that the irresistible grace of God preserves the faith in freedom and freedom in the faith. Upon faith and freedom loyally guarded there fell in due time the fire from heaven,

---

[31] *By His Grace and for His Glory. A Historical, Theological, and Practical Study of the Doctrines of Grace in Baptist Life* (Grand Rapids: Baker Book House, 1986), 107.

the fire of the evangelical revival. Then the Word had free course and was glorified.[32]

No small part of that faithfulness among the Particular Baptists was due to John Gill. His leadership was felt among Christians more widely and if we believe that Dissent has played a significant part in the maintenance of the faith in England, then surely we must thank God for John Gill.

Further reading

The first sketch of John Gill's life and writings appeared in 1773 as an anonymous preface to the first edition of Gill's *Collection of Sermons and Tracts*. It was entitled *A Summary of the Life, Writings, and Character, of the late Reverend and Learned John Gill, D.D.* It was superseded about thirty years later by the biographical account of Gill by John Rippon, who followed Gill as pastor of Carter Lane Baptist Church. Rippon's study of his predecessor was to be the most substantial life of Gill till 1995 when George M. Ella published a book-length biography of the Baptist divine. Rippon's *A Brief Memoir of the Life and Writings of the Late Rev. John Gill, D. D.* (Repr. Harrisonburg, Virginia: Gano Books, 1992) originally appeared as a preface to the 1809-1810 edition of Gill's *Exposition of the Old and New Testaments*. It is invaluable for students of Gill, for it contains important facts about his career as well as some analysis of his theological views.

In this century, a couple of small biographical booklets on Gill have been published: Graham Harrison, *Dr. John Gill and His Teaching* (London: The Evangelical Library, 1971) and John R. Broome, *Dr. John Gill* (Harpenden, Hertfordshire: Gospel Standard Trust Publications, 1991). And there have been a few excellent articles examining various facets of Gill's life and theology: John W. Brush, "John Gill's Doctrine of the Church" in Winthrop Still Hudson, ed., *Baptist Concepts of the Church* (Philadelphia: Judson Press, 1959), 53-70; B. R. White, "John Gill in London, 1719-1729: A Biographical Fragment", *The Baptist Quarterly*,

---

[32] *Essays in Orthodox Dissent*, 195.

22 (1967-1968), 72-91; and Richard A. Muller, "The Spirit and the Covenant: John Gill's Critique of the *Pactum Salutis*", *Foundations*, 24 (1981), 4-14.

In the last two decades there has definitely been a growing interest in Gill as a theologian: witness the appearance of Curt Daniel's exhaustive examination of whether or not Gill was a Hyper-Calvinist—"Hyper-Calvinism and John Gill" (Unpublished Ph. D. dissertation, University of Edinburgh, 1983); Thomas Ascol's study of Gill's federal theology—"The Doctrine of Grace: A Critical Analysis of Federalism in the Theologies of John Gill and Andrew Fuller" (Unpublished Ph. D. thesis, Southwestern Baptist Theological Seminary, 1989); and the major biography by George Ella— *John Gill and the Cause of God and Truth* (Eggleston, Co. Durham: Go Publications, 1995).

Serious reading on Gill also needs to take into account Thomas Nettles' study of Gill as a Calvinist in his *By His Grace and for His Glory. A Historical, Theological, and Practical Study of the Doctrines of Grace in Baptist Life* (Grand Rapids: Baker Book House, 1986), 73-107; Timothy George's study of Gill as a theologian: "John Gill" in his and David S. Dockery, eds., *Baptist Theologians* (Nashville, Broadman Press, 1990), 77-101; and the collaborative study by ten scholars of most facets of Gill's life and thought: *The Life and Thought of John Gill (1697-1771): A Tercentennial Appreciation*, ed. Michael A. G. Haykin (Leiden/New York/Koln: E. J. Brill, 1997).

The Baptist Church 1765 - 1875. Bourton on the Water

BENJAMIN BEDDOME (1717-1795)[1]

Michael A. G. Haykin

John Newton (1725-1807), the well-known eighteenth-century evangelical leader and author of the ever-popular hymn "Amazing Grace," had the opportunity to meet and hear many of the leading evangelicals of his day. It is intriguing, therefore, to read some remarks that he penned in his diary on August 7, 1776, after he had heard Benjamin Beddome preach at the ordination of John Sutcliff (1752-1814), the close friend of William Carey (1761-1834), in Olney, Buckinghamshire.[2] Beddome's text on this occasion was Zechariah 11:12, the verse cited in the Gospel of Matthew with regard to the amount of money Judas Iscariot received for the betrayal of Christ. "He is an admirable preacher," Newton observed after hearing the sermon, "simple, savoury, weighty."

This was not the first time that Newton had heard Beddome preach. The Anglican evangelical had heard him speak the previous year on 2 Corinthians 1:24. Of that occasion Newton later recorded: "[the sermon] gave me a pleasure I seldom find in hearing. It was an excellent discourse indeed, and the Lord was pleased to give me some softenings and relentings of heart."[3] For one who often heard the greatest preacher of

---

[1] I wish to acknowledge the tremendous help that Susan J. Mills, the Archivist of the Angus Library, Regent's Park College, Oxford, and Derrick Holmes of Gloucester, England, have given me in this study of Benjamin Beddome's life.
[2] For details about John Sutcliff, see Michael A.G. Haykin, *One Heart and One Soul. John Sutcliff of Olney, his friends and his times* (Darlington, Durham: Evangelical Press, 1994). Discussion of his ordination may be found on pages 118-120.
[3] John Newton, Diary (1773-1805), entries for 7 August 1776 and 27 June 1775 (Princeton University Library).

the day, George Whitefield, these words are high praise indeed. Robert Hall, Jr. (1764-1831), one of the greatest English preachers during the first half of the nineteenth century, once said of Beddome that he was "on many accounts an extraordinary person," for even though "he spent the principal part of a long life in a village retirement, he was eminent for his colloquial powers." "As a preacher," Hall continued, "he was universally admired...[and] as a religious poet, his excellence has long been known and acknowledged in dissenting congregations."[4]

Yet, like the names of a number of other eminent eighteenth-century Baptists, that of Beddome is known by few Baptists today. By contrast, he was prominent in the memory of the transatlantic Baptist community up until the end of the Victorian era, which raises the question as to why he has been so neglected by Baptists in this century. Possibly it is due to the fact that up until the start of this century a goodly number of his hymns were still being sung. In the twentieth century, however, his hymns have largely fallen into obscurity, and with them interest in their author.

Beddome and Bourton

Bourton-on-the-Water, where Beddome pastored for fifty-five years lies in the Cotswolds, one of the most beautiful regions of England. Bourton itself, due to the River Windrush that flows through the town centre, is often described in tourist literature today as the "Venice of Cotswolds." Known Baptist witness in the village dates from 1655. But between that date and the coming of Beddome to Bourton in 1740, the Baptists seem to have made relatively little progress. In fact, Beddome would later describe this situation before his coming to the village in 1740 as one in which the Bourton Baptists had been "for a long time...unsettled and

---

[4] "Recommendatory Preface" to Beddome's *Hymns adapted to Public Worship, or Family Devotion* (London, 1818).

divided."[5] With the coming of Beddome to the village, though, this long period of uncertainty for the Baptist cause in Bourton was at an end.

Beddome was the son of a Baptist minister named John Beddome, pastor of the Pithay Baptist Church in Bristol for much of his life, and Rachel Brandon, a wealthy heiress and a descendant of Charles Brandon, the first Duke of Suffolk and brother-in-law to Henry VIII. The elder Beddome was said to be "remarkable for his spiritual winning discourse, especially to young converts and enquirers."[6] John Beddome's preaching was obviously an important influence on the development of his son as a preacher of the first magnitude.

Beddome was also convinced of the rightness of singing hymns at the church's public worship. Whether or not hymns could be sung in worship was an issue upon which Baptists were sharply divided for much of the first half of the eighteenth century.[7] The stand that John Beddome took upon this issue is not without significance, for it meant that young Benjamin was exposed at an early age to hymn-singing and thus a foundation laid for his extensive hymn-writing during much of his ministry at Bourton.

Now, although Benjamin regularly sat under his father's preaching in the Pithay as he was growing up, he showed little interest in the things of Christ, and understandably his parents were deeply concerned about his state. In fact, not until he was twenty years of age did the preaching of the Word strike home to his heart, and his parents see the fruit of many years of prayer for their son's conversion. On August 7, 1737, a visiting

---

[5] Letter to Prescot Street Baptist Church, November 22, 1750 [in Thomas Brooks, "Ministerial Changes a Hundred Years Ago", *The Baptist Magazine*, 51 (1859), 427].

[6] Cited Roger Hayden, "Evangelical Calvinism among eighteenth-century British Baptists with particular reference to Bernard Foskett, Hugh and Caleb Evans and the Bristol Baptist Academy, 1690-1791" (Unpublished Ph.D. thesis, University of Keele, 1991), 113-114.

[7] For an excellent discussion of the early stages of this controversy, see Murdina D. MacDonald, "London Calvinistic Baptists 1689-1727: tensions within a Dissenting community under Toleration" (Unpublished D. Phil. Thesis, Regent's Park College, Oxford University, 1982), 50-66.

preacher to the Pithay by the name of Ware spoke on Luke 15:7. So deeply was Beddome affected by the sermon that for some time afterwards he would be in tears when his father preached, and he would hide himself in one of the galleries so that his weeping would not be widely seen.[8] Beddome would later generalize his experience thus in one of his hymns:

> Faith, 'tis a precious grace,
> Where'er it is bestowed;
> It boasts of a celestial birth,
> And is the gift of God.
>
> Jesus it owns as king,
> An all-atoning priest,
> It claims no merit of its own,
> But looks for all in Christ.[9]

Being led to consider pastoral ministry soon after his conversion, Beddome spent a couple of years in theological training in Bristol, and then further time at a school called the Fund Academy in Tenter Alley, Moorfields. It was during this sojourn in London that Beddome became convinced of the necessity of believer's baptism. Accordingly he was baptized by Samuel Wilson (1702-1750), the pastor of Prescot Street Baptist Church, on September 27, 1739 in the baptistery of a church called the Barbican. Few Baptist churches at that time had an indoor baptistery, most of them preferring to baptize in lakes, rivers, or ponds.

At the time of his baptism, his father, in many ways Benjamin's spiritual mentor, wrote to him to express his joy about the step that his son was taking. "I am pleased to hear that you have given yourself to a Church of Christ," he wrote, "but more, in that I hope you first gave up

---

[8] S. A. Swaine, *Faithful Men; or, Memorials of Bristol Baptist College and Some of its Most Distinguished Alumni* (London: Alexander & Shepheard, 1884), 43.

[9] *Hymns*, #165, "Faith the gift of God."

yourself to the Lord to be his servant, and at his disposal."[10] When, in the following year the London church took steps to formally recognize God's hand on Benjamin's life for pastoral ministry and to set him apart for that work, the elder Beddome told his son: "The Lord will help you to make a solemn dedication of yourself to him, and enter on the work of the Lord with holy awe and trembling."[11]

Beddome's father continued to give his son sage counsel up until his death in 1757, deeming "nothing unimportant that stood related to the ministry, and might therefore either help or hinder its success."[12] The younger Beddome's preaching in his early years was often strident and harsh, and his sermons far too long. John Beddome thus told his son in a letter that he wrote on May 17, 1742: "If you deliver the great truths of the gospel with calmness, and with a soft, mellow voice, they will drop as the gentle rain or dew. For the good of souls, then, and for your own good, be persuaded to strive after this." A few weeks later he again urged him: "soften your voice, and shorten your sermons ...Let *two hours* be the longest time you spend in the pulpit at any place"![13]

Beddome first visited Bourton-on-the-Water in the spring of 1740. Over the next three years he laboured with great success in the Bourton church as well as among the Baptists of Warwick. Significant for the shape of his future ministry was a local revival that took place under his ministry in the early months of 1741. Around forty individuals were converted.[14] It may well have been this taste of revival that made Beddome a cordial friend to those who were involved in the evangelical revivals of the mid-eighteenth century, men like George Whitefield and the

---

[10] Cited Thomas Brooks, *Pictures of the Past: The History of the Baptist Church, Bourton-on-the-Water* (London: Judd & Glass, 1861), 23.

[11] Letter to Benjamin Beddome, May 21, 1740 (cited Brooks, *Pictures of the Past*, 23).

[12] Brooks, *Pictures of the Past*, 24.

[13] Letters to Benjamin Beddome, May 17 and August 6, 1742 (cited Brooks, *Pictures of the Past*, 24-25).

[14] William Newman, *Rylandiana: Reminiscences Relating to the Rev. John Ryland, A.M.* (London: George Wightman, 1835), 3.

Mohegan Indian preacher Samson Occom (1723-1792),[15] and gave him an ongoing hunger to read of revival throughout the English-speaking world.[16]

Eventually, in 1743, the Bourton church extended an invitation to Beddome to become what they called their "preaching elder."[17] Readily acceding to their request, he was ordained in September of that year. Unhappily, due to ill-health John Beddome could not be present. But he hoped, he wrote to his son, that

> what you are about to take upon you, will be a stimulus to you, to walk more closely with God than ever, and make you more sincerely and simply concerned for the good of the souls of men. I desire, with my whole heart, that an unction of the Holy Spirit may be poured out upon you at the laying on of the hands of the Presbytery; and that your faith therein may be strong.[18]

When Benjamin Beddome became the pastor of this congregation, it consisted of about eighty members spread out in villages and hamlets around Bourton, places such as Upper Slaughter and Lower Slaughter, Stow-on-the-Wold, Upper Swell and Lower Swell, and Moreton-in-Marsh.[19] Some lived as far away as Hook Norton, more than fourteen

---

[15] For Beddome's association with Whitefield, see Geoffrey F. Nuttall, "George Whitefield's 'Curate': Gloucestershire Dissent and the Revival", *The Journal of Ecclesiastical History*, 27 (1976), 382-384. Samson Occom seems to have been converted under the preaching of James Davenport (1716-1757) around 1740, prior to Davenport's period of fanaticism [W. DeLoss Love, *Samson Occom and the Christian Indians of New England* (Boston/Chicago: The Pilgrim Press, 1899), 34]. Occom preached at Bourton in April, 1767, during an extensive trip that the Native American evangelist made to Britain (Hayden, "Evangelical Calvinism", 152).

[16] Hayden, "Evangelical Calvinism", 152.

[17] Bourton-on-the-Water Church Book 1719-1802 (Angus Library, Regent's Park College, Oxford University), 67.

[18] Cited Hayden, "Evangelical Calvinism", 26.

[19] John Rippon, "Rev. Benjamin Beddome, A.M. Bourton-on-the-Water, Gloucestershire", *Baptist Annual Register* (1794-1797), 2:322.

miles distant to the north-east. In Beddome's day, this was a considerable distance to travel to worship, especially when it was either raining or snowing, for many of the roads in the Cotswolds were well-nigh impassable when wet. In 1768 Arthur Young (1741-1820), an important agriculturalist who wrote a number of travel narratives, described the main road from Burford to Gloucester, which was only a few miles south of Bourton, as "the worst I ever travelled on; so bad that it is a scandal to the country."[20] Beddome himself chose to live in nearby Lower Slaughter, where he resided till his engagement in 1749 to Elizabeth Boswell (1732-1784), the daughter of Richard Boswell (d.1783) and his wife Hannah (d.1765), a wealthy jeweller in Bourton and one of the deacons of the Baptist church..[21]

In view of his upcoming marriage, Beddome decided to relocate to Bourton. A large manse was subsequently built that year for a cost of £324 17s 6½d, no small sum, the bulk of which was raised by the members and adherents of the Bourton church. Beddome himself gave close to £31. Today the manse is a local hotel and pub, with the latter recalling its former owner in its name, the "Beddome Bar"!

These early years of Beddome's ministry saw great numerical growth in the membership of the church. Between 1740 and 1745 the church received 73 new members. By 1764 Beddome reckoned that 176 had been received into the church since he had first come to it in 1740.[22] Describing the state of the church members in 1750, Beddome could thus declare: "my labours have been, and are still, in a measure, blest unto them, above a hundred having been added since my first coming amongst them."[23]

---

[20] Cited David Rollison, *The Local Origins of Modern Society: Gloucestershire 1500-1800* (London/New York: Routledge, 1992), 58.

[21] See Rippon's description of Elizabeth Beddome, "Rev. Benjamin Beddome", 318-319, footnote †.

[22] Brooks, *Pictures of the Past*, 50.

[23] Letter to Prescot Street Baptist Church, November 22, 1750 (Brooks, "Ministerial Changes", 427). For the figures, see also Bourton-on-the-Water Church Book 1719-1802, pages 19-20.

The last thirty years of Beddome's ministry, though, actually saw
decline in the church membership. Between 1765 and 1795, 53 new
members were added by conversion and baptism. But in this same period
105 of the members died, 12 were dismissed to other Baptist works and
2 were excluded. Thus, by 1795, the year that Beddome died, the church
had 123 on the membership roll, sixty less than in 1764.[24]

It is quite clear from letters that Beddome wrote on behalf of the
church to the local Baptist association that he lamented this lack of
growth in church membership. The size of the congregation maintained
its own, probably around five or six hundred, to the end of his life, but
that vital step of believer's baptism leading to full church membership
was taken by far fewer in the final three decades of his ministry than in
the first two and a half.[25] Thus, the poignant prayer of Beddome in the
church's 1786 letter to the association: "Come from the 4 winds O
Breath & breathe upon these slain that they may live. Awake O North-
wind & come thou South, blow upon our Garden that the Spices may
flow out."[26] Nevertheless, there is no hint that Beddome thought of ever
abandoning his post.

Yet, these years were not without their joys. Let me choose one, the
baptism of Ann Wakefield in 1777 and her reception into the membership of the church. Ann was a domestic servant who, around 1772, began to be convicted that she was a sinner in need of salvation. She was
in great distress about her soul's state for about a year till she heard a
sermon by Beddome on Mark 5:19—"Go home to thy friends, and tell
them how great things the Lord hath done for thee." As she listened to
Beddome preach on this text she said "it was as if God was pouring the
Glory of all his Perfections upon her Soul. She saw her sins washed
away in the Blood of Christ." Despite a fear that she might not be able

---

[24] Brooks, *Pictures of the Past*, 50, 55.

[25] See these letters in the Bourton-on-the-Water Church Book 1719-1802,
pages 232-317. For the fact that the size of the congregation listening to Beddome maintained its own during the final years of his life, see the letters for
May 15, 1785 and June 4, 1786 (*ibid.*).

[26] Bourton-on-the-Water Church Book 1719-1802. The punctuation has
been added.

to persevere in the Christian life and thus bring disgrace upon the church if she became a member, by 1777 she had what she called "a strong conviction of her Duty to join in Church-Fellowship." One particular Sunday, as she was walking home from the meeting-house and meditating on Luke 10:37—especially the words of Jesus, "Go, and do thou likewise"—she was given the courage to commit herself to joining the church. So it was on September 28, having been baptized previously, she was "receiv'd into full Communion" with the church.[27]

His ministry also had its challenges, though. Again, one example will have to suffice. "Sister Hardiman," baptized in 1778, lived four miles north of Bourton at Stow-in-the-Wold. Beddome conducted a service there on a number of Sundays a month, but when the Lord's Table was celebrated at Bourton she would come down from Stow to take it at Bourton. She appears to have been either single or widowed and had come to an age when she needed financial support. She insisted that the Bourton church completely support her financially. When the church did not comply she began to publicly criticize Beddome. Theologically, she also appears to have held "erroneous Opinions bordering on Quakerism, Antinominaism and Mysticism."

Well, things came to a head between 1784 and 1786. On September 17, 1784, she came to Bourton for the Lord's Supper. Afterwards, not being invited to stay over in anyone's house, she told Beddome that she was going to sleep the night in the church. He tried to persuade her not to, but she insisted and eventually it appears she did stay the night in the church. That week Beddome and the leadership of the church determined that if she did not behave herself in the future they would have to exercise discipline by asking her to refrain from taking communion. She must have behaved herself for a while at least, since it was not until March of 1786 that she was finally asked to withdraw from communion. She refused, but came to church when the Lord's Supper was being celebrated. And as the bread was being distributed, she brazenly snatched a piece and ate it, but the cup was not given her. Afterwards, before the afternoon worship service, she came into the church and went

---

[27] Bourton-on-the-Water Church Book [F.P.C. F.1(a)], July 6 and September 28, 1777.

into hysterics in the vestry, and had to be carried out.[28] Such are the challenges of ministry!

A Scriptural Exposition of the Baptist Catechism (1752)

Beddome was thoroughly convinced that vital Christianity is a matter of both heart and head. And like fellow Baptists of his day, Beddome found the use of a catechism helpful in matching head knowledge to heart-felt faith.[29] Indeed it is noteworthy that "one considerable instrument" of Beddome's success at Bourton during the 1740s was his use of catechetical instruction.

Catechisms had been central to the Baptist movement from its origins in the 1630s.[30] The most widely-used catechism among the Baptists was commissioned by a national meeting of the denomination in June, 1693. Although a pastor by the name of William Collins (d.1702) was asked to draw it up,[31] many would later know it as *Keach's Catechism*, and it would appear that the prolific Baptist author Benjamin Keach was mainly responsible for it.[32] Formally called *The Baptist Catechism*, this catechism was primarily a Baptist revision of the Presbyterian *Shorter Catechism* (1648)—the catechism which begins with that well-known question, "What is the chief end of man?"—and was still being reprinted well into the nineteenth century.[33]

---

[28] *Ibid.*, September 17 and 26, 1784; March 3 and 5, 1786.

[29] Hayden, "Evangelical Calvinism", 259.

[30] For the importance placed on catechetical literature by the early Nonconformist tradition, see Richard L. Greaves, "Introduction" to John Bunyan, *Instruction for the Ignorant, Light for Them that Sit in Darkness, Saved by Grace, Come, & Welcome, to Jesus Christ*, ed. Richard L. Greaves (Oxford: Clarendon Press, 1979), xxxiii-xliii.

[31] Joseph Ivimey, *A History of the English Baptists* (London, 1811), I, 533; *idem, A History of the English Baptists* (London, 1814), II, 397.

[32] J. Barry Vaughn, "Benjamin Keach" in Timothy George and David S. Dockery, eds., *Baptist Theologians* (Nashville: Broadman Press, 1990), 66.

[33] For a recent printing of the catechism, see *The Baptist Catechism*, revised Paul King Jewett (Grand Rapids: Baker Book House, 1952).

During the early years of his ministry Beddome used *The Baptist Catechism* widely, but clearly felt that the questions and answers of the catechism needed to be supplemented by further material. So he composed what was printed in 1752 as *A Scriptural Exposition of the Baptist Catechism by Way of Question and Answer*, which basically reproduced the wording and substance of the catechism drawn up by Keach, but added various sub-questions and answers to each of the main questions. The *Scriptural Exposition* proved to be fairly popular. There were two editions during Beddome's lifetime, the second of which was widely used at the Bristol Baptist Academy, the sole British Baptist seminary for much of the eighteenth century. In the nineteenth century it was reprinted once in the British Isles and twice in the United States, the last printing being in 1849.

Something of the flavour of Beddome's *Scriptural Exposition* can be seen in his treatment of the question, "What is the word of God?" He begins by citing the answer of *Keach's Catechism*: "the holy scriptures of the old and new Testament are the word of God, and the only certain rule of faith and obedience." Beddome then asks various questions of each of the aspects of this statement and provides Scripture verses by way of answers. For example, here is the way that Beddome deals with the description of God's Word as "the only certain rule of obedience and faith."

Is the Word of God a rule? Yes. It is *a light to our feet, and a lamp to our path*, Ps. cxix.105. Do we need such a rule? Yes. For *we all like sheep have gone astray*, Isa. liii.6. Is the word of *God* a sufficient rule? Yes. *The law of the Lord is perfect*, Ps. xix.7. Is it a plain rule? Yes. *The words of his mouth are all plain to him that understandeth*, Prov. viii.8, 9. Is it an extensive rule? Yes. *The commandment is exceeding broad*, Ps. cxix.96. Is it an abiding rule? Yes. *The word of the Lord endureth for ever*, 1 Pet. i.23. And is it the only rule? Yes. *For if any man shall add to these things, God will add to him the plagues written in this book*, Rev. xxii.18.

Are not unwritten traditions a rule? No. *Ye have made the commandment of God of none effect by your traditions*, Mat. xv.6. Is the authority of the church a rule? No. For our *faith should not stand in the wisdom of men*, 1 Cor. ii.5. Are the sentiments of great men a rule? No. *The prophet and the priest have erred*, Isa. xxviii.7. Is the light of nature a sufficient rule? No. For it is said of those that were guided by it, *The way of peace they have not known*, Rom. iii.17. Is the light within a certain rule? No. *The way of man is not in himself*, Jer. x. 23. Are not the examples of many a rule? No. *Thou shalt not follow a multitude to do evil*, Exod. xxiii.2. Are not the examples of the good a sufficient rule? No. We must *be followers of* them *only as they are of Christ*, 1 Cor. xi.1. May not what angels say be depended upon as a certain rule? No. *Tho' an angel from heaven preach any other gospel to you, let him be accursed*, Gal. i.8. Or a voice from heaven? No. For *we have a more sure word of prophecy*, 2 Pet. i.19.[34]

While a modern interpreter of God's Word might differ with Beddome over some of the texts that he cites to prove a point, there is little doubt the *Scriptural Exposition* is, as Beddome's early biographer John Rippon put it, "a compendium of Divinity."[35]

Earthly trials

The final three decades of Beddome's life were fraught with earthly trials. In 1762 he wrestled with what a fellow Baptist pastor, Daniel Turner (1710-1798), termed "a nervous disorder, attended with spiritual darkness and distress."[36] Three years later his eldest son, John, died at the age of fifteen. A second son, Benjamin, died in 1778 of what Rippon calls "a putrid fever." It is notable that the very day the younger Benjamin died, his father, little suspecting the news he would receive the next

---

[34] *A Scriptural Exposition of the Baptist Catechism* (Bristol: W. Pine, 1776), 11-12.

[35] "Rev. Benjamin Beddome", 322.

[36] Daniel Turner, Letter to Benjamin Beddome, September 4, 1762 ["Spiritual Darkness", *The Baptist Magazine*, 7 (1815), 9].

morning, wrote the following hymn to be sung at the close of the morning service that day.

> My times of sorrow, and of joy,
> Great God, are in thy hand;
> My choicest comforts come from thee,
> And go at thy command.
>
> If thou should'st take them all away,
> Yet would I not repine;
> Before they were possess'd by me,
> They were entirely thine.
>
> Nor would I drop a murmuring word,
> Tho' the whole world were gone,
> But seek enduring happiness
> In thee, and thee alone.
>
> What is the world with all it's store?
> 'Tis but a bitter-sweet;
> When I attempt to pluck the rose
> A pricking thorn I meet.
>
> Here perfect bliss can ne'er be found,
> The honey's mix'd with gall;
> Midst changing scenes and dying friends,
> Be *thou* my all in all.

Six years later a third son, Foskett, drowned in the Thames at Deptford. His dear wife had died earlier that year.

From the mid-1770s on he began to suffer from gout and experience tremendous difficulty in walking.[37] Eventually it got to the point that he had to be carried to the church, and he would preach to his congregation seated. Despite his physical infirmities, though, Beddome simply refused

---

[37] Thomas Purdy, Letter to John Sutcliff, April 11, 1775 (Sutcliff Papers, Angus Library, Regent's Park College, Oxford).

to give up preaching. At the heart of this refusal lay a deeply-held conviction about the vital importance of preaching.

Convictions about preaching

Like most eighteenth-century Particular Baptists Beddome believed that it was through preaching to the mind that God appealed to the hearts and wills of human beings. He brings this out most clearly in a sermon that he preached on 2 Corinthians 5:11a—"Knowing therefore the terror of the Lord, we persuade men." Beddome was convinced that the word "persuade" lay at the heart of preaching. Since men and women are "endowed with reason and understanding," they are "capable of being persuaded" and reasoned with. Thus, we find the Apostle Paul reasoning "with the Jews out of the Scriptures," that is, laying before them "the evidences of truth" and endeavouring to "remove their prejudices against it by solid argument." Consequently, a "minister is not to address himself to the passions, but to the understanding of his hearers."[38]

Beddome, of course, did not disapprove of the presence of emotions. Sermons must be delivered, he argued, with "warmth of affection, earnestness of expression, and unwearied assiduity." As such, they will undoubtedly kindle the affections of the hearers. But, it must be recognized that emotion is also quite fickle, and can "quickly vanish away, and leave no permanent effect." It simply cannot form the foundation of a Christian lifestyle, let alone serve as the basis for believers' "life together."[39]

It needs to be noted that Beddome never lost sight of the fact that it is the Spirit who alone can empower the words of the preacher and make them efficacious to the winning of the lost and the building up of God's people. In Beddome's words: "Ministers lift up their voice, and God makes bare his arm; ministers persuade, and God enables, nay, con-

---

[38] "Sermon V" [*Short Discourses adapted to Village Worship, or The Devotions of the Family* (London: Burton, Smith and Co., 1820), VIII, 49-50].
[39] *Ibid.* (*Short Discourses*, VIII, 50).

strains, men to comply. ...Ministers stand at the door and knock; the Spirit comes with his key, and opens the door."[40]

Publications

At the time of Beddome's death in 1795, almost his sole publication was his *Scriptural Exposition*. In the years that followed, though, a good number of his sermons were published, as was a volume of 830 hymns. It is noteworthy that close to one hundred of these hymns were still appearing in hymnals at the end of the nineteenth century, though today, only a handful are still being reprinted. Among them is the one whose first stanza begins "Father of mercies, bow thine ear" It is a prayer for those called to the preaching of God's Word. Its third stanza is written out of Beddome's own personal experience and is a fitting conclusion to this study of a faithful pastor:

Teach them to sow the precious seed,
Teach them Thy chosen flock to feed;
Teach them immortal souls to gain,
Souls that will well reward their pain.

Further reading

The earliest biographical account of Beddome's life is an extensive obituary written by John Rippon: "Rev. Benjamin Beddome, A.M. Bourton-on-the-Water, Gloucestershire", *Baptist Annual Register* (1794-1797), 2:314-326. This account was largely reproduced by Joseph Ivimey in *A History of the English Baptists* (London: Isaac Taylor Hinton/Holdsworth & Ball, 1830), IV, 461-469. Two significant biographical studies that appeared in the course of the nineteenth century

---

[40] "The Heavenly Calling" in *Sermons Printed from the Manuscripts of the late Rev. Benjamin Beddome, A.M.* (London: William Ball, 1835), 111, 116. The final sentence of this quotation is taken directly from the Puritan author Thomas Watson (d. *c.*1686). See his *A Body of Divinity* (1890 ed.; repr. London: The Banner of Truth Trust, 1965), 221.

are the "Memoir" attached to *Sermons printed from the manuscripts of the late Rev. Benjamin Beddome* (London: William Ball, 1835), ix-xxviii, and the lengthy account of Beddome's ministry in Thomas Brooks, *Pictures of the Past: The History of the Baptist Church, Bourton-on-the-Water* (London: Judd & Glass, 1861), 21-66.

In this century relatively little has been written about Beddome. There are really only four studies worthy of notice: Derrick Holmes, "The Early Years (1655-1740) of Bourton-on-the-Water Dissenters who later constituted the Baptist Church, with special reference to the Ministry of the Reverend Benjamin Beddome A.M. 1740-1795" (Unpublished Certificate in Education Dissertation, St Paul's College, Cheltenham, 1969); Kenneth Dix, " "Thy Will Be Done": A Study in the Life of Benjamin Beddome", *The Bulletin of the Strict Baptist Historical Society*, 9 (1972) [this article occupies the bulk of the *Bulletin* and is lacking pagination]; Roger Hayden, "Evangelical Calvinism among eighteenth-century British Baptists with particular reference to Bernard Foskett, Hugh and Caleb Evans and the Bristol Baptist Academy, 1690-1791" (Unpublished Ph.D. thesis, University of Keele, 1991), 140-160, 287-293; and J. R. Watson, *The English Hymn: A Critical and Historical Study* (Oxford: Clarendon Press, 1997), 198-202.

A

SCRIPTURAL EXPOSITION

OF THE

BAPTIST CATECHISM

BY WAY OF

QUESTION and ANSWER.

By BENJAMIN BEDDOME, M. A.

SECOND EDITION, corrected.

Περὶ ὧν κατηχηΘης. Luc. i. 4.
Κοινωνείτω δὲ ὁ κατηχέμεν⊙· τον λόγον τῶ κατηχῦνli, ἐν
πᾶσιν ἀγαθοῖς. Gal. vi. 6.

BRISTOL:
Printed by W. PINE, 1776.

Benj.ᵒ Beddome

JOHN COLLETT RYLAND

JOHN COLLETT RYLAND (1723-1792)

Peter Naylor

A s John Rippon drew his funeral oration for John Collett Ryland to a
close, he prayed, "God grant that when we come to die, our defects
may be as few as his, and our Christian virtues half as many. Amen."
According to Robert Hall, Jr., Ryland was "a most extraordinary man, and
rarely, if ever, has full justice been done to his character."[1] These
observations imply that the subject of this chapter remains a "must" for
students of the eighteenth-century English Particular Baptists.

Ryland's life

Volume 3 among the books of the College Lane Baptist Church,
Northampton, summarizes John Collett Ryland's life thus:

He was born at *Lower Ditchford* in Gloucestershire   Oct. 12, 1723
Join'd the B Ch. [= Baptist church] at *Bourton on the
Water*, then, and still, under the Pastoral Care of
Revd. B. *Beddome*   Oct. 4, 1742
Went to study at *Bristol* under Revd. *Bernard Foskett* Feb. 18, 1744
Was invited by the B. Ch. at *Warwick* to visit them   April 18, 1746
Rec'd a Member at *Warwick* by Dismn. from *Bourton*   July 8, 1750
(Just one Week after the celebrated Jonath. Edwards preach'd his
farewell sermon to the Ch. at Northampton, New-England.)
Married *Eliz. Frith* daughter of *Sam.* and *Anna Frith*   Dec. 23, 1748
Removed to *Northampton*   Oct. 5, 1759
Removed to *Enfield* near London   1786

---

[1] Cited by W. Newman, *Rylandiana: Reminiscences relating to the Rev. John
Ryland, A.M.* (London: George Wightman, 1835), 198.

Removed to eternal Glory   July 24, 1792[2]

A convinced Baptist, John's grandfather incurred heavy fines for not attending his parish church. John's father married Freelove Collett, whose family claimed as a kinsman Dean John Colet (c.1467-1519), an early reformer. Losing his mother at the age of five, the lad tasted the sins of youth but came to know the Lord in 1741 through the ministry of Benjamin Beddome, pastor of the Bourton-on-the-Water Particular Baptist Church. Scars remained, though, and in later years he would write that it is "dangerous to read any impure book: you'll never get it out of your faculties 'till you are dead. My imagination was tainted young; and I shall never get rid of it, till I get into heaven."[3]

Now a member of the Bourton congregation, John was intent upon entering the Bristol Baptist Academy, and he did so in 1744. His diary records his determination upon entering:

> if God don't bless me with abilities for the ministry, I'll get me a place to be an outrider for a Bristol, Coventry, or London tradesman. When the year is finished with Mr [Bernard] Foskett I shall partly see how the matter will go, and if I don't engage in the work of the Ministry I'll endeavour to return the Money paid for my Board, and any more expended on my account.[4]

He found Bristol and the Principal, Bernard Foskett (1685-1758), difficult:

> Foskett should have spared no pains to educate our Souls to Grandeur and to have enriched and impregnated them with great and generous Ideas of God in his whole Natural and Moral character, relations and actions to us and the Universe. This was

---

[2] In the original, the italicized words are underlined, not italicized.

[3] Newman, *Rylandiana*, 79.

[4] "Diary", June 15, 1744 (Ms. 6.e.27, Angus Library, Regent's Park College, Oxford). The "Diary" is composed of nine notebooks.

thy business, thy duty, thy honour. O Foskett! and this thou didst totally neglect.[5]

Later, Ryland would counsel students to "avoid tea-drinking parties (when at Bristol)." Even so, these formative years gave him a foundation, and he showed himself to be an acceptable preacher. Yet inner distresses haunted him: "My Reason almost ruined and had little power to exercise itself… Sermons forgot as soon as heard."[6]

John left the college in August, 1746. Already "called out" to the ministry by the Bourton fellowship, he went to the Castle Hill church in Warwick. Invited to stay for a probationary twelve months, this term extended to nearly four years, when he was ordained as minister. The Warwick Church Minute Book states judiciously that the people welcomed him because they had "had some Benefit from his Ministry constantly exercised among Us."

The letter of transfer from Bourton shows the esteem in which the young man was held.

As it was our Happiness that God should raise up such a Gift as our Bro. Ryland amongst us, so too your Priviledge that You have enjoy'd his Ministry so long; had him restored after a threatening and dangerous Illness (of ye Small Pox in April last) and are now likely to have him settled in Office amongst You.—For this purpose, we Dismiss him from his Fellowship with us and recommend him to you, assuring You that we think it our Honour that we ever had such a Member.[7]

Ryland's near encounter with death was not forgotten, as witness an undated marginal note in his copy of Doddridge's tome on the subject of regeneration: "Sickness, that great Engine of doing Good."

---

[5] Cited Newman, *Rylandiana*, 37, dates this extract as late as 1784, forty years on. The original "Diary" is untidy, but appears to read March 10, 1744. On Foskett, see below, page 216.

[6] "Diary", April, 1744; Newman, *Rylandiana*, 88.

[7] Warwick Church Minute Book, page 26.

The young pastor married Elizabeth, of a family which counted as an ancestor the martyr John Frith (c. 1503-1533). Thus both sides of the family came from convinced Protestant stock. Five children were born, the first being John Ryland, Jr., who in later years would assist and then succeed his father in the latter's second pastorate at Northampton. Still at Warwick, Ryland founded a boarding-school which prospered so well that he took a lease of the local parsonage in order to gain space, and engaged as an assistant Guy Medley, father of Samuel Medley (1738-1799).[8] John Ryland was as modest as he was able. His diary records that in August, 1746 he preached at Bourton:

> Mr Beddome at Abingdon
> And poor me to Supply his Place here.
> In the Morning my heart too dry and dull.

William Newman (1773-1835), a loyal disciple who worked in his teens at Ryland's Enfield school, observed that the Warwick ministry was "not unprofitable to his people; but in his own personal experience he endured temptations uncommonly severe."[9] His son John noted: "My father's usefulness at Warwick was but small, and he had many trials during his residence there."[10]

In 1759 came an invitation to the Independent Church at College Lane (later College Street), Northampton. Not exceeding thirty when Ryland began, the membership grew, and the chapel had to be twice enlarged.[11] In May, 1776, he recalled that "in 16 years and a half We had Added 84 Men, 137 Women, In all 221. Glory be to God we have had but a few Hypocrites and damned Apostates Atheists and Infidels."[12] According to John Rippon,

---

[8] On Samuel Medley, see below, pages 235-249.

[9] *Rylandiana*, 7.

[10] From John Ryland, Jr., "Copies of Autograph Manuscripts" (The Northamptonshire Record Office, Northampton).

[11] John Ryland, Jr., "History of the Baptist Church in Northampton" (Handwritten and undated Ms., The Northamptonshire Record Office, Northampton).

[12] College Lane Church Minute Book, 1697-1761.

"his style was as much his own as his features, and what it was at any time defective of Grace, it generally possessed in Grandeur."[13] Newman commented that "as a preacher, he was unquestionably a star of the first magnitude."[14]

His school, transferred from Warwick, was equally successful. As a back-up to his teaching Ryland kept the printing-press busy, in Newman's estimation regarding it as almost a goddess.[15] In all things Ryland showed himself a "live wire," as witness his letter to the Northamptonshire Baptist Association in 1768, urging that

> you would join with us in imitating *Socinian Diligence* but apply that Diligence to the glorious Purpose of defending and spreading the Glorious Gospel of the blessed GOD,—shall men who take a vast deal of Pains to damn their own Souls, out do us in Activity? Heaven forbid!

Endowed with an earthy wisdom, his maxims were honest and racy. For instance, "When the improbability of success is greater than the probability, it is not prudent to act or venture. N.B. This is the case in all lotteries." Or, "Keep your name in the church as sweet as a rose, and let it not be said after your death, 'There lies a man but little more asleep than when alive'."[16]

He recalled in the year of his death that, like him, the Baptist divine John Brine had confessed that sometimes he was unable to think at all; that Philip Doddridge (1702-1751) revealed that occasionally he could not speak sense; and that he—Ryland—had even heard George Whitefield give rise to nonsense and rubbish. But he loved the ministry:

> Make solemn pauses in your preaching—tell agreeable facts— accustom yourself to short, pointed, pathetic addresses. And in the

---

[13] John Rippon, *The Gentle Dismission of Saints from Earth to Heaven. A sermon occasioned by the decease of the Rev. John Ryland, Senior* (London, 1792), 46.

[14] *Rylandiana*, 12.

[15] *Ibid.*, 11.

[16] *Ibid.*, 76, 83.

last prayer, pray for the people you have been speaking to, with affection, as if they were the only people in the world.[17]

Although Ryland was, in the jargon of the day, "a mixed-communion Baptist" after his transfer to Northampton,[18] it was said that he never shone more than in the administration of baptism. His son John wrote that when the church "strove to keep it [a baptismal service] more secret for the sake of avoiding the Rabble, it generally excited greater curiosity, and brought more Spectators, since the latter made it no Secret at all."[19]

Inner struggles persisted. As late as 1788 Ryland's papers record the temptations by which he was buffeted. And his temper sometimes led him into indiscretions. The loyal Rippon covers up: "our friend *had* Spots, and *Spots* are in the *Sun*."[20]

After marrying Mrs. Stott, the widow of an army officer, in 1782, he transferred in 1785-1786 to Enfield where he opened another no less successful school.[21] Money, though, was a problem. In 1788 John Newton wrote to the younger John that his father ought to be content with his children's aid while he lived, but that his expectations for financial help *after* he died were "not reasonable"![22]

Sadly, he did not survive to assist the formation of the Particular Baptist Mission. But would he have been willing? Of this, more anon. Concerning his own assurance of salvation, on one occasion he stated robustly that were he to find himself in hell he would there announce to the residents that he loved the Lord Jesus Christ, in consequence of which, turned out by the devils, he would find himself in heaven.[23] And listen to these magnificent

---

[17] *Ibid.*, 80-81.

[18] Rippon, *Gentle Dismission*, 46.

[19] From an undated letter by the younger Ryland to an unnamed recipient recorded in "Copies of Autograph Manuscripts."

[20] Rippon, *Gentle Dismission*, 47.

[21] *Ibid.*, 14.

[22] Cited L. G. Champion, "The Letters of John Newton to John Ryland", *The Baptist Quarterly*, 17 (1977-1978), 159.

[23] James Culross, *The Three Rylands: A Hundred Years of various Christian Service* (London: Elliot Stock, 1897), 62.

words which he delivered at the interment of Andrew Gifford at dawn on Friday, July 2, 1784:

> Farewell, thou dear old man! We leave thee in possession of death till the resurrection day: but we will bear witness against thee, oh king of terrors, at the mouth of this dungeon; thou shalt not always have possession of this dead body; it shall be demanded of thee by the great Conqueror, and at that moment thou shalt resign thy prisoner. O ye ministers of Christ, ye people of God, ye surrounding spectators, prepare, prepare to meet this old servant of Christ, at that day, at that hour, when this whole place shall be all nothing, but life and death shall be swallowed up in victory.[24]

His last sermon had as its theme the deity of Christ, probably his favourite subject, as witness his elegant hand-written booklet, now in the Northamptonshire Record Office, entitled "102 Proofs of the Divinity of the Lord Jesus Christ from his bringing the Children of Israel out of Egypt," and dated as late as 1788. Its style and argumentation compel unreserved admiration.

Although Ryland desired to be buried between the graves of John Brine and John Skepp (1675-1721) in Bunhill Fields, London, friends deposited his remains in the family grave in the Northampton meeting-house. With the coffin placed on the communion table, John Rippon preached to a packed congregation.[25]

Ryland's Calvinism

John Collett Ryland was a moderately High Calvinist:

> The word *offer* is not so proper as declaration, proposal, or gift. The gospel is a *declaration* of the free grace of God. It is a *proposal* of salvation by Jesus Christ, and it proclaims Christ as

---

[24] Cited Joseph Ivimey, *A History of the English Baptists* (London: B. J. Holdsworth, 1823), III, 604-605.

[25] College Lane Church Minute Book, III, 138.

the free and absolute *gift* of God.—See *Hussey*'s "Operations of Grace and no Offers," &c.

And:

> Avoid two extremes. Some high Calvinists neglect the unconverted; but Paul left no case untouched. He spoke properly and suitably to Felix, as well as to Timothy. Some neglect to preach the law, and tell their hearers to accept Christ. O sinners, beware! If Christ says, "Depart," 'tis all over. Depart into a thousand Etnas, bursting up for ever and ever.[26]

Newman recounts that

> speaking of the *Modern Question*, he [Ryland] said, Robert Hall, [Sr.,] his son, and Fuller were busied on it. The devil threw out an empty barrel for them to roll about, while they ought to have been drinking the wine of the kingdom. That old dog, lying in the dark, has drawn off many good men to whip syllabub, and to sift quiddities, under pretence of zeal for the truth.[27]

A quiddity is the essence of a thing. Seemingly, Ryland's moorings remained fixed when others, in his view, were bent on voyages of speculative theological discovery.

In 1790, four years after the elder Ryland had departed, the Northampton church disciplined one James Hewitt for complaining about John, Jr.:

> Mr. Hewitt had stopp'd Smith [a College Lane member resident at Enfield] in the street, and after asking him how old Mr Ryland did, he said, "I wish he was here and the other gone, for he *doth not preach the Gospel*...as to the young one, *he is none of my Pastor*,

---

[26] Newman, *Rylandiana*, 50, 73.
[27] *Ibid.*, 78.

for he is a *linsey-woolsey* preacher, but I don't think he will be here long."[28]

"Linsey-woolsey" was a material made of coarse wool woven on a cotton warp—neither one thing nor the other. Apparently, the Hewitts looked back longingly to John, Sr.'s brand of Calvinism.

At this point the celebrated anecdote of Ryland's rebuke to young William Carey might be considered. According to S. Pearce Carey, a great-grandson of William, in 1786 the latter found himself at a Northamptonshire Baptist ministers' fraternal. Ryland, something of a patriarch, made a grand entrance and insisted that Carey and the other new member, J. Webster Morris (1763-1836) of Clipstone, offer themes for discussion. Carey responded by asking whether the Lord's command to teach all nations was binding until the end of the world, and if it had to be taken seriously by the present company. His topic was brushed aside, the enthusiast allegedly being told to sit down.[29] But was the encounter fable rather than fact? On balance, this author would cautiously suggest the latter. S. Pearce Carey disclosed that in 1833 William spoke with his friend and co-worker Joshua Marshman (1768-1837) about his earliest thoughts concerning mission, and how the Lord sustained him even when Andrew Fuller's breath had been taken away by his audacity, and when the elder Ryland had rebuffed his ideas as unscriptural.[30]

Webster Morris, the other young man at the meeting, bequeaths his own version. According to this version, Carey was told by Ryland "that certainly nothing could be done before another Pentecost, when an effusion of miraculous gifts, including the gift of tongues, would give effect to the Commission of Christ as at first; and that he was a most miserable enthusiast for asking such a question!"[31] But Ryland's son protested (not unnaturally) that the "ill-natured anecdote respecting my father and young

---

[28] College Lane Church Minute Book, III, 109.

[29] *William Carey D.D., Fellow of Linnaean Society* (London: Hodder and Stoughton, [1923]), 50.

[30] *Ibid.*, 381.

[31] *Memoirs of The Life and Writings of the Rev. Andrew Fuller* (London, 1816), 96-97.

Carey…is said to have been before the end of 1786; whereas my father had left Northampton before the Ministers'-meeting in 1786." He added: "I must consider it as very unlikely to have occurred" and "I never heard of it till I saw it in print, and cannot give credit to it at all."[32] This is consistent with Newman's note that Ryland moved from Northampton to London in November, 1785, thence transferring to Enfield in 1786, and with the resumé in the College Lane Church Minute Book cited above at the beginning of this chapter. On the other hand, Rippon remarked in his funeral sermon for Ryland that the latter departed from Northampton in 1786, rather than from London, which might imply that at the time Ryland was still circulating in the area.[33]

Whatever the truth of the matter, it was widely held that Ryland had turned on Carey. If so, why? James Culross notes that forty years later Morris suggested that Ryland might well have been indulging in irony, never actually intending to silence Carey.[34] Anyway, if the incident occurred, the rebuff probably says more about a senior pastor's heart and ministerial tribulations than about his theology. How could Ryland have taken seriously poor young ministers in obscure rural churches when they murmured about the evangelization of the heathen? It might be unfair, even grossly so, to attribute his rebuke to his Calvinism.

On Sundays the boys at Ryland's Enfield school were required to listen dutifully to readings from men of note, among whom were John Owen, Stephen Charnock (1628-1680), Herman Witsius (1636-1708), James Hervey, John Brine, John Gill—and George Whitefield.[35] Apparently, their head-teacher would not allow his overall presentation of the doctrines of grace to be defined by individual emphases.

---

[32] *The Work of Faith, the Labour of Love, and the Patience of Hope Illustrated; in the Life and Death of the Reverend Andrew Fuller* (London: Button and Son, 1816), 175, footnote.

[33] Newman, *Rylandiana*, 13; Rippon, *Gentle Dismission*, 48.

[34] *The Three Rylands*, 61.

[35] Newman, *Rylandiana*, 165.

Communion

The College Lane Church Minute Book for the years 1781-1801 announces itself as "belonging to the congregational Church of Baptists and Paedobaptists holding free communion with each other and assembling together in College Lane Northampton." But the Warwick records show that in 1749, when Ryland was beginning at Castle Hill, the people there reissued their articles of faith. The handwriting would appear to be Ryland's:

Baptism and the Lord's supper are Ordinances of Christ, to be continued until his Second Coming *and that the former is Absolutely requisite to the* Latter, that is to say, that those only are to be admitted into the Communion of the Church, and to Participate of all Ordinances in it who *upon profession of their* Faith, *have been baptized by immersion* in the Name of the Father, and of the Son, and of the Holy Ghost.

And Ryland adds:

All and each of these Doctrines, we look upon ourselves under the *Greatest Obligations* to *embrace, Maintain* and *Defend*, believing it to be our Duty to Stand fast in one Spirit, with one Accord, Striving together for the Faith of the Gospel.

When he crossed over to Northampton, the dismissal sent by Castle Hill and recorded in their church book announced to

...all whom it may Concern that Mr. John Ryland has been a member of our Church for several years past: and as far as we know has not acted altogether inconsistent with the grace of God and the profession he Made amongst us. We do therefore at his own Request dismiss him from his Relation to us as a member of our Church—to Joyn in Christian Fellowship with such people as shall appear to be most for the Glory of God and the peace and welfare of his own Soul.

Newman comments that the obvious coldness of this statement was due to Ryland's difference with the church about the terms of communion.[36] Perhaps, but in any event why the shift? If it was the case that much of his income derived from his schools and publications, might he not have then realized early on that Northampton would offer professional inducements superior to anything at Warwick?

Be this as it may, after the move John could not live with strict communion. Under the pseudonym "Pacificus" he contributed to the tract *A Modest plea for Free Communion at the Lord's Table: between True Believers of all Denominations: In a Letter to a Friend*, issued in June, 1772. That the matter had been bothering him for some time is proved by a lengthy note which he inserted in the College Lane Church Minute Book in October, 1768.

Putting aside financial considerations, it is conceivable that there was another, more fundamental explanation for the volte-face. For six years during the Warwick pastorate Ryland spent his annual holidays—a fortnight at Christmas and another at midsummer—with James Hervey, Rector of Weston Favell, near Northampton.[37] Thence he visited College Lane to preach, and from this came a call to the pastorate. Could it have been that the benign influence of the rectory and contact with evangelical celebrities weaned Ryland from the closed-communion system?

Hervey, who died in 1758, was an establishment pluralist, and no doubt conveyed the impression that Dissent was second-best. That some Nonconformists *did* incline to grovel might be detected by Newman's eulogy to the effect that John "must have been a young man of extraordinary excellence to gain the affections of the seraphic Hervey, in the last and best part of his life too!"[38] It may just be that in Ryland's mind enlarging prospects and early dogmas were deemed incompatible.

But we ought not to be over-critical. For instance, although College Lane had no problem with mixed communion, the congregation entertained severe heart-searchings about permitting friendly Presbyterians to break bread with them. In 1783 they were asked to consider whether or not they ought to

---

[36] *Ibid.*, 11.
[37] *Ibid.*, 17.
[38] *Ibid.*, 7.

"exclude from all Fellowship and particularly from the table of the Lord, all such persons of whose real piety we have no doubt, who yet are not exactly of our Judgment concerning Congregational Order?"[39] In the event they decided to admit these "weak" brethren to "occasional" communion. The welcome did not extend to the Church of England.

The classroom

In the 1700s not a few Nonconformists operated schools. Doddridge, also of Northampton, was a prime example. Assured of a sale of their textbooks to their pupils, the ministerial proprietors tended to produce their own materials, and in this Ryland was second to none. A surviving cover for his 1778 prospectus, "A Plan of a truly Liberal Education...by John Ryland, A.M. of Northampton, & proper Assistants," was expensively engraved and printed in Paris. It was meant to impress. The entry fee, exclusive of boarding and tuition charges, was one guinea, no mean sum. Newman tells us that more than £25,000 passed through Ryland's hands when he was at Northampton, and this on the school account alone.[40] We can imagine the contrast between so many in the College Lane congregation who could hardly read and write, and John's pupils, the polished offspring of affluent parents, who were taught, among other subjects, French, Greek, Latin, mathematics and astronomy.

Ryland must have been a superb teacher. Augustus Toplady wrote that he "possesses, in a very distinguished degree, the happy art of simplifying and familiarizing to young minds, the most valuable branches of useful and ornamental knowledge." Here are two typical maxims for a Christian schoolmaster: "Always begin school with prayer and Scripture," and "keep the end of education in view, which is to repair the ruins of the fall. The objects you have to work upon are the mind—the heart—the manners."[41]

The "living orrery" was one of Ryland's favourite educational helps, an "orrery" being a clockwork model of the solar system. Required by his pedagogue to represent a heavenly body, each personified planet clutched a

---

[39] College Lane Church Minute Book, III,75.
[40] *Rylandiana*, 11.
[41] *Ibid.*, 87, 183.

placard and ran in a prescribed orbit within a largish play area. The boy representing the sun had to be more rotund than his satellites. One such card read "My name is red-faced Mars. My diameter is 5,400 miles. I move round the Sun in 686 days, at the distance of 145,000,000 miles, and at the rate of 55,000 miles an hour."[42]

Was the pulpit or the classroom Ryland's priority? In 1770 he published a work designed to refute Deism and Socinianism, the forty-five-word title being followed by the author's name: "John Ryland, A.M. Master of a Boarding-school in Northampton." The American Master's degree had been given him just one year earlier, and he must have deemed it highly useful. Note that Ryland does not mention his church, a possibly significant omission. "Candour," Newman asserted, "will acknowledge that Mr. Ryland would have done more, had he done less." Toplady and Hervey proffered similar advice.[43]

An appreciation

Why did John Ryland surrender his ministry in 1785 to move elsewhere? The College Lane Minute Books studiously omit any reference to the underlying reasons for Ryland's departure from the church. The final minute to be signed by both Ryland Sr. and Jr. is dated 20 July, 1782. The next, dated 20 July, 1783, allows a two-line gap for both men to append their names, although only the younger Ryland did so. From that time only the latter appears as a signatory. It might seem that there were problems even though the elder Ryland was still living in Northampton.

John, Jr. writes about his father's second marriage in February, 1782, commenting darkly that "many unpleasant consequences follow'd which are best omitted. He went to London, Nov. 11, 1785, and never returned to Northampton, till he was bro't down to be burried."[44] That not all was well is shown by John Rippon's delicate remark in his funeral address for Ryland:

---

[42] *Ibid.*, 121.

[43] *Ibid.*, 136; Culross, *The Three Rylands*, 57.

[44] From "Copies of Autograph Manuscripts."

In the year 1786, when he removed from Northampton, this luminary, which had emitted so much light to the region of his connexions, was clouded...on which I make but one remark; it is this, If the Sun is eclipsed *one* day, it attracts more attention than the shining of it for FORTY YEARS.[45]

Was money the straw which broke the camel's back? Or the "Modern Question," that is, how and to whom to preach the gospel? Or was the classroom a primitive love which endured to the end? What of the new Mrs. Ryland? All that Newman elects to tell us about the lady is that she was "admirably qualified for her new situation" at Enfield. He refrains from endorsing her as suited to being a pastor's wife and we may read into that what we will.[46] One thing is tolerably certain: at this length of time we cannot tell why Ryland left. Perhaps we do not want to know.

How does one estimate this loveable and larger-than-life servant of the Lord? A blustering man, it may be that he did not always know how to be cautious, thus landing himself in difficulties. Fortunately, his stature almost always saved him. It might not be unfair to say that he was never an original thinker, although this need not be taken as a defect. He did a noble work. Perhaps—and it is a large "perhaps"—another of his weaknesses was a defective churchmanship. With his family background and the indelible stamp that Benjamin Beddome, his pastor, placed upon him, plus his love for God's Word, how could he have shifted from a strict-communion pastorate to a church which was, on its own admission, non-Baptist? "Pacificus" protests the open-communion position too much, and we might suspect that Ryland was never totally satisfied with his ecclesiological gymnastics, even though a swelling congregation would probably have anaesthetized any twitches of conscience.

In his late twenties John suffered from what appears to have been acute depression. A letter written in 1751, soon after his ordination at Warwick, reveals that "I have known what it is to be under the hidings of the Lord's face for eighteen months together, and through all that time I have not had

---

[45] *Gentle Dismission*, 48. The ellipsis in the citation is original to Rippon.
[46] *Rylandiana*, 14.

one hour's spiritual consolation."[47] This is alarming. Would we care to record that, perhaps as pastors, we felt that the face of God had been hidden for us for a precious year and a half of our short lives? Even so (to repeat), Ryland was a master preacher. Robert Hall, Jr. wrote that "when, for instance, he exhibited the face and convulsions of the terrified Belshazzar, and traced the handwriting on the wall, expounding at the same time its awful import, his hearers were breathless, petrified with horror."[48] The imagination boggles. When preaching at the grave of a one-month-old infant, he told the mourners that God sometimes takes away little children to put us in mind of Adam's treason, to show the Lord's sovereignty, to remind us of our own deaths (if God only took aged people, young folk would never contemplate death), and to lead us to think about the general resurrection.[49]

Webster Morris tells us that

> for zeal and fidelity he had few equals, and none could surpass the bold and daring nature of his eloquence. His eccentricities were numerous and remarkable, his piety unquestionable; to a stranger his manners were sufficiently terrific, though in reality no man possessed more genuine kindness, or more enlarged and disinterested benevolence. With all his failings, and without any written memorial of his life and labours, he was one of the brightest ornaments of the last century.[50]

The Warwick Record Office retains an extract of what is said to be a "very rare book," *An Historical and Descriptive Account of the Town and Castle of Warwick*, by a William Field and published in 1815. The author comments that Ryland

> was possessed of considerable abilities, but a strong and ardent imagination was not controlled by equal soundness, or strength of judgement; and a great degree of what is called ECCENTRICITY

---

[47] *Ibid.*, 8.
[48] *Ibid.*, 200.
[49] *Ibid.*, 80.
[50] *Ibid.*, 196.

marked not only the manner of his public services, but even his conduct in private life.

When we read through church books, diaries and biographies, John Collett Ryland appears to have been a giant in the land. Yet it seems that he tore Carey to pieces at the 1786 ministers' meeting. Perhaps the older man ought to have pondered issues which at the time some of the newer generation knew could not be suppressed, and to have given less attention to his day-schools. The holy ministry will not brook rivals.

Further reading

William Newman, *Rylandiana: Reminiscences relating to the Rev. John Ryland, A.M. of Northampton* (London: George Wightman, 1835), and James Culross, *The Three Rylands: A Hundred Years of Various Christian Service* (London: Elliot Stock, 1897), 9-66, have written the only major studies of the elder Ryland. The Congregationalist William Jay has a marvellous sketch of Ryland's character: see *The Autobiography of William Jay*, eds. George Redford and John Angell James (1854 ed.; repr. Edinburgh: The Banner of Truth Trust, 1974), 286-296.

Ph.ᵉ Van Dyke. Pinx.ᵗ   T. Trotter. sculp.ᵗ

THE REV.ᴰ M.ʳ ROBERT HALL,

late of Arnsby,

Leicestershire.

Publish'd as the Act directs Aug.ᵗ 1ᵗ 1792.

ROBERT HALL, SR. (1728-1791)[1]

Michael A. G. Haykin

In his day, Robert Hall, Jr. was renowned as one of the most eloquent preachers of Great Britain. In fact, Thomas R. McKibbens has recently written that in his preaching there was displayed "a natural pulpit eloquence that has seldom been known before or since."[2] Without wishing to gainsay such a judgment, the use of the word "natural" can easily obscure the formative role that Hall's father, Robert Hall, Sr. had upon his son, and which, as we shall see, the son later acknowledged. As Graham W. Hughes has written: "To have so profoundly influenced the mind of one of the most brilliant figures in the history of the Christian pulpit...was no mean achievement for one whose whole ministry was spent in a small country pastorate."[3]

The following sketch of the elder Hall's life and thought, seeks to display the rock from which his son's "pulpit eloquence" was hewn.

Conversion

Like John Bunyan, the elder Hall was deeply distressed from a very early age by his own sinfulness. When Hall was but twelve years old, he was filled with "black despair... continually...accompanied with horrid

---

[1] Much of this chapter originally appeared as "The Elder Robert Hall and His *Help to Zion's Travellers*: 1", *The Banner of Truth*, 343 (April 1992), 17-20, 27. Used by permission.

[2] *The Forgotten Heritage: A Lineage of Great Baptist Preaching* (Macon, Georgia: Mercer University Press, 1986), 62.

[3] *Robert Hall (1764-1831)* (London: Independent Press Ltd., 1961), 4. See also Graham W. Hughes, "Robert Hall of Arnesby: 1728-1791", *The Baptist Quarterly*, 10 (1940-1941), 444-447.

temptations and blasphemies which ought not to be uttered."[4] From this
state he found no lasting relief until he read Paul's statement in Gala-
tians 4:4-5 that God sent Christ into the world to redeem those who were
under the law. This text fully convinced Hall, now in his twenties, that,
sinner though he was, he was not outside the bounds of Christ's saving
work. Not long after his conversion, Hall received a call to the ministry,
and in 1753 was invited to become the pastor of a small Baptist work in
the village of Arnsby, Leicestershire.

Throughout Hall's ministry at Arnsby, the church found it difficult to
provide adequate financial support for him, his wife, and fourteen children. Consequently, Hall often thought he would have to leave his
charge, but he said:

> I found my heart so united to the people, that I never durst leave
> them.... I trust the Lord was with us of a truth, and the fifth chap-
> ter of the First Epistle of Peter was habitually impressed on my
> mind. It appearing pretty clear to myself and my wife, that we were
> where God would have us to be; this sense of duty, and a willing-
> ness to live honestly, made us resolve in the strength of the Lord,
> that we would not run into debt, let us live as hardly as we might:
> which resolution he enabled us to keep. But many and unknown
> difficulties we grappled with: however, I am thankful I have been
> enabled to continue with the people to this day, of whom I can say
> with truth, I love them in the Lord.[5]

To help supplement his income Hall kept a small farm, and on a number
of occasions he acknowledged that the Lord undertook for him through
generous gifts from friends. For instance, in 1775 John Newton, then
pastoring the parish church at Olney, Buckinghamshire, only a few miles

---

[4] John Rippon, "The Rev. Mr. Robert Hall", *Baptist Annual Register*
(London, 1793), 1:226-227.

[5] Cited Joseph Ivimey, *A History of the English Baptists* (London: Isaac
Taylor Hinton/Holdsworth & Ball, 1830), IV, 603-604.

away, sent him a gift of £10, at which he declared, "This is the Lord's doing and Marvellous in my eyes. O to be found worthy of favours."[6]

Teaching on the Trinity

In time Hall became a respected member of the Northamptonshire Association of Particular Baptist Churches and occasionally he was asked to write the circular letter which the Association would send out annually to its member churches. One of these letters especially worthy of note is that of 1776 in which Hall presents a very able defence of the doctrine of the Trinity. It was occasioned by what he describes as "awful departures from, and artful oppositions made to, the fundamental doctrine of a Trinity of Persons in the Godhead."[7] This denial of orthodox trinitarianism was a prominent feature of the religious landscape of eighteenth-century England.[8] For instance, Joseph Priestley (1733-1804), a well-known Unitarian minister, rejected the worship of the Lord Jesus as idolatrous and regarded the Spirit as a power, not a person.

Over against such views Hall asserts on the basis of Scripture that the Son and his Spirit are "persons properly divine" and, together with the Father, "are the one living and true God."[9] Consider, for instance, his defence of the Spirit's personality and deity. In seeking to demonstrate that the Holy Spirit is a person Hall has recourse to those Scriptural passages where the Spirit is said to have a mind and a will (Romans 8:27; 1 Corinthians 12:11), where he is said to speak (1 Timothy 4:1; Ezekiel 3:24; Acts 8:29; 10:19-20; 13:2), and where he is spoken of as one with whom believers have fellowship (Ephesians 4:30). That the Spirit is divine Hall shows from the fact that he is involved in the creation of the heavens, the world and its inhabitants (Job 26:13; Genesis 1:2; Job 33:4), and that he is (implicitly) called God (Acts 5:3-4; 1 Corinthians 3:16; 6:19). Moreover, Scripture depicts the Spirit as om-

---

[6] Robert Hall Warren, *The Hall Family* (Bristol: J. W. Arrowsmith, 1910), 17.

[7] *The Doctrine of the Trinity Stated* (2nd ed.; Coventry, 1776), 2.

[8] See above, pages 148-150, 153-157, *passim.*

[9] *Ibid.,* 4.

niscient (1 Corinthians 2:10), omnipresent (Psalm 139:7), and eternal (Hebrews 9:14), all of which are divine attributes.[10] Ending on a practical note, Hall concludes that the believer's

> obligations to the Lord the Spirit are great. He is the author and inditer of your Bible... He is the Lord of the harvest, who prepares and sends forth labourers. He is the author of all edifying gifts to the Church. It is owing to him that you are renewed and strengthened in your minds. Look to him to create in you a clean heart and renew a right spirit within you.[11]

This small work proved to be of such help to Hall's fellow Baptists that a second edition was called for and printed in the same year. But of even greater import was Hall's *Help to Zion's Travellers*, published five years later in 1781.

Help to Zion's Travellers

The immediate origins of *Help to Zion's Travellers* lay in a sermon which Hall had preached before the Northamptonshire Association in May 1779 on Isaiah 57:14: "Cast ye up, cast ye up, prepare the way, take up the stumbling block out of the way of my people." In this sermon, and later in its published form, Hall sought to remove what he described as "various stumbling blocks [for the believer] relating to doctinal, experimental and practical religion."

The first section of the work dealt with doctrinal difficulties relating to such matters as the deity of Christ, the nature of God's love, election and the atonement. Hall then grappled with what he termed experimental difficulties: difficulties such as not knowing the precise time of one's conversion, the lack of spiritual joy, and the believer's experience of indwelling sin. Finally, Hall focused on practical difficulties arising "out of the sinful conduct of professors of religion, the enmity of the world and the heresies of false religionists."

---

[10] *Ibid.*, 20-23.
[11] *Ibid.*, 32.

The most significant contribution of the book probably lies in its assertion that, contrary to the canons of Hyper-Calvinism, which was then regnant in some Particular Baptist quarters, "the gospel proclamation is 'whosoever will, let him come' to Christ." As Hall put it:

> If any one should ask, Have I a right to apply to Jesus the Saviour, simply as a poor, undone, perishing sinner, in whom there appears no good thing? I answer, Yes; the gospel proclamation is, "Whosoever will, let him come." "To you O men, I call, and my voice is to the sons of men." Prov. viii.4. The way to Jesus is graciously laid open for every one who chooses to come to him.[12]

Hall clearly intends that the preaching of the gospel not be restricted in any way, but that men and women everywhere and in every condition be exhorted to repent and believe on Christ for salvation.

Given this perspective on evangelism, it is hardly surprising that William Carey, who frequently walked from Olney to Arnsby to hear Hall preach, would later declare of his first encounter with this book: "I do not remember ever to have read any book with such raptures."[13] Carey was well aware that there were some, presumably Hyper-Calvinists, who called the book "poison." But Carey declared, "It was so sweet to me that I drank it greedily to the bottom of the cup." Many years after he first read it, he could still state that its "doctrines are the choice of my heart to this day."[14]

Nor was his experience an isolated one. Joseph Ivimey, the Baptist historian of the following century, saw in the preaching and subsequent publication of Hall's sermon the "commencement of a new era" of ad-

---

[12] In Charles G. Sommers, William R. Williams and Levi L. Hill, eds., *The Baptist Library* (New York: Lewis Colby and Co., 1846), III, 87.

[13] Raymond Brown, *The English Baptists of the Eighteenth Century* (London: The Baptist Historical Society, 1986), 116. On Carey's indebtedness to Hall, see also Reginald H. Spooner, "Northamptonshire Ministers' Meetings, 1770-1816", *Baptist History and Heritage*, 11 (1976), 90.

[14] Eustace Carey, *Memoir of William Carey, D.D.* (London: Jackson and Walford, 1836), 16-17.

vance and spiritual prosperity for the Particular Baptist denomination.[15] And Hall's own son, in a preface which he wrote for a later edition of *Help to Zion's Travellers* in 1814, declared:

> To this treatise, and to another on a similar subject by my excellent and judicious friend Mr. Fuller,[16] the dissenters in general, and the Baptists in particular, are under great obligation for emancipating them from the fetters of prejudice, and giving free scope to the publication of the gospel.[17]

Hall's piety

A couple of years after the publication of *Help to Zion's Travellers*, a singular occurrence took place in connection with Hall's eldest daughter Ann (d.1802) which well reveals Hall's piety.

In July of 1783 Ann had been married to a Colonel James Cotton and the newlyweds left England for a tour of Spain. One night while they were on this tour Hall dreamt that they were in great danger. When the dream was repeated and Hall had awoken, he spent the rest of that night in prayer for them. The following morning he made a record of the night this had taken place. Later he learned that it was that very night they were in great danger of their lives at a small rural inn in Spain, and that in fact a murder had taken place in the inn during the night.[18]

Hall died rather suddenly on Sunday, March 13, 1791. In the morning he had preached a sermon on John 4:10 with particular vigour. In the late afternoon he complained of feeling sick and having a violent pain in his chest. To a friend who had come to see him he remarked, "Friend Looms, fear nothing: do not be afraid of trouble, trials, nor even death: if

---

[15] *History*, IV, 41.

[16] Hall is referring to Andrew Fuller's *The Gospel Worthy of All Acceptation*, which was first published in 1785.

[17] "Preface" to *Help to Zion's Travellers* [*The Works of the Rev. Robert Hall, A.M.*, eds. Olinthus Gregory and Joseph Belcher (New York: 1854), II, 452].

[18] Warren, *Hall Family*, 22-23.

the Lord is but with you, you will do."[19] Somewhat later he said to two other members of his congregation who had come to see how he was faring: "I have not lived so long in the world as to be weary of it, nor am I afraid to die. I don't care whether I live or die."[20] That evening, when being helped into the parlour of his home, he said, "I shall swoon," and immediately collapsed and died without another word or sound.

Reflections on Hall's character and ministry

Shortly after his death, Hall's close friend, Andrew Fuller, described his ministry and character with these words:

> His ministry in the hands of God was effectual to the conversion of great numbers; and in this particular he was distinguished in a manner not very common, for the last years of his life were the most successful. But it was not only in the pulpit that he shone; in his private sphere of action as a christian, his virtues were not less distinguished than his talents as a minister. Deep devotion and unaffected humility entered far into this part of his character. ...Great abilities are often allied to pride, but the character of the deceased was an illustrious exception to this rule. His talents and virtues were in some measure concealed from the world, and almost entirely from himself, by a veil of the most unaffected modesty. He was never so happy as when he was permitted to sit in the shade, though the high opinion entertained of his abilities seldom allowed him that indulgence. It would be difficult to conceive a human mind more completely purged from the leaven of pride or of envy, than was that of our deceased friend. In this particular his magnanimity was so great, that he seemed, on all occasions, desirous of sinking the recollection of himself in the reputation and applause of his contemporaries. To cultivate the seeds of reflection and improvement in the minds of his inferiors, to behold the growing talents and virtues of his brethren, to draw merit from its obscurity and give

---

[19] Ivimey, *History*, IV, 604.
[20] *Ibid.*, IV, 605.

confidence to timid worth, formed some of the highest satisfactions of his life. ...

He had failings, no doubt, (for who is free?) but they were scarcely ever suffered to influence his conduct, or to throw even a transient shade over the splendour of his character. Upon the whole, if a strong and penetrating genius, simplicity of manners, integrity of heart, fidelity in friendship, and all these virtues consecrated by a piety the most ardent and sincere on the high altar of devotion, have any claim to respect, the memory of the deceased will long be cherished with tears of admiration and regret by those who knew him.[21]

These words form an excellent conclusion to this sketch of the life and thought of Robert Hall, Sr. But it would be appropriate to finish where we began, that is, with his son, the younger Robert Hall. Concluding his "Preface" to his father's *Help to Zion's Travellers* in 1814, the son added this personal note: "Gratitude and veneration compel me to add, that...I shall ever esteem it one of the greatest favours an indulgent Providence has bestowed upon me, to have possessed such a father, whom, in all the essential features of character, it will be my humble ambition to imitate."

Further reading

The earliest biographical study of Hall is John Rippon, "The Rev. Mr. Robert Hall", *Baptist Annual Register* (London, 1793), 1:226-241. Robert Hall Warren, *The Hall Family* (Bristol: J. W. Arrowsmith, 1910), 5-33, a very rare volume, has what is the most recent study of the elder Hall. For Hall's written corpus, see *The Complete Works of the Rev. Robert Hall*, collected J. W. Morris (London: W. Simpkin and R. Marshall, 1828).

---

[21] *Ibid.*, IV, 606, 607-608.

The DOCTRINE *of the* TRINITY *stated:*

IN A

CIRCULAR LETTER

FROM

The Baptist Ministers and Messengers,

ASSEMBLED

AT OLNEY, BUCKS, MAY 28, 29, 1776.

Maintaining the important Doctrines of Three equal Persons in the Godhead; Eternal and Personal Election; Original Sin; Particular Redemption; Free Justification by the imputed Righteousness of Christ; Efficacious Grace in Regeneration; the Final Perseverance of the Saints; and the Independency, or Congregational Order, of the Churches of Christ inviolably.

> To the several Churches they represent, or have received Letters from, meeting at *Nottingham, Sheepshead, Leicester, Sutton, Arnsby, Foxton, Okeham, Spalding, Soham, Kettering, Walgrave, Northampton, Road, Olney, Carleton,* and *St. Albans:* As also to the many Churches not yet in this Association, who, notwithstanding, countenance it, by the Attendance of their Ministers and Members :——

> *Grace be unto you, and Peace from God our Father, and from the Lord Jesus Christ.*

THE SECOND EDITION.

To which is added,

THOUGHTS ON THE CAUSES

OF

SALVATION AND DAMNATION.

COVENTRY:

Printed by J. W. PIERCY: And sold by G. ROBINSON, in Paternoster-Row, *London*; G. KEITH, Grace-church-street; and J. MATHEWS, in the Strand. [Price 6d.

L. Bateman pinx.   J. Fittler sculp.

The Reverend Caleb Evans D.D.

VIRTUS PRÆSIDIUM DECUSQ.

Publish'd as the Act directs, Dec.r 1790.

CALEB EVANS (1737-1791)

Kirk Wellum

Caleb Evans only lived for fifty-four years, but he lived in such a way as to be missed when he was gone. Born in 1737, he was the son of Welshman Hugh Evans (1713-1781), who was called to be the pastor of Broadmead Church in Bristol and the president of Bristol Baptist Academy after the death of Bernard Foskett in 1758. Caleb loved the Lord Jesus Christ and distinguished himself as a hard-working servant who was faithful in his generation. Shortly after his father took up his new responsibilities at Broadmead, a call was extended to Caleb, who was then only twenty-one years of age, to come and serve as his assistant, which he did to the benefit of the church and particularly the Academy. He remained faithful to his Savior until the end of his life and when he lay paralyzed from a stroke from which he never recovered it is recorded by John Rippon that with rapture he exclaimed: "O the breadth and length, and depth and height of the love of Christ which passeth knowledge. Behold what manner of love the Father has bestowed upon us that we should be called the sons of God, and it doth not yet appear what we shall be."[1]

Early years and early ministry

Caleb was part of a large family of which only he and two sisters outlived their father. He lost his mother, Sarah, when he was just fourteen years old, but had a good relationship with his father's second wife and his step-mother, Ann. In a sermon preached at her funeral he described

---

[1] Norman S. Moon, "Caleb Evans, Founder of The Bristol Education Society," *The Baptist Quarterly*, 24 (1971-1972), 189.

her as "a most faithful and affectionate wife, a kind and tender mother, not only to her own children, but likewise to those of us she generously took charge of in our early years."[2]

Caleb grew up in Bristol at Broadmead Church and was first educated by Bernard Foskett and his father Hugh Evans. Believing in the importance of more formal education and hoping that his son might want to serve God in the proclamation of the gospel, his father sent him to Mile End Academy in London in the fall of 1753. There he attended the Little Wild Street Church which was being pastored at the time by Samuel Stennett who also baptized him.[3]

The time of his conversion is unclear, but he does tell us that he heard and responded to the gospel as he listened to the preaching of his father. "When I was only a youth I beheld with admiration my father in the pulpit, and was delighted with the heavenly sounds which flowed from his lips. Hearing the awful terrors of the law and the astonishing grace of the Gospel, I was brought into the very dust before the throne of a holy God, and enabled to magnify the riches of free grace."[4]

During his time at the Little Wild Street Church his gifts of ministry were recognized and upon receiving proper authorization to preach the gospel on June 12, 1757, he began preaching in another London Particular Baptist Church, Unicorn Yard, where he was eventually asked to assist the pastor of that work. But no sooner was he situated there, than the call came from his father and the church at Broadmead asking him to come and labor there as the assistant pastor, a call which he eventually accepted on March 25, 1759.

His first sermon at Broadmead as the new assistant was preached on June 17, 1759, but it was not until eight years later that he was officially recognized as an elder and co-pastor alongside his father, a decision that was unanimously approved by the members of the church on July 19, 1767, and formally accepted by Caleb on August 2, 1767. He was ordained about two weeks later on August 18, 1767. Between the time when he returned to Broadmead as an assistant, and the time when he

[2] *Ibid.*, 176.
[3] On Samuel Stennett, see above, pages 140-143.
[4] Moon, "Caleb Evans", 176.

was ordained as a co-pastor, he married Sarah Jeffries of Taunton in 1762. They had five children together before she died in 1771. Three years later he married another Sarah, Sarah Hazel, who is said to have been "the daughter of a very respectable family in Bristol."[5]

The Bristol Baptist Academy

Without doubt the most important contribution of Caleb Evans to the advancement of the kingdom of God was his re-organizing of the Bristol Baptist Academy and his role in founding the Bristol Education Society in 1770. The Academy can trace it's roots back to the Clarendon Code of 1661-1665 which banned Dissenters from Oxford and Cambridge Universities. Recognizing the need for educated ministers who were theologically prepared to wrestle with the issues of the day, a group of ministers led by Andrew Gifford, Sr. met in London in 1677 to talk about what they could do to meet this challenge. Nothing concrete came out of that meeting, although the persecution which was ongoing at that time and for the next eleven years would have made it difficult for any plans to have been put into action.

However, while nothing seemed to be happening outwardly, during this time a ruling elder at Broadmead, Edward Terrill (1635-1686), was moved by the Lord to write a will (dated June 3, 1679) that bequeathed his wealth, which was considerable, to the church for the training of future ministers. In the words of the relevant portion of the will:

> For the glory of God and the propagation of the Gospel of our Lord Jesus Christ, and for the true love and affection he hath and beareth unto the congregation of which he is a member. Mr. Terrill empowered his trustees to devote the proceeds of his estates to the maintenance of a holy, learned man, well skilled in the tongues (Greek and Hebrew), and doth own and practice the truth of believers' baptism as a pastor or teacher of the congregation.[6]

---

[5] *Ibid.*, 188.
[6] Cited *ibid.*, 180.

This was the beginning of the Bristol Baptist Academy, although the idea as Terrill envisioned it did not really get off the ground until a man by the name of Caleb Jope was appointed by Broadmead to train ministers and was supported by the Terrill fund from 1714-1719. He was followed by Bernard Foskett in 1720, who trained Hugh Evans and who succeeded him in 1758. Hugh, in turn, was joined by his son Caleb at the Broadmead Church and the Baptist Academy in 1759.

During the Foskett years, the quality of education at Bristol was adequate, but not all that it would be when Hugh, and especially Caleb, took the helm. John Rippon, who studied at Bristol after the Foskett era but before the restructuring of 1770, later said: "If it be conceded that Foskett's method of education was limited rather than liberal, severe rather than enchanting, employing the memory more than the genious [*sic*], the reason more than the softer powers of the mind... in a word, if it be granted that Mr. Foskett is not the first of tutors... it is a debt of honor to acknowledge that some good scholars and several of our greatest ministers were educated by him."[7]

In spite of these deficiencies in the previous administration, when the Evanses took over in 1758-1759, things did not take off right away. In fact, from 1759 until 1764 only 5 students came to study at Bristol and only 12 more attended between 1765 and 1768. From these statistics it appears that there were growing pains and some degree of uncertainty during this time of transition. According to Roger Hayden, part of the problem was in the way that the Terrill Trust fund was being managed.[8]

During the 1760s new people were put in charge who were better qualified to administer the fund. Then, in June 1770, Hugh and Caleb Evans launched the Bristol Education Society. They were not alone in this initiative, but they certainly provided the necessary leadership and drive to see it become a reality. Both believed in the need for an educated and a converted ministry, and both saw the need to have a solid fi-

---

[7] Cited *ibid.*, 182.

[8] "Evangelical Calvinism among eighteenth-century British Baptists with particular reference to Bernard Foskett, Hugh and Caleb Evans and the Bristol Baptist Academy, 1690-1791" (Unpublished Ph.D Thesis, University of Keele, 1991), 222.

nancial base of support if the Academy was going to have the resources it needed to prepare men to minister effectively in the changing times in which they lived. The Bristol Education Society was formed to meet these needs and at the same time the Bristol Academy was re-organized so that it was independent of the Broadmead Church although there continued to be a close working relationship between the church and the Academy. To try and ensure, as far as is humanly possible, that those who came for training were indeed genuine Christians, none were received into the Bristol Academy who did not come recommended by their local churches.

In a sermon to the Bristol Education Society in 1773, Hugh Evans rehearsed for those present the concerns and convictions that were shaping the structure of things at Bristol in those days.

The able minister needs to possess a tolerable share of natural endowments...and he needs the improvements of human learning. No profession needs this more than the ministry—when such learning is sanctified and humbly devoted to the service of God. But such a ministry depends on God, whose calling should be confirmed by a man's home church, and the minister must be evangelical, one who is led into the true spirit of the Gospel, who preaches Christ and Him crucified.[9]

We also need to bear in mind that these were days of enormous change. Norman S. Moon rightly reminds us that:

The eighteenth century was a time of intellectual and political ferment. The growth of scientific knowledge, in astronomy, in medicine, and in the explorations of men like Captain Cook, who set foot in Australia in 1770, (the year the Bristol Education Society was born), continued to expand the horizons of men's minds. It is interesting to think of some of the books that influenced Caleb Evans' generation. *Christianity not Mysterious* by Matthew Tin-

[9] Hugh Evans, "Sermon Before Bristol Education Society," cited by Moon, "Caleb Evans," 178-179.

dal, the so-called 'Bible of Deism' appeared seven years before Caleb's birth; Butler's *Analogy* was published just before his birth. When Caleb was 20, David Hume wrote his *Natural History of Religion*, Edward Gibbon's *Decline and Fall of the Roman Empire* appeared in 1776, as did Tom Paine's *Common Sense*, which stimulated radical politics in the American Revolution. In the year of Caleb's death, Paine's *Rights of Man* defended the principles of the French Revolution.[10]

Hugh and Caleb Evans understood that this was not a time for Christians to run and hide from the issues that were being raised, nor could Christians advance the cause of Christ through mere intellectual reasoning alone—the head and the heart must come together. The need was for clear thinking combined with heart-felt passion for the Lord. They felt that those whose calling it was to provide leadership in the churches had to study languages, logic and rhetoric; they had to be aware of what was going on in the areas of geography, astronomy and natural philosophy; they needed to read the best of books; but they also needed the time and freedom to meditate and to integrate what they were learning with the wisdom of God found in the Bible.

To this end, Caleb traveled about raising financial support and spreading this vigorous gospel vision among Baptist churches. And he challenged those who came to study at the Academy to make sure that their motives and priorities were right before the Lord. Here is part of one such address that is still in the possession of the College.

> Reflect on your views in devoting yourselves to this sacred employ. Was it merely to have an opportunity of pursuing different branches of literature to which you had a strong inclination? Was it that you might lead an easy, genteel life, which you might be ready to support a minister's life to be? Was it to obtain popular applause and fame, which you might fondly hope your abilities would procure you? Or was it from the principle of unfeigned love to Jesus Christ and to the souls of men? The question the Lord put to

---

[10] *Ibid.*, 182-183.

Peter, 'Lovest thou me?' is a question I would earnestly entreat you to consider. Let me exhort you to the vigorous pursuit of your studies in general. There is scarcely any branch of knowledge but what may be useful. Whatever hath a tendency to enlarge our ideas of the divine perfections, to give us a clearer view of the meaning of Scripture, and enable us to express our thought... is worthy of the attention of every candidate for the ministry.[11]

The intellectually and spiritually balanced nature of his vision for the College can also be seen in the concern that he expressed for missions. Where there were funds available this money would be put toward the encouragement of "evangelical and popular ministers as missionaries and itinerant preachers in those places where there is an opening for the Gospel, but not the ability to support the necessary expense attending it."[12] And again: "The education of pious candidates for the ministry is the first object of the Institution, the encouragement of missionaries to preach the Gospel wherever providence open a door...is the next."[13] Barren intellectualism, or a run-and-hide approach to the new ideas and evils of the world, does not produce this kind of intense missionary desire and determination to take the gospel *wherever* God opens a door.

That his message was heard by those who studied at Bristol in those years and that it was embodied in Caleb himself can be seen in the comments of his students when speaking about him. For instance, Thomas Langdon (1755-1824), who was a student in the late 1770s and early 1780s, said of Caleb: "Never was a man better qualified for the station which he filled in the Academy... He was a person of extensive information, a refined taste, and sound learning. In fervent piety, warm and active benevolence, ardent and disinterested friendship and unwearied zeal in promoting the interest of religion."[14]

And then there were others, like John Ash (1724-1779), who was

---

[11] Cited *ibid.*,182.
[12] Hayden, "Evangelical Calvinism among eighteenth-century British Baptists", 223.
[13] *Ibid.*, 229-230
[14] *Ibid.*, 229.

trained by Foskett and Hugh Evans before the re-organization, but who was a close friend of Caleb and undoubtedly reflects what was going on at Bristol in those days. Speaking to the Society in 1778 he said: "my brethren, if we have not our commission and our qualification from Christ, and if he be not with us in the discharge of our ministry, alas! our learning, our labour, our preaching is in vain. But enlivened by his grace, qualified by his Spirit, directed by his providence and blessed with his presence, wherever we go, wherever we are stationed, whether Israel be gathered or not gathered, we shall be glorious in the eyes of the Lord and our God shall be our strength."[15]

So we find that Caleb Evans built on the labors of those who had gone ahead of him. He and his father advanced what Bernard Foskett had been doing and fulfilled the vision of Edward Terrill who had been stirred by God to lay the financial foundation in the first place. In a special way, Caleb understood his times and had the foresight to see what would be required if the Church of Jesus Christ was going to bring every thought into captivity to her Master. History shows that God blessed their words, their dedication and their endeavors. Between 1770-1780 Caleb and Hugh Evans trained 48 ministers, and Caleb himself was involved along with other tutors in training 32 more before 1790 arrived.[16]

In terms of missions, the Society raised money to fund the labors of former and present students in Cornwall, like Bristol-trained evangelist Benjamin Francis (1734-1799), who eventually settled at Horsley, Gloucestershire, in 1757. He enjoyed a long ministry there in which he baptized 450 new members while continuing to take the gospel into the surrounding countryside whenever he had the chance. We get some idea of the extent of his work from the words of Thomas Flint, his son-in-law and assistant in ministry.

His manner was to set out on Monday morning and return on Friday evening, after taking a circuit of 90 miles and preaching every evening. In Wiltshire...he established a monthly lecture at Malm-

---

[15] *Ibid.*, 231-232.
[16] *Ibid.*, 234.

esbury which he supplied from 1771 to 1799 so that he preached 282 sermons and for the latter part he reached as far as Christian-Malford where he preached 84 sermons. He extended his journey frequently as far as Devizes, 30 miles from home, where he preached 56 times, and oftener to Melksham, Frome, Trowbridge and Bradford [on-Avon], at each of which four places he preached 90 sermons. At Wotton-under-Edge, seven miles from Horsley, he kept up a monthly lecture for 30 years and preached there 394 times. At Uley, five miles distant, he maintained another stated lecture for many years and preached 350 sermons there...at Hampton, 802 sermons. On visits to Bristol he preached at Broad-mead 101 times and 28 at the Pithay.[17]

While this is probably the best example of missionary labor, it does give us some idea of the kind of zealous Christian worker that was produced as a result of the labors of Caleb Evans and many others at the Bristol Academy.

Writer, preacher, and pastor

Over the course of his life Caleb published more than 30 pamphlets and sermons. He also worked together with John Ash of Pershore, who had trained under Bernard Foskett and Hugh Evans at Bristol in 1747-1748, to produce what was called *A Collection of Hymns Adapted to Public Worship*. It was published in 1769 and has been called "the first Baptist Hymn Book."[18] According to Hayden, it was a collection of hymns which attempted to give the people of God songs that expressed objective truths about God as well as selections of music that captured "the warmth of evangelical and personal experience."[19] Later in his life he also published four sermons that he preached on the atonement from 1 Corinthians 1:23-24 under the title *Christ Crucified*.

As a preacher, Evans made sure that when he went into the pulpit he

---

[17] *Ibid.*, 225-226.
[18] *Ibid.*, 231.
[19] *Ibid.*, 231.

had something to say. He believed in the importance of preaching. In 1775, when preaching on the theme "Thy Kingdom Come" he said: "It is by the preaching of Christ and him crucified, accompanied with the influences of the blessed Spirit that this Kingdom is formed, subjects brought into it, the privileges of it dispensed, the laws of it enforced, the honours of it established, the extent of it enlarged."[20] In light of these convictions as to the importance of preaching, it is not surprising that a contemporary said of his preaching that "it was solid and judicious, the fruit of mature thought and labour. He did not offer God that which cost him nothing...his discourses were mostly on weighty and serious subjects, composed with judgment in the best order, delivered with manly dignity and becoming warmth and zeal."[21] He often preached from full notes, but there were other times when he deliberately used none. However, whether he did or did not use notes, he was always well prepared and he was particularly known for his unique ability to be able to say something worthwhile on "special occasions." This probably can be attributed not just to his native intelligence, but to his broad reading and his keen interest in what was going on around him both in the church and in the world.

As a pastor, Samuel Stennett tells us that, "His manner was grave, not formal, animated but not affected, commanding but not assuming."[22] Even as the Principal of the Academy he did not cease to be a shepherd to his students. His was not the stance of an aloof administrator, but that of a mentor and friend. When necessary he would not hesitate to get involved in the lives of his students and give them advice that he expected them to obey!

Roger Hayden refers to this aspect of his character as "Caleb Evans' paternalism," and uses his relationship with student Thomas Langdon as a case in point.[23] Before Langdon had finished his studies at the Academy a congregation in Leeds wanted him to come and be their pastor.

---

[20] *Ibid.*, 229.

[21] Moon, "Caleb Evans," 188.

[22] Cited *ibid.*, 188.

[23] "Evangelical Calvinism among eighteenth-century British Baptists", 226.

Langdon wrote to Evans for counsel and was told in a loving but authoritative manner that he should definitely finish his work before considering their offer. Langdon did so and when he graduated he was invited to be the assistant of aging pastor Daniel Turner in Abingdon with a view to his taking over the responsibilities there when the senior man was called home. However, the congregation at Leeds was still interested in Langdon, even though they were only prepared to pay him less than half of what he was being offered in Abingdon. Langdon did not know what he should do. Should he go to Leeds or Abingdon? The latter offer was more attractive for obvious reasons, but was that the right thing to do? Was it the Lord's will? Again he sought the advice of Evans who responded with two letters. In the first, he expressed his frustration with Leeds for offering him such a small salary because he felt they were in a position to give much more. While God's providence had seemed to be moving him in the direction of Leeds in the beginning, Evans expressed his doubts as to whether that was still the case. But in the second letter, written six weeks later, he revealed that he was not sure what was best for Langdon and in the end encouraged him to "seek direction from above." These letters illustrate the sincere affection and concern that existed between teacher and student, for, even though Evans was a very busy man, he still made it his business to pray for, counsel, and worry over his students. It would seem, then, that in Caleb Evans we find a Christian leader who not only looked out for the best interests of his students, but who also was concerned that they were where God wanted them to be in spite of any difficulties that might be connected with their placements.

Theological convictions

To be the kind of leader that Caleb Evans was, required nothing less than a sure foundation beneath his feet. The kind of drive and love for the Lord, the church, the Academy, and the individual students that Evans demonstrated throughout his relatively short life was certainly not built upon nothing. Evans was a man whose thinking and life was constructed upon his personal relationship with his Lord. And that relationship was grounded upon particular theological convictions. What were those convictions?

We get the clearest and most systematic idea of what they were when we look at his statement of faith given at Broadmead on August 18, 1767, on the occasion of his ordination. On that occasion he began by affirming the rightness of such confessions of faith. He believed that every Christian has the right to private judgment in matters of religious faith and practice, but that this right did not rule out the need to articulate the nature of those beliefs and practices. In his day, many were opposed to the need to do so on the grounds that Christ had set them free and therefore they did not have to explain themselves to anyone. Caleb Evans objected because he saw this as a smokescreen to conceal the fact that they no longer believed in those truths which were and still are "the glory and bulwark of the Reformation."[24] Since he was unashamed of those great doctrinal convictions that were re-discovered and proclaimed during the Reformation, he was prepared to spell out exactly where he stood in terms of the "everlasting gospel."

He then went on to express his belief in God, but not just any god. He believed in the God who has revealed himself in his Holy Word. He saw this as a gracious act on the part of God, and, as such, the Scriptures were to be received with proper humility because they are "worthy of God" and "bear his impress."[25] This humble reception of the Scriptures is crucial, for it is only in the Scriptures that we learn that God is a triune being, that he is the creator, that he appointed Adam to be the federal head or representative of the human race, and it is there alone that we discover why men and women, who were made upright, now find themselves entangled in sin and disobedience.

Even more: it is in the Scriptures alone that we learn that from this tragic state of affairs there is only one way out. And what is that way out? For Evans the way out was only to be found in the God of the Bible who takes the initiative, the God who acts on behalf of sinners, the God who has provided salvation for people who could not save themselves. Indeed, for Evans, the only solution to the hopeless plight of humanity is found in the sovereign grace of God. And thankfully, God has been gra-

---

[24] *Ibid.*, 214.
[25] *Ibid.*, 215.

cious; God has taken the initiative in salvation.

Foreseeing the fall of mankind into sin, God, out of his mere good pleasure, decided to rescue a definite number of the ruined race and to exalt them to the privileges of being sons of God in and through the work of his Son. To this end Jesus came to this earth. Here he died as a vicarious, atoning sacrifice for the sins of his chosen people. However, although salvation is ultimately the result of the grace of God in Christ, this does not mean that it comes to men and women without any response on their part. Lost and fallen sinners must experience this salvation personally. They must be regenerated and transformed by the Holy Spirit. In other words, man must experience what Evans called "a spiritual, divine change," having "his understanding enlightened...his will renewed...his affections spiritualized, and [he must be] brought to a spiritual knowledge of faith and love of Christ."[26]

Though Evans stressed the sovereignty of God in salvation, he did not deny that this same God, who created the natural world, was also gracious to his creation as such. While Caleb recognized that it is a "stubborn fact" that God has not chosen to save everyone in the world, and the evidence that this is the case is "irresistible," he nevertheless believed that God is gracious to all people in so many ways that they are morally responsible to him for their failure to seek him and love him as they should.

Furthermore, it is also very important to note that his views on these matters did not hinder him from freely offering the gospel to sinners, nor did they restrict his field of vision and concern when it came to missions or the need to go into all the world with the message of what God has done in Christ. This is because he carefully distinguished between man's natural and moral ability to respond to the gospel. Following the New England theologian Jonathan Edwards (1703-1758), he argued that men and women did not come to God through Christ because they were morally unwilling and rebellious, not because they lacked the natural ability (the thinking, feeling, willing faculties) to respond to the call of God in the gospel. They did not come because they did not *want* to come. They were averse to the true God and would always remain that

---

[26] *Ibid.*, 216.

way unless God in grace performed a life-giving miracle of grace in their hearts. But, God be praised, this is exactly what he does when he stoops to save those who have gone astray, while at the same time assuring them that those who come to him through Jesus will never be turned away.

Evans put it this way when speaking about Christ's invitation to weary sinners to find rest in him:

> Does the doctrine of election teach us to put in, if ye are elected? No... the doctrine of election leaves these and all such passages...in their full force and meaning... All the doctrine of election does in this case is, when the sinner is brought savingly to know Christ, and created anew in him, it teaches him to ascribe it, not to himself, but unto God and his free grace.[27]

When Caleb Evans died, Benjamin Francis wrote an elegy (a poem written on the occasion of a death), in which he beautifully and accurately captured the theological stance of the deceased and the effect that it had upon his life and ministry.

> Celestial truth shone through his inmost soul,
> Illumined, controlled, revived and warm'd the which,
> He felt the doctrine of the Cross, and found
> Life, peace and joy through all his powers abound...
> But wrath divine was not his favorite theme
> He dwelt with joy on the melodious Name
> Ador'd by all the heavenly host above
> The King of glory and the God of love
> Who vanquish'd sin, destruction, death and hell
> In whom alone life and salvation dwell:
> He gazed with rapture on the bleeding cross
> All human worth he viewed as shining dross
> Jesus, whose hand the universe control
> He loved, he preach'd, he serv'd, with all his soul...

---

[27] *Ibid.*, 217-218.

How strong thy faith in the Redeemer's Name!
His cross was still thy sweet, thy darling theme.[28]

Social and political issues

No review of the life and ministry of Caleb Evans would be complete
without some mention of his involvement in charitable causes and his
political views. By some his social and political views were considered
radical, but they were in many respects nothing more than a practical
expression and outworking of his faith. Caleb Evans was not someone
who was only concerned with mankind's spiritual welfare. We have already observed that he was very aware of his social surroundings. Consequently, he was particularly interested in trying to do what he could to
alleviate the poverty and ignorance that were all too prevalent in his day.
To this end he was involved in a project at Downend, a heavily popu-
lated but very needy neighborhood. This project included the preaching
of the gospel with such great success that a large facility was needed to
accommodate everyone who wanted to gather for worship. But it also
included the establishment of a school for the education of 40 poor children who lived there, as well as making sure that they were provided
with adequate clothing. He even spearheaded a co-operative effort between several churches so that the reach and effectiveness of the pro-
gram might be extended to more children who were in need.

Nor was his interest merely verbal or organizational; he gave of himself. Once a week he personally visited the school which was called the
Broadmead Charity School, to pray with and teach the children. All this
did not go unnoticed by others and when he died, there were many moving testimonies about the sincerity and breadth of concern. For example,
one such testimony beautifully captures Evans' heart: "He was always
ready to show kindness of heart, not waiting to be asked, but was fore-
most with his advice, his purse, and his prayers in every design calcu-
lated to relieve distress, instruct the ignorant, give ease to the pained,
and health to the sick, to soothe the miseries of age and rescue giddy

---

[28] Moon, "Caleb Evans," 178; Hayden, "Evangelical Calvinism among
eighteenth-century British Baptists", 221.

youth from the early habits of vice."[29]

Politically, Caleb Evans was a radical in his day, although not among Particular Baptists, many of whom shared his views. Not only did he know his Bible well, but he was also very familiar with the writings of various political philosophers and thinkers whose ideas were shaping the thinking of an entire generation. In 1775, he publicly battled with none other than John Wesley in what has been called "the most publicized clerical debate" of that time.[30] This was over the publication of Wesley's *A Calm Address to Our American Colonies* which defended the right of the British monarch to tax the American colonies even though they had no elected representation in the House of Commons. Evans responded with a pamphlet of his own on October 7, 1775, writing under the pseudonym of "Americanus."

His main point was that the British had no right to impose taxes on the American Colonies without giving them a voice in the government. He did not believe in the divine right of kings to do whatever they wanted, nor did he believe that Christians were to render unto them passive obedience no matter what. In his thinking, there was an important distinction between lawful and unlawful authority with God being the final source of all legitimate authority. Where the authority of the monarch is lawful, he should be obeyed. But where he oversteps his rightful, God-given authority, Christians are not obligated to obey him. In fact, where he is acting unlawfully it is their duty and responsibility under God to resist him, and if needs be, to disobey him.

In the debate with Wesley, and later with his supporter John W. Fletcher (1729-1785), vicar of Madeley in Shropshire, Evans wrote: "if a *lawful* authority, our resistance is *sinful* in a very high degree; but if it be an *unlawful* authority our resistance is glorious."[31] And a few years after the end of the American War of Independence, in 1788, in a ser-

---

[29] Cited Moon, "Caleb Evans," 185.

[30] James E. Bradley, *Religion, Revolution, and English Radicalism. Nonconformity in Eighteenth-Century Politics and Society* (Cambridge: Cambridge University Press, 1990), 127-128.

[31] *A Reply to the Rev. Mr. Fletcher's Vindication of Mr. Wesley's Calm Address To Our American Colonies* (Bristol: W. Pine, 1776), 55.

mon entitled *British Freedom Realized*, he said:

> Nothing can warrant resistance to any established government, but
> an attack upon those principles of liberty, civil or religious, which
> if once destroyed, must necessarily destroy all liberty, and overturn
> the very foundations of all free and lawful government. And in such
> a case to resist is not only lawful but highly virtuous and praise-
> worthy, and will most assuredly be crowned with the approbation
> of God and of all good men.[32]

Although Caleb Evans and John Wesley were on opposite sides of the
debate concerning the American War of Independence or the American
Revolution, they were united when it came to their opposition to slavery.
Bristol was one of three major cities involved in the slave trade, the others being London and Liverpool. According to British Baptist Norman
Moon, "Manufactured goods left Bristol for West Africa, where they
were used to purchase negroes, who were then shipped under appalling
conditions across the Atlantic."[33] After a report was compiled by Thomas Clarkson (1760-1846) on behalf of the Anti-Slave Trade Society in
the summer of 1787, Evans, along with some other prominent individuals in the community, called a meeting at which a committee was formed
to work for the abolition of the slave trade.

Not everyone in Bristol was sympathetic to their cause. Some merely
wanted the slave trade regulated, not abolished, because they feared that
there would be negative economic repercussions. In the end, however, a
thousand signatures were collected in favor of abolishing slavery. And in
1788, a resolution was passed and money sent to help put an end to this
tragic story of human greed and barbarism. Evans himself suffered a
stroke before he eventually died on August 9, 1791, so there is little
doubt that he never had the opportunity to do all that he would have
done to bring about the end of slavery, had he been healthy.

---

[32] *British Freedom Realized* (Bristol: William Pine, 1788), 25.
[33] Moon, "Caleb Evans," 187.

Some lessons from Caleb Evans' life

Though Caleb Evans did not have a long life, he did live one that was extremely active and productive, which, if we are willing to listen, has many lessons to teach us. First, he reminds us about the need for balance in so many areas of our lives. He was balanced in his studies. He was full of the Word of God without being unaware of what was being said and written around him. He realized, in other words, that the Word must address the world. He knew that to be faithful to the Lord in the day in which he had been called to live and serve, and to make a positive impact on his society with the unchanging gospel of God's sovereign grace, he had to not only proclaim and teach God's Word, but he also had to do it in such a way that he addressed his own culture and time. We too need to learn this very important lesson. Furthermore, Evans was also balanced in his recognition that the preaching of the gospel needs to be accompanied by the formation of schools and institutions of higher learning, so that the message may be passed on to faithful men and women who can in turn pass it on to others.

Notice that he never seems to have wrestled with the *spiritual* gospel versus the *social* gospel. He preached Christ while simultaneously feeding and clothing the poor. He defended the politically oppressed and enslaved while he spoke about a glorious spiritual kingdom that would never pass away. Even in the often contentious area of church music, he seems to have understood the importance of having hymns and songs that express objective truth about God and salvation, while at the same time having words and music that give the worshipper a chance to express their love for God, the joy of sins forgiven, and the wonder of being part of the international family of God.

Second, Caleb Evans also has something to say about current educational ideas, particularly when it comes to the training of men for the work of the ministry. As a busy pastor and administrator he nevertheless found time for those who were studying at the Academy. He was involved in their lives, he followed them when they left, he was concerned to do all he could to ensure that they faithfully discharged their responsibilities. All the students of the Academy of which he was principal were integrated into the life of a local church. There they could see first-hand how things operate and there they could refine and sharpen their skills. How different this is from some of the sterile academic settings in which many people are trying to prepare for the Christian ministry today. Though academic credentials are important, no one is ready to serve in the church of Christ who does not love the church and has not already proven by their labors within the church that they have truly been called to the ministry to which they aspire.

Third, Caleb Evans teaches us to view the Scripture and theology as truth. We need to hear him again when he says that "there is scarcely any branch of knowledge but what may be useful. Whatever hath a tendency to enlarge our ideas of the divine perfections, to give us a clearer view of the meaning of Scripture and enable us to express our thoughts...is worthy of the attention of every candidate for the ministry."[34] Do we have the confidence that he has? These are not the words of a man who is running from the battlefield, but of a Christian who is ready for the fight because he knows where his power lies and because he knows the sovereign God who is in control of all things. Indeed, these are the words of a man who believes that the gospel is objective and public truth, because it is rooted and grounded in the God of truth and the Lord of glory who is the way, the truth, and the life (John 14:6).

We need to recapture this in our day. We live in a day in which truth is denied and scorned. But Caleb Evans reminds us that the God whom we serve is the God of authority and truth. No matter what branch of knowledge we may study, it is the God of the Bible who is the very foundation of truth itself. Could it be that we are not as ready for the conflict as we should be because we have lost this vision? Could it be that we have succumbed to the *Zeitgeist* of the day because we are not confident in the Lord of the Word and the Word of the Lord? Mark it well: to have the spiritual vision and vigor of a Caleb Evans in our day of incredible change and unbelief, requires nothing less than full confidence in the sovereign God Evans loved and proclaimed.

If we are to be effective servants of the Lord, we need to seriously consider once again that only the sovereign God of the Bible is able to give us Scriptures that are completely trustworthy. Only he can em-

---

[34] *Ibid.*, 182.

power us for service. Only he can send us out into the fields that are white for harvest. And by his grace, only he can enable us to bring every thought into captivity to him. Caleb Evans' life and thinking should inspire us and gently push us in that direction.

Given his life, it does not come as a surprise that his death at the age of fifty-four came as a real blow to his family, the Broadmead Church, the Bristol Academy, and the Bristol Education Society. Faithful husbands, fathers and leaders like Caleb Evans are not easily replaced and this was eloquently expressed by Thomas Dunscombe (1748-1811), who studied at the Academy after it was re-organized by Evans in 1770. In his *Tribute of Affection to the Memory of the Late Dr. Evans* Dunscombe writes about the loss which the Bristol Society sustained in the death of its "President and Parent":

> The first idea of it was conceived in his mind...the plan of it was his framing; his exertions carried the plan into effect... Like a fond father—a father whose fondness is marked...with truest wisdom—he nourished and cherished the infant institution, till, with a growth that has been great and gradual, it has just reached at the time of his death, the age of manhood...another President we may have, but another Father we cannot have.[35]

Caleb Evans was one of those who, in the words of Hebrews 12:1-3, knew what it was to throw off everything that hinders and the sin that so easily entangles, and to run with perseverance the race that was marked out for him. He knew what it was to fix his eyes on Jesus, the author and perfecter of our faith, and to so consider him who endured such opposition from sinful men, that he did not grow weary or lose heart. May God continue to give us Christian leaders of this caliber until Jesus himself comes in glory and power and all the battles and struggles of this life are

---

[35] Cited Hayden, "Evangelical Calvinism among eighteenth-century British Baptists", 239-240.

finally over.

Further reading

In this century, there have been only two significant studies of Caleb Evans: Norman S. Moon, "Caleb Evans, Founder of The Bristol Education Society", *The Baptist Quarterly* 24 (1971-1972), 175-190; and Roger Hayden, "Evangelical Calvinism among eighteenth-century British Baptists with particular reference to Bernard Foskett, Hugh and Caleb Evans and the Bristol Baptist Academy, 1690-1791" (Unpublished Ph.D Thesis, University of Keele, 1991), 209-240.

The Rev.ᵈ Sam.ᵗ Medley.

SAMUEL MEDLEY (1738-1799)

B. A. Ramsbottom

There was a time when Dissenting congregations in England delighted to sing the hymns of Samuel Medley, with their beautiful last line refrains: "My Jesus has done all things well," or "His lovingkindness, O how free!" Sadly these hymns have fallen into decline—no doubt due to the decline this century in vital godliness—though now through the influence of new popular evangelical hymnbooks[1] they are becoming known and loved once more. It is as a composer of hymns that Medley has been best known. However, in his lifetime he gained great popularity as a preacher, both to his own large congregation in the sea port of Liverpool, and also on his highly-valued annual visits to the large preaching places in London.

Who, then, was Samuel Medley?

Early years, conversion, and call to ministry

It was into a talented and learned family that Samuel Medley was born on June 23, 1738, at Cheshunt, Hertfordshire. As he himself received an excellent education, it seems surprising that he was apprenticed in the cloth trade; no wonder, then, that with such a lively mind he was unhappy. When war with France broke out in 1755, it was with delight he was able to join His Majesty's Navy. Both his brothers were already

---

[1] E.g. *Christian Hymns* (Worthing: Henry E. Walter, 1977). Based on the authors of this hymnbook, Elsie Houghton, *Christian Hymn-writers* (Bridgend: Evangelical Press of Wales, 1982) contains a chapter on Medley (pages 136-139).

in the navy; in fact, both were to lose their lives at sea. Samuel's heart
was set on a glorious naval career. He would not be satisfied till he
became an Admiral!

At the age of seventeen he was serving aboard a 74-gun ship called
the Buckingham, the captain taking special interest in him as he had
been educated by Samuel's grandfather. Soon he was transferred to
another 74-gun ship, the Intrepid, and spent the next years as master's
mate with the fleet of Admiral Edward Boscawen (1711-1761) in the
Mediterranean. There he found wonderful opportunities to improve his
knowledge and education, but also, sadly, opportunities to go to great
lengths in sin. He had been brought up by godly parents, but his
Christian upbringing was soon forgotten. "He gave full scope to his
reigning propensities, acknowledging that he had neither the fear of God
nor man before his eyes."[2]

At the age of twenty-one he reached a crisis in his life. In that year
(1759) one of the famous English sea battles, the Battle of Cape Lagos,
was fought. In this battle Medley's job was to sit on board deck and
write down minutes of the action between the English and French fleets.
The slaughter that day was dreadful. So great was the bloodshed that
barrels of flour were tipped on the decks to stop the men from slipping.
Yet Samuel Medley's conscience was so seared, and his heart so hard,
that he was unmoved by all this—even when the mizzen mast was
shattered by a cannon ball, even when a nearby sailor carrying a
wounded man was hit and both fell headlong into the hold.

As the heat of the battle increased, Medley himself was badly
wounded, the greater part of one of his calves being shot away, so that
he had to be carried to his bed. This terrible day ended in victory for the
British Navy.

As time passed the leg did not heal and gangrene set in. Eventually
the ship's surgeon said there was only one remedy—amputation (a
dreadful thing in the eighteenth century). Medley was filled with horror,
but the surgeon would allow only one more day before he did the
operation.

------

[2] Samuel Medley, Jr., *Memoirs of the late Rev. Samuel Medley of Liverpool* (London: J. Johnson, 1800), 66. Henceforth referred to as *Memoirs*.

So that night Samuel Medley prayed—all night long. He thought of his misspent life. He sent for a Bible that he knew was hidden in his chest. And a miracle took place! Next morning the surgeon was amazed, and declared there was no more need for an operation. But how true:

Judgments nor mercies e'er can sway
Their roving feet to wisdom's way.

As the leg healed, every religious impression wore off. But it was God's purpose that this young man should be an eminent minister of Jesus Christ, not an Admiral, and the time was drawing near "not to propose, but call by grace."

Having to convalesce for a long period, Samuel Medley went to his grandfather's home in London. His old grandfather, William Tonge, was both a godly and learned man. At this time he was one of the deacons in the Particular Baptist church in Eagle Street, Holloway, London, where the eminent Andrew Gifford, Jr. (1700-1784)[3] was pastor. Samuel Medley was surrounded by every comfort, but found his grandfather's solemn warnings and spiritual conversation irksome.

One Lord's day evening, to Medley's disgust, the old man insisted on reading one of Isaac Watts' sermons to him—from Isaiah 42. 6, 7: the opening of the eyes of the blind, the bringing of the prisoner out of the prison. What an entrancing scene: the old man standing there with the manuscript in his hand; the young, proud sailor, bored, angered, yet politely showing respect! Then the Holy Spirit began powerfully to apply the Word.

He heard, he more than heard, for every sentence described his own case, and every word sank deep into his heart. At once convinced of his awful state as a sinner before God, and the imminent danger he was in as such, with a heart broken under a sense of his guilt and impenitence, and the astonishing forbearance of God toward

---

[3] Gifford was also sub-librarian of the British Museum. He is not to be confused with his grandfather of the same name, Andrew Gifford, Sr. (1642-1721).

him, as soon as he was alone he fell down before the Lord, and spread before Him his mournful and dangerous case.[4]

Now there was a difference. There were no more thoughts of being an Admiral! As soon as he could go out, it was his delight to hear such men as George Whitefield and Andrew Gifford. There is no record of how he found peace and pardon, but "he soon received the comforts of the gospel by a believing view of the fulness and sufficiency of the atonement of the Lord Jesus."[5] Shortly afterwards he copied out three verses (altered from Watts) in his manuscript book, dating them in a special manner. They include the couplet:

> The sure foundation of my hope
> Is in a Saviour's blood.

In December 1760, at the age of 22, Samuel Medley was baptized by Andrew Gifford, and became a member of the Particular Baptist church in Eagle Street, London.

A period of convalescence was still necessary, but Samuel Medley was not idle. Day by day he studied in his grandfather's excellent library, learning to read Hebrew and Greek, but especially prayerfully studying the Word of God. From this time dates the remarkable knowledge of the Scriptures for which he was renowned. His months of convalescence were like Moses' forty years in the backside of the desert, a gracious preparation for his life's work. Eventually Samuel Medley commenced a school of his own (which greatly prospered) near Seven Dials in London. On April 17, 1762, at the age of 23, he married, and removed to King Street, Soho, London.

Just over four years later his pastor mentioned the matter of preaching, and Samuel Medley could not deny the burden of his heart. Being forgiven much, he loved much, and there was a desire to speak to sinners of the glories of his Saviour. On August 29, 1766, the church publicly called him to the work of the ministry.

---

[4] *Memoirs*, 76-77.
[5] *Ibid.*, 77-78.

Call to Liverpool

At first he preached at various places in and around London, where great numbers came to hear him. A year later he became pastor of the Particular Baptist church at Watford. Not much is recorded of his four and a half years there. Though favoured with some success, he was troubled by a spirit of disunity in the church and also because the church could not completely support him. He was worn out by the labours of his preaching and the pastorate along with being compelled still to carry on a school during the week.

In 1771, in the mysterious providence of God, he happened to meet one of the deacons of the Particular Baptist church at Liverpool, in the north of England. Things at Liverpool were in a poor state, few attending, and the pastor recently dismissed because of open sin. Yet they were wrestling in prayer for the Lord to appear for them in their sad condition, and to send them a pastor after his own heart. The result of the unexpected meeting was that Samuel Medley was asked to preach two Lord's days at Liverpool at the end of the year, and early in 1772 he moved there to settle as their pastor. Liverpool by this time had developed from a ragged fishing village into a leading sea port and the sixth largest town in England.

Here he stayed for the remaining twenty-seven years of his life. Humanly speaking, things seemed impossible, but the gospel was so blessed that during the first few weeks between twenty and thirty people were added to the church. Very quickly this number doubled. The year following, the old meeting house in Byrom Street had to be enlarged, and was filled with attentive hearers. With passing years there was continued prosperity, sinners being converted and added to the church. In 1789 a completely new chapel had to be built (in the same street), this chapel being one of the largest in the British Isles.[6] Here Samuel Medley

---

[6] J. Gadsby, *Memoirs of Hymnwriters and Compilers* (London: Gadsby, 1882), 98. Samuel Medley, Letter to John Fawcett: "Yesterday evening I preached as it is supposed to near 2,000 people in it" (November 14, 1790) [cited B. A. Ramsbottom *Samuel Medley: Preacher, Pastor, Poet*, (London: Fauconberg Press, 1978), 18].

continued with the Lord's blessing and increasing success till his death in 1799—one interesting feature being that his congregation found his preaching as profitable as ever—even more so—during the final months of his life.

The preacher

The conclusion of Robert Halley, the Congregationalist historian, was that Medley was "a great preacher but a small poet."[7] Whatever can be said of the latter, the former certainly seems to be true.

Unhappily, we have only two of Medley's complete sermons in print—one preached at Moorfields Tabernacle in London, and the other at a gathering of an Association of Baptist churches in North Wales. Besides this, there are a number of "skeletons"—detailed notes—of sermons that he preached. So we have some impression of the kind of preacher he was.

There is something of eighteenth-century formality about his sermons (almost inevitably so), but there is also a warmth permeating them. With delight he would exclaim, "O the height and breadth and depth and length of the love of Christ!" The "skeletons" show us how ably he handled his text, dividing and sub-dividing it, as was the custom at that time. Curiously, he often preached a sermon on one word, for instance, "But," or, "Not," or "Him."

His preaching was marked, as was his conversation, by pointed, pithy sayings. For instance:

> We have one instance of a malefactor converted at the eleventh hour that none may despair; and only one that none may presume.

> The door of life shuts with more than common violence against those who have long sat under a faithful ministry and die impenitent.

---

[7] *Lancashire: Its Puritanism and Nonconformity* (London: Hodder and Stoughton, 1869), II, 480.

Psalm 46 is my pocket ammunition. I draw supplies, or stand on my defence against my enemies, by the powerful and gracious assistance of the truths it contains.

Do not be afraid of the fiery trial of persecution. Those saints whom God employs in wintry seasons, He always clothes in winter garments. He can put heaven into the soul before He take you there.

W. T. Whitley speaks of Samuel Medley's "exceptional abilities,"[8] and the *Dictionary of National Biography* records "remarkable and increasing popularity."[9] But above all it was the blessing of the Lord that attended the Word. "It pleased God powerfully to attend the Word preached by the influences of His Holy Spirit to the revival, comfort and encouragement of His people, and for the conversion of many others; and this success, blessed by God, was uniform to the last year of his life."[10]

As well as preaching at home, he annually visited London, being one of the popular "Tabernacle preachers." Large numbers came to hear him at Tottenham Court Road and at Moorfields. His popularity in London was immense, and it is recorded that he had "reason to believe that several, more or less, were called to a knowledge of the truth under his ministry in these places every journey; and he often heard of many pleasing seals to his ministry after his return home."[11]

The question may be asked: exactly what was Medley's degree of eminence in the Baptist denomination, and outside? This, of course, though interesting, is a difficult question. Most biographers overemphasise the importance of their subject! But two somewhat

---

[8] *Baptists of North-West England 1649-1913* (London: Kingsgate Press, 1913), 135.

[9] Alexander Gordon, "Samuel Medley", *The Compact Edition of the Dictionary of National Biography* (London: Oxford University Press, 1975), I, 1360.

[10] *Memoirs*, 90.

[11] *Ibid*, 92

unusual things throw a degree of light on the question. It is recorded that John Hirst of Bacup had once travelled purposely to preach at Chester— a considerable distance. Medley happened to be present as a hearer, but he was invited to preach and Hirst to stand down—a rather thoughtless act, but showing the veneration in which Medley must have been held, as John Hirst was a much-loved and eminent minister himself.[12] Second, the evangelical "Eclectic Society" in London (John Newton was a leading member of this body) discussed on January 21, 1799—while Medley was still alive—popularity among ministers, and Samuel Medley's name was mentioned along with sixteen others including Whitefield, William Huntington (1745-1813), William Romaine (1714-1795), John Berridge (1716-1793), Rowland Hill (1744-1833), William Jay (1769-1853) and John Wesley![13]

Yet Samuel Medley had no great thoughts of himself. He had such overpowering views of his own unworthiness and sin, and of the riches of God's grace towards him, that he felt himself to be nothing. Severely tempted by Satan, he would say, "Mine is a religion of necessity, for Thou, Lord, alone hast the words of eternal life, and 'though He slay me, yet will I trust in Him.' If I perish it shall be at the foot of the cross, and blessed be God, I shall be the first to perish there."[14] His daughter Sarah noted that he had "a tormenting fear that he who had preached the gospel to others, should be himself a cast away, and fall through the presence of sin and temptation."[15]

During the latter years of Samuel Medley's ministry the "modern question" arose among the Baptists concerning the right way to address the unconverted. Medley, always noted for his "zealous attachment to the distinguishing truths of the gospel" (i.e. Calvinism), was in no doubt: "Either fallen man is dead in trespasses and sins, or he is not; and if he

---

[12] J. Hargreaves, *Life and Memoir of Rev. John Hirst* (Rochdale: Little-wood, 1816), 193-196.

[13] *The Thought of the Evangelical Leaders: 1798-1814* (Repr. Edinburgh: Banner of Truth, 1978), 90-91.

[14] Sarah Medley, *Memoirs of the late Rev. Samuel Medley* (Liverpool: J. Jones, 1833), 35.

[15] *Ibid.*, 35.

really is dead in trespasses and sins, it is utterly impossible that he should either will or do anything towards his own salvation. For my part, I should think it far more optional to go decidedly to the Arminian conclusion upon the question than to attempt to shake hands over the wall."[16]

From his surviving sermons we see his method of addressing the unconverted:

Ye poor Christless sinners, may you bless God for sparing goodness, that you are yet out of hell; and O may a sense of this lead you to true repentance so that you may bless Him for Christ and salvation to all eternity.[17]

May the good Spirit of God quicken and renew your souls, and enable you to flee from the wrath to come to a dear and precious Jesus, while you are on mercy's ground, under mercy's sound, and within mercy's reach.[18]

Samuel Medley was no Fullerite, that is, a follower of Andrew Fuller.[19] When Richard Davis (d.1832), whose views coincided with those of Andrew Fuller, became pastor after Medley's death, a great portion of the church left, including Medley's widow.[20] Those who had loved Medley's ministry became lovers of William Gadsby.[21]

---

[16] *Ibid.*, 33.
[17] *Memoirs*, 239.
[18] *Ibid.*, 259-260.
[19] The biography of Andrew Fuller may be found in *The British Particular Baptists 1638-1910*, Volume II.
[20] John Davis, *A Brief Memoir of the late Rev. Richard Davis* (London: G. Wightman, 1833).
[21] J. Gadsby, *Memoir of William Gadsby* (London: Gadsby, 1851), 67-71, 72-73. These pages contain an account of how popular Gadsby was in the Liverpool congregations which had seceded following Medley's death, and also of Richard Lord of Bury who loved Medley and later found the same di-

The pastor

No account of Samuel Medley's life would be complete without considering him as a pastor. How interesting it would have been to spend a day with Samuel Medley! A typical day was something like this. We should find him rising at four o'clock and, while the rest of the family were asleep, going across the yard in all weathers to his study. In winter the fire would have been laid the night before and would soon be blazing brightly. Here in quietness and solitude Samuel Medley would commit himself to the Lord and hold sweet communion with him.

After these private devotions, the early hours of the day would be spent profitably—meditating on the services before him, or writing a few letters, or composing a hymn or poem. After about ten o'clock he would set out on a round of various pastoral visits and duties.

Samuel Medley appears to have been a wonderful pastor, loving, warm, affectionate. He used to say, "I can never bear so much with anyone as the Lord bears with me!" He rejoiced in his congregation's prosperity, sympathised in adversity, warned, exhorted, encouraged in times of trial, putting up "weeping supplications to heaven on their behalf." The greatest tenderness and forbearance were shown to the weakest of the flock and even after his death his pastoral visits were remembered with tears.

Specially appreciated were the monthly addresses on prayer he gave in the vestry of his meeting house. Here he appeared as a father with his family, "opening his soul with the most unreserved frankness, while solemnity and sweetness united in every sentence."[22] He specially encouraged them to pray for the poor and needy, and for the rich to help the poor. Also, at times of joy and sorrow, he had a habit of speaking impressively from some portion of Scripture in the homes of his people.

In a number of his excellent letters and poems we see the heart of a pastor—on the occasion of the loss of a child; or the death of the wife of

---

vine truths in Gadsby's preaching. The biography of William Gadsby may be found in *The British Particular Baptists 1638-1910*, Volume II.

[22] *Memoirs*, 93.

one of his members; or an aged deacon falling from a horse; or the launching of a ship belonging to two Liverpool captains.

Naturally, because of his past life, he had a great interest in sailors and, of course, Liverpool afforded him many opportunities for witness to such folk. Some attended his chapel; but he would speak to any he met in the streets or on the wharves, telling them of his own experiences in the navy and enquiring concerning the state of their souls. Occasionally, at the request of the Seaman's Society, he would address a large gathering of sailors (often using nautical terms in his preaching). It was noticed how tears would flow down the weather-beaten faces of these seemingly hard seamen. One such occasion was when the subject was Paul's shipwreck and Samuel Medley spoke of a greater shipwreck, a greater deliverance, and the greater mercy of being saved from sinking into hell.

Also, he was specially interested in young people. "He seldom enjoyed himself more than in conversing with young people and instructing them, either publicly from the pulpit or privately in the parlour."[23] He was both faithful and tender, and would sternly rebuke sin, especially Sabbath-breaking. He always gave a special address on New Year's day. Many traced their spiritual beginnings to Samuel Medley's loving interest in them in their early days.

A beautiful order was maintained in the church under Medley's pastorate, open sin always being dealt with in a desire for the Lord's glory. It was always a great delight when any were blessed with repentance and restored. There were interesting difficulties in the church. Some were seafaring men, sailing as far away as the West Indies—yet their pastor always felt it his loving responsibility to watch over them. Those who had moved to London received pastoral visits when Samuel Medley went down annually to preach. There was even the unusual case of a church member going to live in the Isle of Man. She could neither read nor write, nor had any godly friend to help; but the church made every effort to keep in contact with her.

---

[23] *Ibid.*, 94.

Very interesting is the way in which "Zion's solemnities" were kept. For instance, the church minute book gives an account of a whole day (April 7, 1777) spent on the ordination of deacons.

One last point concerning Samuel Medley the pastor needs to be mentioned. The article on him in *The Dictionary of National Biography* erroneously states that Medley practised open communion and that his church order was little different from that of a Congregational church. Why this error has been made is hard to understand. It is clear that both in his Watford and Liverpool pastorates Medley was a strict or closed communion Baptist—both concerning membership and visitors. About forty years after Medley's death there was a legal issue at Byrom Street concerning open communion, but on that occasion (1837)[24] both sides publicly agreed that what was suggested was a complete innovation, and that throughout its whole history Byrom Street had been a strict communion church.

The poet

Though Robert Halley said he was "but a small poet," and J. C. Philpot complained of "poverty of thought,"[25] it is as a poet that Samuel Medley is best known today. People who *admire* other hymnwriters say how much they *love* Medley.

Medley's hymns are gospel hymns, full of Christ and the riches of his grace—the suitability of Christ to meet the sinner's need. As a learned writer Kenneth Howard has put it: "He seems to strike the note of authentic Christian joy with never a suspicion of hollowness or effervescence."[26]

---

[24] Legal document in the hands of the present Shaw Street Particular Baptist church: "Case: Baptist Chapel, Byrom Street, Liverpool" (February 15, 1837). See also James Stuart *Beechen Grove Baptist Church, Watford. Memorials of Two Hundred Years and More* (London, 1907).

[25] *Reviews by J. C. Philpot* (London: Frederick Kirby, 1901), II, 11.

[26] Personal letter from K. W. H. Howard, September 27, 1975.

There is usually a refrain in each verse—such as "His lovingkindness O how great!," or "Jesus my Sanctuary is," or "Nor shalt thou seek His face in vain." In most hymns the next to the last verse is on death, and the concluding verse on heaven. An old preacher once said that Medley was his favourite hymnwriter "because he always lands you in heaven in the last verse."

Many of his hymns were specially written for the services at Byrom Street, the refrain being the substance of the text on which he was to speak. Some were written in the quietness of the early morning hours; others were hastily finished, with his hat and great coat on, just before he set out for the service.

In former days the custom was for hymns to be announced and sung two lines at a time—partly because of the shortage of hymnbooks. Medley was one of the first to try to break with that system. He had some of his hymns printed on broadsheets and handed out to the congregation so that they could be sung straight through. (They must have possessed above average literacy.) When "Awake, my soul, in joyful lays" was first composed, it sold by hundreds in leaflet form in the streets of Liverpool.

He wrote many poems as well—some of inferior quality. His letters to friends were often in verse. Among those published are poems of thanks for the gift of a hare, or for an inkstand, or for a present of salt fish and twelve bottles of cider from America. In the case of the latter he does not scruple to mention his well-known antipathy to rebellion, especially the rebellion of the American colonies. Also there are sympathetic poems written to his congregation in their times of trouble.

Samuel Medley's best known hymn is undoubtedly:

> Awake, my soul, in joyful lays,
> And sing thy great Redeemer's praise;
> He justly claims a song from me;
> His lovingkindness, O how free!

This appeared in Rippon's *Selection* in 1787 while Medley was still alive. So before his death, his hymns were in common use. In the various Baptist hymn selections of last century, 48 of Medley's hymns appeared in Denham's, 31 in Gadsby's, and 30 in Stevens's. Recently the beautiful hymn, "I know that my Redeemer lives," has become better known again. It is said that the hymn, "God shall alone the refuge be/And comfort of my mind," was written after the tragic loss of a tiny child.[27]

It was among the Baptists in England that hymn-singing began during the later years of the seventeenth century—yet the strange fact has been commented on that the greatest hymns seem to have been written by Episcopalians, Methodists and Independents, but not by Baptists! Arguably, Samuel Medley may be considered the finest of the Baptist hymnwriters.

Final days

When Samuel Medley came to die, he was wonderfully blessed, though he had been sorely tempted by Satan. The desires of his beautiful hymns were fulfilled. Among his death-bed sayings were:

> You see me now on my dying bed and a sweet bed it is to me. What mercies I am now enjoying in it! I never saw so much of my own unworthiness, or so much of the excellency, glory and the suitableness of Christ as an all-sufficient Saviour.

> That Jesus whom I have so long recommended to poor sinners is my only comfort in my dying hours. His salvation is in every way perfect and complete. Remember, I die no Arminian, Socinian or Arian. I die a poor sinner saved by sovereign, rich and free mercy.

> I am now a poor shattered bark just about to enter the blissful harbour; and O how sweet will be the port after the storm!

---

[27] Oral tradition handed down among the older members at Shaw Street Particular Baptist Chapel, Liverpool.

Then at the end: "Dying is sweet work! sweet work! My heavenly Father! I am looking up to my dear Jesus, my God, my Portion, my All in all." His last words were: "Glory! Glory! Home! Home!"

So died Samuel Medley on July 17, 1799, aged 61. He had prepared a Latin inscription for his gravestone, leaving the date of his death to be fitted in. In translation it reads:

S. M.
A MOST UNWORTHY PREACHER OF THE GOSPEL,
FORMERLY PASTOR OF THIS CHURCH OF CHRIST,
BY NATURE AND PRACTICE A GREAT SINNER,
BUT REDEEMED BY GRACE AND THE BLOOD OF THE SAVIOUR,
HAS HERE LAID DOWN HIS BODY,
WAITING FOR THE BRIGHT AND MORNING STAR.
COME THEN, LORD JESUS!"[28]

Further reading

There are two book-length memoirs of Medley, one by his son Samuel and the other by his daugther, Sarah: Samuel Medley, Jr., *Memoirs of the late Rev. Samuel Medley of Liverpool* (London: J. Johnson, 1800) and Sarah Medley, *Memoirs of the late Rev. Samuel Medley, formerly minister of the Baptist Chapel in Byrom Street, Liverpool* (Liverpool: J. Jones, 1833). In her volume, Sarah does not conceal her hatred of her brother. Joseph Ivimey, in his *A History of the English Baptists* (London: Isaac Taylor Hinton/Holdsworth & Ball, 1830), IV, 590-602, almost exactly follows the life by Medley's son.

More recently, B. A. Ramsbottom, on the basis of considerable original research, has written an excellent work on Medley: *Samuel Medley: Preacher, Pastor, Poet* (London: Fauconberg Press, 1978). This chapter was based to a considerable extent on this study.

---

[28] *Memoirs*, 125.

THE BRITISH PARTICULAR BAPTISTS
1638-1910

Volume II

Table of Contents

Also Available From

Particular Baptist Press

*The Life and Works of
Joseph Kinghorn*

in four volumes

*The Life and Ministry of
John Gano*

in two volumes

*The Annual Register of Indian Affairs
1835-1838*
by Isaac McCoy

All are edited by
Mr. Terry Wolever

and are Hard Bound on
Acid-Free paper

**Particular Baptist Press
2766 W. Weaver Road
Springfield, Missouri 65810**